China Streetsmart is the only book I have read that explains practical and effective secrets learnt from on-the-ground experience coupled with a deep understanding of Chinese history and ideology. This book provides you with a framework on how to deal with problems, how to make profits and how to set the long-term risk and investment strategy.

China Streetsmart is not only meant for new or western investors, but it also stimulates executives with several years of China experience to rethink their issues in a different way. The book is original in approach, written for people who want to capitalise on the opportunities that exist in China today and the next decade.

Henry Luk
Regional Director and CFO
The Economist Group, Asia Pacific

China Streetsmart tells you pretty much all you need to know to outfox your competitors in the superhighways – and back alleys – of China's labyrinthine commercial world. Based on the author's personal experience as a businessman as well as painstaking research, this innovative work offers practical tips in areas ranging from choosing joint venture partners to negotiating deals. A must for understanding – and profiting from – the post-WTO China market.

Willy Lam
Senior China Analyst at CNN's Hong Kong Office
and author of *The Era of Jiang Zemin*

For any foreign investor aspiring to succeed in China's fast-growing, complex and intensely competitive marketplace, *China Streetsmart* offers the essential survival kit and insightful winning tips.

Dr Fred Hu
Managing Director
Goldman Sachs

China Streetsmart is a professional thriller for smart businessmen and women to read, understand and learn from. The book is based on practical experiences that can help to create a long-term sustainable and profitable model.

Amitava Chatterjee
President
Greater China
Household & Body Care Division
Sara Lee Douwe Egberts

China Streetsmart is an essential guide for investors to assess the benefits versus operational risks of investing in China. Taking a macro (top-down) view of the Chinese business environment, John Chan's unique guide to investing in China is easy to read and follow by providing practical tactics based on best business practices. This book shows both new and seasoned corporate strategists how to deal with China's various pitfalls.

Jun Ma
Director and Senior Economist
Deutsche Bank Hong Kong

China
Streetsmart

**What You MUST Know
to be
Effective and Profitable
in China**

John L. Chan

Singapore London New York Toronto Sydney Tokyo Madrid
Mexico City Munich Paris Capetown Hong Kong Montreal

Published in 2003 by
Prentice Hall
Pearson Education Asia Pte Ltd
23/25 First Lok Yang Road, Jurong
Singapore 629733

Pearson Education offices in Asia: *Bangkok, Beijing, Hong Kong, Jakarta, Kuala Lumpur, Manila, New Delhi, Seoul, Singapore, Taipei, Tokyo, Shanghai*

Cover illustration by PhotoDisc/Getty Images

Printed in Singapore

4   3
06   05   04

ISBN 0-13-047488-6

China Streetsmart® is a registered trademark of John L. Chan

For Coco
Keep the torch bright

People's Republic of China
Founded 1949

Heilongjiang

Ningxia Hui
Autonomous
Region

Beijing

Jilin

Xinjiang
Autonomous
Region

Liaoning

Gansu

Inner Mongolia
Autonomous Region

Tianjin

Hebei

Shanxi

Shandong

Qinghai

Shaanxi

Henan

Jiangsu

Tibet
Autonomous
Region

Anhui

Shanghai

Sichuan

Hubei

Zhejiang

Chongqing

Hunan

Jiangxi

Fujian

Taiwan

Guizhou

Yunnan

Guangxi Zhuang
Autonomous
Region

Guangdong

Hong Kong
Macau

Hainan

General Information

(Excludes Hong Kong/Macao/Taiwan)

Total population (2001)	1.28 billion
Area in square kilometres	9.6 million
GDP (2001)	1,166.1 billion USD
Trade exports (2002)	325.6 billion USD
Trade imports (2002)	295.2 billion USD
Retail sales (2002)	494.0 billion USD
Foreign exchange reserves (30 December 2002)	286.4 billion USD
Foreign direct investment (2002)	52.7 billion USD
Unemployment estimate (2002)	4.0%
Consumer price increase over previous year (2002)	– 0.7%

1 USD = 8.28 RMB

Contents

About the Author

Born and raised in the small town of Saint John, New Brunswick, Canada, John L. Chan's cultural and business backgrounds are a blend of East and West, and rural and big city influences and perspectives; coupled with working for regional based Asian companies to the largest multinational companies in the world. He has been developing his *China Streetsmart* experience since he came to China in 1993 when he spent his first two years as a consultant assisting multinational companies enter the China market. He then  spent five years in China's beer industry in positions ranging from Chief Representative to National Marketing Director, marketing and selling international brands such as Foster's from Australia, Beck's and Holsten from Germany, Steinlager from New Zealand and a host of leading local brands all across China in both urban and rural markets, managing teams of up to 150 people. After leaving the beer industry, he joined the technology sector and was the Director of Marketing for Asia Online. Prior to coming to China, he spent six years with Exxon (Imperial Oil) developing the consumer retail markets across Canada. He currently lives in Shanghai with his Beijing-born wife Mary (Ma Xin) and daughter Coco.

John's passion is using his creative energy and strategic leadership skills to help people and companies better understand China. He welcomes those individuals and companies who seek a better understanding to contact him by sending him an email at johnchan@chinastreetsmart.com or by visiting his website at www.chinastreetsmart.com

List of Figures

List of Tables

Preface

When people heard I was writing *China Streetsmart®*, some people thought the book would contain information such as the "right way" to bribe officials or the "shadier side" of how to get things done. Ken Davies, the former Chief Economist and Bureau Chief for the Economist Intelligence Unit in Asia, now an executive with the Organisation for Economic Cooperation and Development (OECD) examining China's Foreign Direct Investment (FDI) policies, based out of Paris, had a milder view. He said, "Oh I expect your book to have a lot of information on how to not get blind-eyed drunk at the next Chinese business banquet, by telling your local Chinese host you have a medical ailment or something." Which actually works and is good advice if you are ever in this situation, but not what this book is really about. **This book is about adopting an effective approach modelled after the way China business professionals set up and run a profitable business in a complex and fast-developing political economy.** The book is not only meant for new investors, but also for executives already working in China to give them an alternative viewpoint on how to handle common challenges. One could even argue that this book could be applied to investors in other markets, since many of the challenges faced in China are similar elsewhere.

China Streetsmart is all about being practical and effective. If it's going to be practical and easy to use, the ideas in it must be easy to understand and implement. While I respect the intellectual process of how theoreticians and academics develop theories on how to do business in China, such as trying to explain yin and yang and Daoism to the Westerner, my approach is quite different and much simpler. My analysis and recommendations are not based on regression analysis or other heavy-duty statistical processes, rather they are based on interviews and anecdotal information, coupled with what I personally know, having worked in this market for about a decade, in positions ranging from Vice President of International Strategies and Marketing, to Chief Representative, to National Marketing Director for regional Hong Kong-based companies and multi-billion-dollar multinational corporations.

I tell people whom I interviewed for this book to imagine they were sitting in an airport lounge having a drink while waiting for a connecting flight. Along comes a person who is interested in doing business in China, but doesn't really know much about the market. I tell them, "I will bet some of the information you could pass on to that person in those 15–30 minutes will probably be as useful as any high-priced market report. Why? Because your advice comes directly from on-the-ground experience and is easy to understand." Dell Smith, the International Business Development Director for Freser Refrigeration Equipment, which has a plant in Shanghai and sells coolers and dispensing equipment to major clients like Coca-Cola and Pepsi, immediately smiled when I related this scenario to him. "You know," he said, "I had this happen to me very recently. I had just run into this American selling equipment in China to this local Chinese distributor and this guy was quite happy about having made a successful sale on his first trip to China. I then asked him if he got paid, which dumbfounded him and he replied, 'Uh no …' I smiled, and then explained the importance of getting paid versus 'making the sale'. Some people learn the hard way. I certainly have."

However, since anecdotal information is far from perfect science, how you treat and use this information is equally important. *China Streetsmart* is not meant to be a literal do's and don'ts guide in setting up a profitable business, rather you must be the judge in deciding how to interpret the situations presented relative to your own. For example, it is critical to keep in mind the information you receive within the context of time and geography. In China, things change quickly and at different paces over a huge area the size of Europe, so what was true in one location might not be applicable to another. Back in 1979, practically all Chinese businesspeople were unaccustomed to Western business practices and etiquette. Likewise, the foreign businessperson (including the Hong Konger and Taiwanese) had little understanding of the Mainland Chinese side. Often deals were lost over misunderstandings or what the other side thought were major cultural blunders. The Mainland Chinese would wonder why foreign businesspeople, if they were really looking to establish a good relationship built on mutual trust and cooperation, felt they should bring their lawyer to an introductory meeting – not an unusual practice in the West, but differently perceived in China.

Now that more than 20 years have passed since the doors to China first re-opened, Chinese businesspeople today are more familiar with Western business customs, especially in large sophisticated cities such as Shanghai. Barry Friedman, the Chief Commercial Consul for the United States Commercial Service (USCS) based in Hong Kong, has spent more than 15 years in the China market. He comments, "Today I'm amazed to go into Chinese offices on the Mainland to see their executives all decked out in $1,000 suits. They've come a long way from the Mao suits I used to remember." Vangelis Giannakaros, the former China Country Manager for the Economist Corporate Networks based in Beijing, who has more than 20 years of experience in the China market, offers a useful analogy when referring to business practices in the less developed areas of western China: "If you want to know what things were like in Beijing and Shanghai ten years ago, just go to the western interior of China today and you will see."

Anecdotal information should really be used for reference purposes only. **The objective of *China Streetsmart* is to provide you with a framework for how your particular business objectives may be accomplished within a Chinese context by stimulating your thinking through real life examples**, and to let you judge whether these particular approaches or tactics are applicable to your own business situation. If this book has inspired you to think about an issue in a different way, it will have achieved its objectives.

Having managed departments of well over a hundred staff, I am expected to be the leader and teach. Often instead, I find myself the student, as some of the excellent staff in China I have had the privilege to work with have often taught me more than, I am humbled to say, I have given in return. For this reason, I strove to get a good cross section of experiences and differing levels of management. Hundreds of interviews have been conducted with staff ranging from CEO and Regional Managing Director levels, to line management business directors like myself, to sole proprietors and frontline local managers.

China Streetsmart focuses on the valuable lessons learned from on-the-ground experience. The book is not meant to be an exposé highlighting the follies and blunders of companies and individuals. In the beer industry, for example, we certainly made our share of mistakes and I would have to own up to my personal share. I have a high level of respect for my esteemed colleagues and their efforts. In fact, trial and error was often how we learned about the market. Recently, I was in a meeting with the former marketing director at Carlsberg where I was her counterpart when I was working at Foster's a number of years back. Although we had never met previously, we really felt like we knew each other, given the "famous" marketing battles we used to wage against one another on the streets of Shanghai. It was similar to war veterans from both sides of a conflict speaking to each other, years after the battles were fought. You cannot help but develop deep admiration and respect for each other. Often when I get nostalgic about my beer battle days, I'll give Jesper Madsen, the Managing Director for Carlsberg Greater China, or Phil Davis, the Managing Director for Anheuser-Busch Asia, a ring to go out and have a few "cold ones" to reminisce about the good old days.

My objective in speaking with these often high-level executives is to gain from their experience and be able to pass it on in a practical manner. Often, however, I am confronted with the sensitive issue of corporate confidentiality. Many corporations, often some of the most well-known and largest multinationals operating in China, have strict policies on what can and cannot be published and also who can and cannot speak on the company's behalf. It's perfectly easy to understand that companies do not want their dirty laundry being hung out for the public to see – especially if they are publicly listed. If I had to follow corporate guidelines and go through each of their public relations departments, most of the good and valuable experience would not be able to be included in this book. So for example, when I mention that there is this General Manager who works for a major multinational soft drink company, and he learned from this or that mistake, my objective is for the reader to pay attention to the lessons learned, rather than for people to try and figure out whether I am talking about Coca-Cola or Pepsi.

The book is divided into three parts: Part I is *The Approach*, which explains how to be effective in China; Part II is *The Application*, which shows how to be profitable; and Part III is *The Outlook*, which shows how to be strategic. The challenge for any business book on China is to how to summarise all that is said and known about China in a practical, easy-to-use guide. The Approach is built on an observed pattern of action steps which some of the more successful executives follow. **The methods presented are not about getting around the regulations, but rather about how to deal with them effectively using an easy-to-understand framework, based on six action steps.** What really makes an executive or company effective in China may be contrary to some of the stories you hear, which is why it is important to demystify all the talk around much talked-about issues, such as the importance of *guanxi* (relationships) and language, which is why I deal with these topics first.

The Application profiles a detailed case study on how one particular company has effectively followed the *China Streetsmart* approach and as a result has always been profitable in China. Many case studies do not go in-depth enough to allow readers to understand how to effectively handle the specific problems one can expect to face in China. There were many excellent companies and executives I could have profiled in detail, such as Siemens Switchgear and Emil Schlumpf, its General Manager for eight years (who headed arguably Siemens's most successful joint venture in China) or Mark DeCocinis, the General Manager of the Portman Ritz-Carlton, winner of the Best Employer in Asia for 2001, the first ever for a China-based company. The company I chose to highlight is Shanghai Portola Packaging and its General Manager, Michael Colozzi. Shanghai Portola Packaging began as a joint venture, failed to work adequately with their local partner and now operates as a wholly owned foreign enterprise. The key point of Portola is they have always been profitable in China because they followed a *China Streetsmart* approach.

The Outlook takes a much broader view of China and is meant to help foreign investors understand some of the major challenges China faces with the aim of helping them set the right long-term risk and reward investment strategy. Before examining the challenges, one first needs to adopt the appropriate perspective of looking at China. Understanding the motivations of the government will also help predict how they may react to issues that affect investments in China. Furthermore, it is critical for the investors to have a degree of confidence that the data presented is reliable and if not, what is the best way to utilise the myriad of facts and figures being presented.

Not everyone has an optimistic view of China's future. In fact, there are some who predict many troubles ahead. I take a contrarian view to critics I refer to as harbingers of doom who predict scenarios such as China's entry into the World Trade Organisation ultimately bringing about the collapse of China. Nevertheless, to be Streetsmart it is important to understand their arguments to prevent forming blind optimism about China – a mistake made by many of the earlier foreign investors. To create a more balanced perspective, one should take note of the very many positive trends also emerging. How one views these positive and negative trends emerging in China is very much dependent on one's perspective of looking at the facts. **Streetsmart investors are generally cautious optimists.** While it is important to acknowledge the real risks and dangers of investing in China, within every crisis is an opportunity and it will be those who can think out of the box that will benefit most.

No one can accurately predict which direction China will ultimately take. Even the best China hands have been surprised, therefore it would not be realistic to say the contributors know better. One of my favourite sayings is **"There is no such thing as a China Expert, only people with varying degrees of ignorance ..."** But one thing for certain is that foreign investment will play a role in shaping that ultimate outcome. Following the *China Streetsmart* approach, foreign investors will ensure they profit from China and China will profit from the wealth of experience they bring – an ideal win-win scenario. The positive effects FDI has had and will continue to have on China's future generations, who are far more open-minded and adaptable than their predecessors, suggest a re-emerging China that is open to the world. This openness will not only be good for its own citizens, but also for the world.

Acknowledgements

A book that is the result of interaction with hundreds upon hundreds of contributors, participants, influencers and supporters, it becomes almost impossible to try and mention and thank each person specifically. Some books try to mention everybody and the acknowledgements section ends up as streams and streams of names, but inevitably there are always key people that should be thanked, but for some reason get missed. I certainly want to avoid upsetting those who have helped so much and to be fair, I'm not quite sure where to draw the line, since a real thank-you would mean going beyond just the formal interviewees. *China Streetsmart* is really the culmination of efforts by people who have not only explicitly offered their valuable China knowledge, but also those who supported and influenced me over the years to reach this exciting point of fulfilling a lifelong dream. For example, one of the first people I want to mention is Professor Victor Falkenheim, Chair of the East Asian Department at the University of Toronto, for getting me started.

Next I want to thank my former bosses throughout my career who have taught me a great deal and have had a great influence on my life. Specific mention goes to Dave Thomson of Imperial Oil (Exxon), who gave me my break to come to China; James Cheng, who gave me my first consulting contracts in China; Alan Reid, Jim King and Mark Prechelt, whom I'd learned so much from while at Foster's; Jim O'Mahoney, for his leadership while at Lion Nathan; and Kiron Chatterjee and S.I. Lee for their support and for making the topsy-turvy life in the dot-coms interesting and fun while at Asia Online.

Special thanks go to Jerry McLean and Mark Langhammer, who helped me establish critical initial contacts; Willy Wo-Lap Lam of CNN, who helped me find my publisher; Lois Dougan-Tretiak of The Economist Group; Patrick Powers of the US China Business Council and Ken Davies of the OECD, who offered me great advice for proofreading the manuscript; Gillian Chee, Irene Yeow and Pauline Chua at Pearson Education Asia; and of course the hundreds of interviewees, participants and supporters, a fraction of whom have been mentioned publicly in the book due to space and confidentiality. You certainly know who you are and I not only thank you for taking the time to contribute, but also for your friendship and continuing support.

Finally, I wish to thank my family and friends for their support. Fred Armentrout, the Publications Manager for the American Chamber of Commerce in Hong Kong, with more than 20 years in the publications business, was explaining to me what it is like to write a book when I first began my life-fulfilling project: "Do you know why guys always thank their wives? Because writing a book is really tough and the dedication, discipline and support required is tremendous." The writer often feels he is bobbing alone in a great open sea, but in reality it's usually his wife that keeps the ship afloat and the sextant pointing in the right direction. So the final special mention I need to make is to my dear wife, (Mary) Ma Xin, whose support has truly made this book possible. For this support, Xin, I can tell you with people around the world reading this, with love *thank you!*

1 | Introduction

Avoid making the same mistakes of past foreign investors.

Being *China Streetsmart*

What's the definition of being *China Streetsmart?* Well, the dictionary defines being streetsmart as possessing and exercising the knowledge and ability to survive in a hostile urban environment. Substitute *China* for the word *urban* and you've got the meaning and purpose of the book *China Streetsmart*.

Is China that hostile? Certainly in the early to mid-90s, most foreign companies didn't appear to think so. I find it amusing that in 1992, Barton Biggs, the Chief Economist at Morgan Stanley, made a statement that became famous when he said he was "maximum bullish" about China. The statement was a watershed in foreign investment in China. Soon after that remark was published, foreign direct investment (FDI) soared with FDI growing from 3 billion USD in 1991 to 53 billion USD in 2002 (see Figure 1.1). Today, China is the largest recipient of FDI in the world surpassing the US for the first time. A.T. Kearney's FDI Confidence Index which surveys the CEOs and CFOs of the top global 1,000 companies also supports this fact. An accumulative of more than 448 billion USD in FDI have been invested in China since the Open Door Policy began.[1] With China's entry into the World Trade Organisation (WTO), the lead-up to the 2008 Olympics in Beijing and the 2010 World's Fair in Shanghai, some experts are predicting FDI to soar to 100 billion USD each year between 2006 and 2010.[2]

---

[1] Ministry of Foreign Trade and Economic Cooperation, Foreign Direct Investment Statistics: http://www.chinafdi.gov.cn/english/O1/f/22/12.htm

[2] *China Daily*, 2 January 2003, "Annual FDI to hit US$100 b", http:/www1.chinadaily.com.cn/cndy/2003-01-02/99823.html

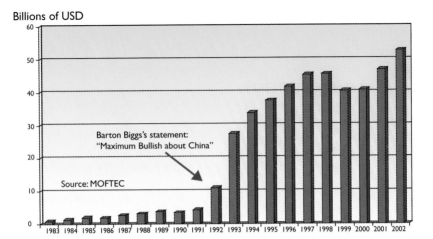

Billions of USD

Barton Biggs's statement:
"Maximum Bullish about China"

Source: MOFTEC

Figure 1.1   Foreign Direct Investment in China

The 80s: New Beginnings, New Challenges

It is amusing to note how easily we forget our history lessons regarding FDI in China, which officially has 662 cities (see Figure 1.2).
Wave after wave of companies entered China over the past two decades, not bothering to learn from the lessons of the past. The first
wave began soon after the Open Door Policy was promulgated at
the Third Plenum of the 11th Communist Party of China (CPC) Central Committee in December 1978, to re-allow foreign investment
in China. Foreign companies numbering in the thousands came rushing into China. The promise of one billion "anything" was the
catchphrase of the day. Executives would spout the common phrase,
"Can you imagine if everyone in China bought, consumed, or used
this or that?" What really happened, after these companies started
actual negotiations with Mainland Chinese companies and got past
the "new friend of China" rhetoric, was a very tough and drawn-out
negotiation process. Contracts often got cancelled at the last moment in favour of another (foreign) competitor, who was willing to
undercut their contract terms, once the Chinese leaked the terms of
their offer.

However, some companies in this first wave were successful.
Having persevered through difficult negotiations and tough business conditions, they are now benefiting from their efforts. One of
the best examples is the American International Assurance (AIA)
Insurance group, a wholly owned subsidiary of American Interna-

China Streetsmart

Figure 1.2   Major Cities in Greater China

China officially has 662 cities with 166 cities with populations over 1 million. Most of the listed cities in this map are actually prefectures that also have several satellite cities under their administration. Four cities (Beijing, Tianjin, Shanghai and Chongqing) carry national administration status equivalent to a province.

tional Group, Inc. (AIG). In the 90s, most foreign insurance companies were struggling to get a licence and lobbying the government by spending millions to show they were a "good friend" of China. They invested in university programmes, training projects and other large-scale infrastructure projects. AIG enjoyed a virtual monopoly from foreign competition in Shanghai to sell life insurance policies because they were one of the early entrants in China. In 1994–1995, I was a consultant helping Lincoln National Life Insurance Co. from Fort Wayne, Indiana, lobby the central government for a licence to sell life insurance. We were all envious of AIG, as we saw them taking a huge market share and making huge inroads into China, while Lincoln sat on the sidelines in their lonely representative office. Why was AIG so successful? There are a number of reasons, but two key factors Maurice "Hank" Greenberg, CEO of AIG, often gives are patience and a step-by-step approach, so that one does not blindly rush into China.[3] Other large multinationals, such as Coca-Cola and Pepsi,

---

[3] John B. Studdard, 2000. *The New Silk Road*, p. 40, New York: John Wiley & Sons.

remain the kingpins in China's soft drink industry. Guy Chambers, General Manager of Customer Development at Swire Beverages, the largest Coca-Cola bottler in China, estimates that [the equivalent of] 25 million cans of Coke are consumed every day. McDonald's and Tricon's Kentucky Fried Chicken (KFC) and Pizza Hut are other model success stories. Today, every day, somewhere in China, a new McDonald's, KFC or Pizza Hut opens its doors.

Yet in the early 80s, quite a few companies walked away from China empty-handed. Many complained about the lack of business ethics in leaking their quotes to competitors to get the best price. Others complained about the utter confusion within the government bureaucracy and how long it took to get things done, while others were simply shocked as to how tough it was to negotiate with the Mainland Chinese. Even Chinese businesspeople from Hong Kong, Taiwan or Singapore, for example, would experience similar frustration. Foreigners were even more culture-shocked and often stunned by the negotiation tactics of the Mainland Chinese, which ranged from continual cancellation or postponement of the meetings, to outright emotional outbursts by the Chinese negotiation team and their walking out of meetings. The fact that there were huge language and cultural differences, coupled with the fact that there were few competent translators at the time, only exacerbated the issue. Was China a hostile environment to do business in then? While I would not consider it hostile, the China market was certainly very, very difficult.

Photographs by John L. Chan

These pictures show the first KFC and Pizza Hut stores to open in China (Beijing) during the early 90s. KFC's three-storey flagship is located just south of Tiananmen Square, while Pizza Hut's first store is located in the Embassy District.

In the 90s, a decade after the Open Door Policy, the FDI climate, while still tough, improved dramatically. Flourishing were Special Economic Zones (SEZ), such as Shenzhen, and Open (Coastal) Cities, such as Shanghai, that attracted the bulk of FDI in China (see Figure 1.3). However, during the 90s, a new problem emerged in China, which I can directly relate to from my time working in China's beer industry – hyper-competition and massive oversupply. Working in China's beer industry from 1996 to 2000, I witnessed firsthand the explosion of foreign brewers onto the scene. Prior to 1990, there were less than a handful of foreign brewing joint ventures (JVs). By 1997, there were more than 100. In the early 90s, China's beer sector was growing at 30% a year. During the early half of the 90s, Chinese breweries could not produce enough beer to meet the burgeoning demand. Foreign brewers, who had made huge capital investments with an estimate of more than 2 billion USD invested in China,[4] saw the answer to profitability was simply to increase capacity. However, like the old adage that one person standing up in a movie theatre might get a great view, if everybody does it, there is a potential for chaos. By the end of the 90s, China's beer sector went from a situation of undersupply to one of massive oversupply. In markets like Shanghai, production capacity was up to three to four times the market demand and chaos ensued.

The beer industry was not the only industry to suffer from hyper-competition and massive oversupply. Colour television sets, air conditioners and white good appliances, for example, suffered from this fate as well. During the 80s, television sets were the first large ticketed item people bought with their newfound wealth. Today, out of the 351 million registered households in China, on average, every household has a television set (see Table C.4 in Appendix C), yet manufacturers continued to produce and the overproduction has

---

[4] These estimates are based on conversations with China beer expert Glen Steinman. My personal knowledge can attest that the investments of Foster's, Lion Nathan and Anheuser-Busch alone total about half a billion USD. When you then add South African Breweries, Asahi, Suntory, Carlsberg, APB, San Miguel and Suntory, for example, which all have invested in multi-breweries, 2 billion USD is probably a very conservative figure.

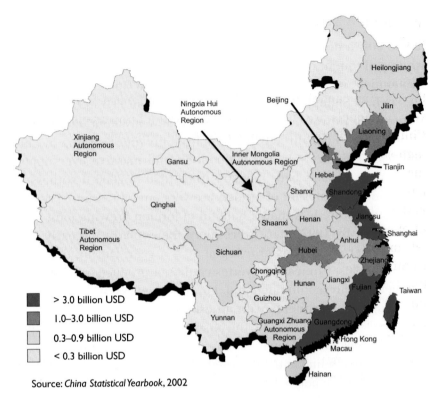

Source: *China Statistical Yearbook*, 2002

Figure 1.3   Foreign Direct Investment in China by Area

Guangdong province attracts a quarter of China's FDI (25%) while the city of Shanghai is the single largest recipient (9%), more than double that of Beijing (4%).

led to vicious price wars. In fact, in many sectors, including almost every consumer goods category, there is oversupply. Industry analysts in many sectors do not know when the situation will improve. The problem of overcapacity in the beer industry, for example, is not expected to improve for at least another five to ten years. Professor Philip Kotler, Distinguished Professor of International Marketing at the Kellogg School at Northwestern University, talks about the Rule of Three, that in any competitive sector you cannot have more than three major competitors in any given segment.[5] The rest,

---

[5] I finally got to meet the famous Professor Philip Kotler, known as the "Father of Modern Marketing" at a marketing seminar in Shanghai on 24 October 2001. He spoke about the theory of the Rule of Three, which is actually sourced from Jagdish N. Sheth and Rajendra S. Sisodia, *The Rule of Three: Surviving and Thriving in Competitive Markets*, The Free Press, 2001.

China Streetsmart

in order to survive, must either become niche specialists or "get out".

In the case of the beer industry, rationalisation means consolidation and/or the closing of doors. Becoming niche players, when the original capital investment was geared on mass-market, high-volume models, was not sustainable. Foreign brewers operating in China and realising this danger during the mid-90s began a very high-stake poker game of bluffing to become one of the surviving three: "I can sustain huge losses because I have deep pockets and am committed to China's long-term potential. I will continue to invest in China for however long it takes, so you had better fold." One by one, foreign brewers folded or scaled back their investments and left millions on the table. Having worked in this industry on the frontlines, battling these worthy competitors, I can attest firsthand that the China market was hostile. So hostile were these battles that literally physical fights would break out among beer promotion or push-girls between competing brewers across various cities in China.

Whether one refers to China as a hostile environment or simply a very tough market to do business in, Streetsmart advice learned from real life experiences will help tremendously. **The contributors to *China Streetsmart* show clearly, that with the right approach, it is possible to set up and run profitable businesses in China's challenging political economy both in the short and long term.**

Managing Information: Deciphering What's True and Relevant

Vet the stories you hear about China using a simple four-step process.

One of the biggest challenges with doing business in China is knowing how to decipher the plethora of information and keep up with the continual change. Infrastructure, regulations, laws, consumer habits and business culture, for example, change rapidly and at differing rates across a huge geography. As a result, varying levels of understanding about China and interpretation based on personal biases can create a lot of misinformation and misunderstandings, resulting in contradictions and paradoxes. China is so complex that overgeneralisation or oversimplification can be dangerous. **The first mistake many uninformed people and books make about China**

is to treat it as if it were a single market. A common theme stressed throughout this book is that China's differences in language, culture and geography are as diverse as Europe's. Therefore, before analysing the specifics of what is being said, the *China Streetsmart* approach is to judge whether those statements being made are true or more importantly, relevant. To do this, people need to ask four basic questions:

Question 1: When did the story or information received happen?

The first question to ask is what period the story or information refers to. For example, those who complain about how they had to "bribe" people or treat people to lavish banquets and give expensive gifts to get major deals signed and licensing approvals issued are often referring to the early days of the Open Door Policy, where for bureaucrats, still "fresh" from the cultural revolution, going through the back door, or *houmen* (pronounced "ho-men" in Mandarin), was often how things got done. **To assume China is a corrupt culture where bribes MUST be made in order for things to get done is FALSE.** Unfortunately, graft and corruption still exist throughout China, but as you will learn, regulations and penalties have tightened up significantly, making it far more difficult than it used to be. Another common complaint heard, which is less relevant today, is the difficulties foreign companies have in working with their local JV. In the past, the only investment option available was through a local JV partner and unfortunately, there were limited experienced or suitable JV partners to choose from. Today, after more than 20 years of exposure to FDI, a vast selection of JV partners are available, ranging from experienced state-owned enterprises (SOEs) to a growing number of sophisticated local private companies. Furthermore, wholly owned foreign enterprises (WOFEs) or "Woofies", as they are affectionately known, are permitted in many sectors, bypassing the need for local partnership and as WTO regulations take effect, this will only improve.

This picture of Shanghai shows the enormous change China has undergone over the past decade. The areas in yellow show the height of the original buildings in Shanghai prior to 1992. Everything else was built over the past ten years. The areas in red are new construction sites about to be filled with new high-rise buildings. This picture looks north away from the downtown core where there are even more impressive buildings and high-rises.

Question 2: Where does this story or information take place?

Understanding the differences in China's geographical markets is an important theme of *China Streetsmart*. It is important to determine if a story applies to a large urban setting, where officials and businesspeople are more sophisticated, compared to a rural area, where education levels and exposure to international business practices are low, as the outcomes can be quite different. Cultural differences also vary widely over China's vast geography. Guangdong province, in the South of China, which has attracted about 30% of China's total FDI,[6] is very much influenced by Hong Kong businessmen who like to move fast and cut corners. In Beijing, the bureaucracy is very different and whom you know often plays a critical role in getting things approved, especially in areas where policy is often vague and confusing. Shanghai is perhaps the most sophisticated and most familiar to Western business practices. It is no surprise that Shanghai is the single largest urban recipient of foreign investment, about double that of Beijing[7] (see Figure 1.3).

---

[6] CEIC Asian Economic Database. In 2000, FDI and other investments totalled 13 billion USD for Guangdong vs 42 billion USD for the total China market.

[7] CEIC Asian Economic Database. In 2000, FDI and other Investments totalled 3.2 billion USD for Shanghai vs 1.7 billion UDS for Beijing.

Question 3: Who are the Mainland Chinese involved?

People also need to understand how the generational differences in China affect the information received. Those over 40 years old in China, and now in leading positions in companies and the government, were all veterans or victims of the Cultural Revolution. Many lost their chance of a formal education and got to their senior positions through a self-learned process of opportunistic survival. This group has developed a very different mindset from those in their 20s and 30s, who barely remember or care to remember the Cultural Revolution. Many of the younger generation don't even care to think about the Tiananmen student uprisings in 1989. This younger group, or children of the single-child policy or the S-generation, are the new wave of an open China that will set the tone for future generations. Growing up in a narrowly confined space with not two parents, but up to six (counting two sets of grandparents) catering to their every whim, creates a new generational attitude of "Little Emperors and Empresses" who are far more open, optimistic and demanding than their parents' generation and who are now impacting how China cooperates with the West. **Therefore, the stories of the past, referring to an older generation's thinking and management style will unlikely affect the future.**

Question 4: Who are the foreigners involved?

A final note about understanding the people dynamics in the stories you hear about China is to keep in mind who is being represented on the foreign side. To say the Chinese are prejudicial against a certain race or country is wrong, but the natural fact is that inexperience in dealing with foreigners by most Mainland Chinese can cause them to behave differently towards a "foreign face" compared to a Chinese face, like myself. Stereotypes also affect behaviour. Not all American men are Sylvester Stallones and American women, Madonnas, but Hollywood does have a powerful influence on local impressions – especially if movies are the only link with the West. As a result, false impressions and double standards are ripe in China that could influence behaviour towards foreigners either favourably or unfavourably. For example, some Mainland Chinese have the impression that America often tries to suppress China with constant accusations of human rights and political abuses. As a result, those who feel this way may take a tougher stance to show Americans they can also be tough and will not be pushed around. Politics can influence a deal either favourably or unfavourably – especially as the value of the investment grows, such as the case when China deals with Boeing and Airbus. These cases are certainly not the norm, but business can be influenced by the political climate at the time. For example, after the NATO bombing of the Chinese Embassy in Belgrade, American products were briefly boycotted and American advertisements pulled off the air. Regardless of right or wrong or the political view, it is good to keep in mind these potential biases by developing a deeper understanding of the Mainland Chinese by looking at China's past, which is covered in Appendix B – A Historical *China Streetsmart* Primer.

A Practical Approach to a Constantly Changing China

The more information you can sieve through using this four-question approach, the better you are able to piece together the complex puzzle China is. While I would partially agree that most China business books become dated after only a few years because the economy develops so quickly and rules and regulations change so often, a practical streetsmart common-sense approach to China should be less capricious. My guidepost for the book is the word *practical* and to be practical, the information must not only be easy to use and adopt, but also relevant for some time to come. You do not need to become a Sinologist to be effective in China. The *China Streetsmart* approach suggests that **you do not need to become something different to be successful in China; rather, the common element needed is what everyone, regardless of background or nationality, already possesses – and that is common sense.**

Therefore, the book can be summed up in a single sentence:

"The biggest secret of doing business in China is – there is no secret; it is just plain common sense."

PART I

The Approach

In this section you will learn how to be effective in China, specifically:

- To follow the action steps based on the best practices of some of the most successful business leaders in China.

- To clarify myths and misperceptions regarding much talked-about facets of doing business in China, such as *guanxi*.

- To understand why some companies fail or succeed.

- To understand the differences between Western and Chinese management and negotiation styles.

2 | The Practical *China Streetsmart* Approach

An Easy-to-Use Toolkit for the Foreign Executive

To develop the *China Streetsmart* approach, I conducted hundreds of interviews with successful (and not-so-successful) business leaders in China. Interestingly, many of these executives would begin the interview by saying, "Well, I think my situation is quite unique ..." when in reality they were quite similar to others and paralleled my own business experience in China. After about 50 interviews and hearing a similar story and situation repeated over and over, definite patterns began to emerge as to what were the more successful universal practices or action steps business leaders operating in China followed. The conclusion to my findings is what I call the *China Streetsmart* approach, which consists of six universally applicable easy-to-follow action steps that are based simply on common sense. While these common-sense action steps may seem too basic to mention as a serious business strategy for companies to follow, examining each step closely will explain why many of the companies who are complaining about how difficult it is to do business in China have failed. While the logic in pointing out why they failed now appears obvious on hindsight, apparently it wasn't so clear for these original investors, and one of the goals of *China Streetsmart* is to prevent repeating their mistakes.

The six universally applicable common-sense action steps the most successful executives and companies practise to be effective in China are simply:

1. Maintain management consistency – own up to mistakes and manage expectations
2. Be flexible and adaptable – develop based on local needs
3. Be patient and thorough – wait for the right moment to strike
4. Think win-win – but develop respect and trust first

5. Be detailed – clarity prevents problems
6. Maintain a healthy attitude – choose your battles carefully

To think of these six universally applicable action steps as good habits or business practices to adopt, not only as a major strategy, but also a daily approach to living and working in China, will increase your effectiveness tremendously and set the basis on how to build a profitable company.

A key word to note is the word *universal*. The determining factor in deciding what made the list of universally applicable action steps to follow was judged on practicality and universality, i.e., good for business executives regardless of ethnic background or origin. There are a number of other important business practices or seemingly obvious skills to have that did not make this universal list, highlighting a lot of the myths and misunderstandings of what people really need to succeed in China. For example, a non-Chinese Western expatriate, in China for only a short period of time, may deal with issues of *guanxi*, language and listening skills differently from one who has Chinese roots like myself and is committed to being in China for the long term. As a result, it is not surprising that many Hong Kong businesspeople place far more importance on *guanxi* than Westerners. To overgeneralise and set these business practices or skills as "universal" action steps that everyone needs to follow in the same way is wrong.

Before beginning the explanation of the six universal action steps, it will help your understanding of China to first focus on the common myths and misunderstandings surrounding *guanxi*, language and listening skills. They have often been touted to be *the* most important skills every business leader needs to have to be able to be effective in China – which is not necessarily true. It is important to understand how these myths and misunderstandings developed, because they all have elements of truth. To avoid the dangers of overgeneralisation, clarification is needed when discussing the need and application of good *guanxi*, language and listening skills in a Chinese context. *China Streetsmart* clarifies these misunderstandings and enables one to decide whether to include these practices as part of their overall strategic approach to China. For most non-Chinese executives, these business practices or skills to develop often fail the universal practicality test.

Finally, whether you believe that *guanxi*, language and listening skills or the six *China Streetsmart* action steps are what should constitute your basic toolkit to be effective in China, it is important to keep in mind that they are all still merely tools. **The ultimate goal remains to set up a profitable business – which is accomplished by developing the best products and services suitable for the local market – and to find and develop the best people to carry out the plans.**

3 | The Importance of (Demystifying) *Guanxi*

Debunking the Myths and Misunderstandings Surrounding One of the Most Talked-about Features of Doing Business in China

What is *guanxi* (pronounced "gwan shee" in Mandarin)? The word simply means relationships. People often highlight the building up of *guanxi* or relationships in China as *the* single most important skill for businesspeople to develop while doing business in China. In fact, a survey was conducted where a number of leading Hong Kong businesspeople were surveyed and *guanxi* often ranked the most important business practice they felt they needed to develop to be successful in China.[1] I have listened to many businesspeople talk about the secret to doing business in China, saying that "it all boils down to *guanxi*". But is *guanxi* really at the heart of all business transactions in China? The short answer is often yes, but to be *China Streetsmart*, this answer requires clarification and explanation to avoid the wrong assumptions, such as if you've got good *guanxi* you will be able to run a profitable company – this is *wrong*. As the previous chapter emphasised, *guanxi* is basically a tool or a means rather than an end. **The real factor that will determine whether you are able to run a profitable business remains in your company being able to develop the best products and services that best meet the local needs.** Without this, not even the best *guanxi* will save you. Therefore, there is more to *guanxi* than a simple sweeping statement. In fact, if not fully understood, *guanxi* can work against you and your company.

---

[1] Irene Y. M. Yeung and Rosalie L. Tung, Autumn 1996, "Achieving Business Success in Confucian Societies: The Importance of Guanxi (Connections)", *Organizational Dynamics*, p. 60.

Since *guanxi* is at the heart of (almost) all business transactions in Chinese society, why not add practising *guanxi* to the list of six universally applicable *China Streetsmart* action steps for a foreign executive operating in China to follow? The major reason is that it is difficult and takes time to develop, and people have been successful in China without having to practise it religiously. **Many people do not understand what real *guanxi* is.** Some people think of *guanxi* as simply a reciprocation of favours through a network of contacts. Worse still, others think you can "buy" *guanxi* and often complain when it doesn't seem to work. While there is an action of reciprocation of favours, it is not based on "tit for tat" or simply a process of "I'll scratch your back if you scratch mine". One of the key elements not clearly understood by foreigners is the importance of "respect" in the context of Confucian values, which contain elements of hierarchy, obligation and "face".

I am not saying *guanxi* is not important; on the contrary, **if real *guanxi* is built up in its proper sense, *guanxi* could very well prove to be the most valuable tool for a person to have in China.** But the foreign executive is unlikely to learn this ancient practice quickly as it often takes years of understanding and practice to master. Over time, foreigners are as capable as anyone to learn the art of practising real *guanxi*. For example, Laurence Brahm, an American lawyer, political economist, writer and friend, is a great practitioner of *guanxi* and a significant contributor to this book. But Laurence has been here since the 80s and now has excellent *guanxi* – good enough that he could ask Prime Minister Zhu Rongji and other top government officials to contribute to his books. I jokingly call him China's modern-day Edgar Snow.

The misunderstandings and myths stem from the fact that on the surface, *guanxi* does appear to be very straightforward. But after having interviewed a lot of foreign executives on this important subject, many do not really seem to understand that *guanxi* is more than a reciprocal act; but as just mentioned, it contains the Confucian elements of respect, hierarchy, obligation and face. Having grown up in the West for most of my life, I can understand why many Westerners would find these Confucian-based values difficult to accept, let alone grasp, because this is not the way they were likely raised. Complicating this slightly foreign concept is the fact

Long-time China hand Laurence Brahm runs the Red Capital Club and Residence in Beijing. Two classic courtyard houses have been converted into a popular restaurant (the Red Capital Club) whose menu contains the favourites of China's past leaders and a small boutique hotel (the Residence) furnished with classic Chinese furniture and paraphernalia from China's recent past. The photo on the right is the must-see underground bomb shelter now converted into a bar at the Red Capital Residence. Each of his guestrooms is uniquely styled and named after a modern historic figure in China. Not surprisingly one of his guestrooms is called the Edgar Snow Room.

that Mainland Chinese culture and society have, over the past 30–50 years, been subjected to ideological thinking quite different to the original values upon which real *guanxi* principles were built. **Some people have confused the practices of real *guanxi* with giving short-term favours and playing the back door game.**

Guanxi and Confucianism

I promise not to get too theoretical, but one cannot avoid the challenges and need to explain Confucian values when trying to explain Chinese thinking and how it differs from thinking in the West. If practised and learned properly, *guanxi* could be your most valuable tool in China – it is just not practical for the non-Chinese businessperson operating in China for only a short period and not absolutely necessary if he sticks to the six universally applicable *China Streetsmart* action steps discussed shortly. Here is my simplified, but formal way of explaining *guanxi*:

> *Guanxi* is a relationship built on a practised form of respect and obligation that adheres to Confucian hierarchical values where favours are given and received only when there is mutual benefit involved and in accordance to how people conduct themselves based on the five sets of formal relationships set out by Confucius: Man

and the state; Man and his wife; Man and his siblings; Man and his children; and Man and his friends. Each relationship has its own set of social rules and conduct. If one side benefits too much, then it is the obligation of the other to correct it or not proceed with taking the benefit since it is always the obligator who loses face when things are not balanced.

While growing up, I had no idea my parents were teaching me Confucian values; rather, simply because I was "Chinese" this is what we did. For example, to this day I feel it is improper to address my older siblings by their given names and will feel like I was doing something wrong, similar to addressing the Queen of England as "Liz". Instead, it is proper to only address those older than you by their title *Gege* (Older Brother) or *Jiejie* (Older Sister), while my older siblings can refer to me as John, "Johnny Boy", "Meathead", or whatever name they can think of. Although they could get away with picking on me, as they often did when I was a kid (and still do), they were also obligated to look after me, and my welfare was their responsibility. I had to serve them, but they had to look after me. The parent-child relationship also develops along similar lines in Chinese society, which is why few parents of Chinese children eventually live in senior citizen homes – to do so would cause great shame and loss of face to the whole family. More importantly, this ancient practice also extends to traditional Chinese management practices. The practice of loyal service to your boss (not the company) in return for being taken care of is still very much imbued in Chinese business circles.

The practice of *guanxi* is not necessarily exclusive to the Chinese either. It may be called by a different name in other cultures, but my European friends tell me that this practice is quite common. Guy Bouchet, from France, Vice President and General Manager of A.T. Kearney in China, has lived and worked in Africa, Europe, North America, and now Asia. He comments, "Only in Anglo-speaking cultures such as North America, UK and Australasia is *guanxi* really unfamiliar. I was born in Casablanca, North Africa, and many of the practices I was brought up with, I find here in China. These ancient practices started in the East, and flowed west gradually. America is actually at the end of mankind's civilised development, not the beginning."

Photograph by Guy Bouchet

Guy Bouchet, Vice President and General Manager of A.T. Kearney, China.

However, even growing up in North America, I often think about stories from the small farming communities where if one farmer needed help, all the other local farmers would naturally assist, be it to rebuild a barn or plough a field. Confucianism is a form of living one's life in society, where if everyone follows these principles, everyone can live in harmony. There are no rules or written contracts among these American farmers that state, "If I help you rebuild your barn, then you've got to come over to plough my field." People just remember the good deeds and favours bestowed upon them and should there be a day when they would need a favour, they could always count on the others coming to their aid. In Chinese and other Asian cultures there are strong similarities. "I only wish we had this practice more in the cities," sighed one American executive. "These were the values [of helping out your neighbour] I believe America was built upon."

Practising Real *Guanxi* vs Buying Short-Term Favours and the Back Door Game

Not all Westerners have experienced real *guanxi* in China, which confuses their understanding. I was explaining this practice to an American friend, Richard Tomlinson, a former senior Boeing engineer and who now runs a software development company between China and the US. He has been in China for about three years and is married to a local Shanghainese woman who works at an American law firm. "I hate this obligation thing," he exclaimed. "I have had so many times people here in China take you out for dinner and the next week they are on the phone asking me if I can get them or their kids a visa to go to the States." My reply was he was under no obligation to try and get them visas since the reciprocation was clearly out of balance and that individual should have been ashamed for asking in the first place.

My personal example involves Marshall Xu Xiangqian, one of the "ten legendary" military leaders of the Chinese Revolution who eventually went on to become Vice Premier and Minister of Defence of China, and his family. His son and son-in-law both did their postgraduate studies in Canada and while they were in Canada, because of my family's *guanxi*, they stayed with my family and my father was their guardian. Now that I am living in China, would I attempt to use that relationship for personal gain or business advantage? No, because this would be an abuse of the relationship. There certainly would not be mutual benefit involved because I know I would not be in the position to repay such a favour and I would be the one to lose face. Practising real *guanxi* involves understanding and respecting the positions and benefits of both sides.

I thought about the situation Richard complained about and concluded that the actions by the local Mainland Chinese he encountered could either be a possible corruption of Confucian principles, given the Communist era of opportunistic survival people learned during the Cultural Revolution, for example, or they simply might be following a double standard, believing they could get away with not following the "proper rules of conduct" simply because he was a foreigner. As shocking as it may sound, I often come across Mainland Chinese, with very little outside exposure to foreigners, treating foreign faces differently, either overfavourably or the opposite – simply out of ignorance. The main point is this practice is *not* real *guanxi*.

Practising real *guanxi* is really an art that takes time for people to understand if they have never been exposed to it before, since there are no crystal-clear rules how we need to conduct ourselves in any given situation. It is this lack of transparency that often bothers a lot of foreigners coming to China. But with that being said, **if you have true *guanxi*, there will be nothing stronger in China, going beyond any contractual piece of paper.** Once again, the key words to keep in mind are mutual benefit, respect, understanding and obligation.

Foreign businesspeople often come across local or overseas Chinese businesspeople boasting about whom they know and how they can get things done more quickly than most people. Sometimes this is true; often this is not. A person with real *guanxi* will rarely talk about whom they know. The *China Streetsmart* approach when a *guanxi* peddler approaches you with an offer that says they can get things processed through the bureaucracy in a much quicker time for a "fee" is to walk away – unless you like to gamble. What that person is really often suggesting is that he or she knows whom to bribe or pay off to get things done. This is not real *guanxi*; this is the buying of short-term favours and the results are at best mixed – and a gamble. China is changing so rapidly that those who are in power and authority to grant certain approvals or "chops" might not be there the following year. There are a lot of short-term opportunists out there trying to make a quick buck and I have unfortunately come across many situations when money was given to an individual with supposedly great *guanxi* to be used for "entertainment" purposes, only to have the deal take as long as they originally anticipated. If that person had real *guanxi* he would likely not have to really need to entertain (bribe/pay off) in the first place. But the foreign manager will never really know what happened. *Guanxi* peddlers are often no more than paid lobbyists who often haven't a clue nor real care about your business objectives, rather what they can get out of the deal for themselves.

How to Develop *Guanxi* as an Effective Tool

Taking a slight tangent away from *guanxi*, let's try to understand why people need to employ so-called "well-connected" individuals in the first place. Most foreign companies coming to China for the first time view the Chinese bureaucracy much like people look at sending e-mail through the Internet. You just press the "send" button and it eventually gets to the target computer and when it doesn't, you haven't a clue what happened. Getting a business started, especially for complicated projects, often involves multi-ministries with different and occasionally competing departments. The Ministry of Foreign Trade and Economic Cooperation (MOFTEC), the State Administration for Industry and Commerce (SAIC), and the tax and customs bureaus are all under different departments and ministries, but are all critical to getting your business up and running. The hapless foreign company often has no idea where the delays are. Today the trend is for many ex-government bureaucrats to utilise their skills and connections to help companies navigate through the complex web of bureaucracy. Often top legal firms and other leading service companies employ these "true experts". A good example of this trend is Wang Lei, a locally educated lawyer who worked with MOFTEC from 1986 to 1996 and was a negotiator for China's entry into the World Trade Organisation (WTO) in Geneva (formerly the General Agreement on Tariffs and Trade (GATT) when he began working for MOFTEC from 1988 to 1994). He has been a Partner at both international and local law firms and now spends most of his time advising clients on exactly what he is an expert at – how to navigate and interpret China's complex bureaucracy and laws. Given China's entry into the WTO and his background as an actual WTO negotiator representing the Chinese side, I suspect Mr Wang will be busier than ever.

However, rather than hiring short-term intermediaries or worse still, *guanxi* peddlers, **the *China Streetsmart* approach to effectively manage governmental *guanxi* is to develop the capabilities in-house.** Employees with a good sense of the company's objectives are best able to ensure that the company is able to navigate through the complex bureaucratic web to meet its goals. Beware of people who say, "Oh you need to get 'such and such' done? Well I can introduce you to 'so and so' and (for a fee) he can help you get things done, the 'Chinese way' (wink wink)." Another effective way of working with the Chinese bureaucracy is to find a good local Chinese partner – this is a good reason why some foreign multinational corporations (MNCs) still prefer to maintain their local joint venture (JV) partnerships rather than move to wholly owned foreign enterprises (WOFEs).

Avoiding Over-Reliance on *Guanxi* by Buffering Enough Time

Another *China Streetsmart* approach would prefer to emphasise better planning or buffering of time. Often companies that resort to taking shortcuts by buying short-term favours to get things approved faster are doing so because their initial time schedules were not allocated correctly in the first place. **The *China Streetsmart* advice is to develop the skills of *Managing Expectations*** – an important skill for *China Streetsmart* business executives to practise, which is outlined in Action Step 1. Managing expectations in the time it takes to complete a project or get a project under way relieves a lot of pressure and temptations to take unnecessary shortcuts. Long delays can be expected in any developing economy where rules are fast changing and vague, and bureaucrats are afraid of making the wrong decision. For businesses setting up in new or sensitive areas such as telecommunications, banking and insurance, delays in approvals are common. The key is to plan or buffer enough time for these uncertainties.

Risks and Dangers of *Guanxi* in the Workplace

In terms of employee relationships, *guanxi* can damage a company if not managed properly. Given the importance of *guanxi* in Chinese society, it is not difficult to realise that personal loyalty goes far beyond company loyalty. Often what happens is the senior local Chinese managers cultivate strong relationships with their direct reports and should that senior local manager leave, he or she is likely to take a large portion of their staff with them on to their next assignment, suddenly leaving huge gaps of employees to fulfil, disrupting the business.

As I was relating this story to a sales director of a famous biscuit manufacturing company, he suddenly became very animated and said that was exactly what had happened to them as they were starting their operations a number of years back. They had hired this senior local sales manager who had his training with one of the major soft drink companies and could speak fluent English, which appealed to the overseas executives. The local senior sales manager then proceeded to build up the staff directly with his own *guanxi* network. In a short time, he had built up this sales force with people who were directly loyal to him, not to the company. Most of the employees came from his previous company. The company was originally pleased with the speed he built up the sales force, but later suspected the senior sales manager was making personal side deals with local distributors to get kickbacks. After being confronted and accused, the manager left and within one month, so did a majority of their sales force. In the end, the company was left with a huge disruption in sales and angry distributors not getting what they were promised from the company, since the sales manager had made all kinds of "hidden" promises the company simply could not honour.

The company was left to "sort out the mess". "In fact," the new sales director said, "it took us up to two years to completely recover and sort through the mess. It wasn't just the sales manager who caused all the problems, but his staff were likely in on the take as well." Hence an internal *guanxi*-oriented support group developed within this company, but for purposes contrary to the company's objectives.

Preventing companies from allowing employees to build their own "kingdoms" was a challenge for human resource (HR) executives in China during the 90s, given the lack of skilled employees available. Furthermore, even if only a single individual leaves, people need to keep in mind the strong *guanxi* that may have developed between the various employees, since this is one of the most frequent ways in which sensitive company information and trade secrets leave the company and get passed around to the competition. I have been both a victim and beneficiary of this practice of *guanxi*. If you want to know the sales of a competitor or what it is like to work for a competitor from the inside, all you need to do is to tap into one's *guanxi* network. This problem and practice often happens in the West as well and the steps to address them are no different.

Checks and balances need to be in place to prevent *guanxi* from potentially hurting the business. These methods include leaving the hiring decision to more than just the direct report, changing managerial heads to allow for greater experience among developing employees and increasing company-oriented activities to increase company loyalty and participation. The good news is that these principles are already practised in the West and so are not new for foreign managers to implement. Frankly speaking, I was amazed how even some of the largest and most reputable MNCs failed to set up these basic checks and balances when they first came to China, even though they have these policies in their home country. My guess is that because they were under so much pressure in the 90s to get the business going, frequent delays and being behind schedule, coupled with the shortage that existed for qualified staff, caused too many shortcuts to be made. One of the six *China Streetsmart* action steps to follow is avoid rushing into things before you are ready.

4 | The Importance of (Demystifying) Language

Is learning Mandarin essential or enough to survive and succeed in China?

There is a school of thought that strongly believes that one's ability to speak Mandarin is the key to one's success in China. In fact, some people I interviewed believed language skills to come ahead of *guanxi* as a determining success factor. "How can you be effective if you don't understand what's being said?" argued one executive. There is no question that knowing the local language can help, but it is not a guarantee for success. There are many businesspeople from Hong Kong and Taiwan, for example, who are fluent in Mandarin, but have not been successful. On the other hand, I have interviewed plenty of foreign executives who could not speak Mandarin but were successful in China. For a senior foreign executive to take the time to learn Mandarin is very difficult, since it often takes years just to master the basics, and it is usually not necessary (unless you are in sales – see box on page 29), which is why the ability to speak Mandarin does not make the universal list of action steps for executives to follow.

After thinking carefully about what was being said around the issue of learning Mandarin, I believe they were really referring to the importance of language as a significant communication tool. Thus language, like *guanxi*, becomes a means, not an end, to determining one's success. Fortunately, many examples exist where people can communicate and be understood without being a fluent Mandarin speaker. One of my favourite stories is of Phil Davis, the Managing Director of Anheuser-Busch Asia, describing his situation at home. Phil has been in China since 1996 and is one of the many successful foreign executives who can't speak Chinese, but is a skilled

Phil Davis salutes his staff during a conference.

communicator in getting his point across. His wife is from China and they live in Shanghai with their two children.

"Recently my mother-in-law was visiting us so when I go home, the only language being spoken is Chinese. Although I can't speak directly to my mother-in-law, I communicate with her through gestures, smiles and nods. What really makes things interesting is when a 'disagreement' ensues between my wife and her mum. I've got to be superobservant with the action and body language because sometimes I may need to step in to smooth things over and keep everybody happy. Sometimes not speaking the language is an advantage because I can't be blamed for saying the wrong things, but I can pretty much pick up on what is happening by being very observant. Also, it helps that they are all terrified of me, even though I've never done anything to let them think otherwise. They must think of me like the big teddy bear they don't want to get angry with," he says, with a huge grin on his face.

Cultural and Regional Issues in the Sales Environment

Language is not the only obstacle in being an effective salesperson. Cultural and regional differences also need to be taken into account. For example, one might argue that the reason customers or distributors choose not to voice their real feelings to a senior sales manager could be more a function of the position; they may prefer to voice their concerns only to a lower ranked salesman, since direct confrontation, especially to an executive, is frowned upon in traditional Chinese culture.

Another element to keep in mind is regional issues across China. In Shanghai, for example, local Shanghainese may feel it "beneath them" to take orders from a sales manager from Anhui or Jiangxi, which are known for its poverty and lack of sophistication, compared to Shanghai. The real issue is locals like to deal with locals. When I was at Foster's we would send Shanghainese salesmen down to Wenzhou, a smaller, less sophisticated city, about 500 km south of Shanghai in Zhejiang province. The Wenzhou distributors had little time or respect for these "big city boys" and would continually play their games and sales tricks. We were never really successful in developing the market for a sustainable period of time using Shanghainese. The local dialect in Wenzhou is called *Minnan hua* (pronounced "me-nan hwa" in Mandarin – *hua* means language), which is also the local dialect spoken in parts of Fujian and Taiwan. Once again, while everyone may speak *Minnan hua*, regional accents and variations of *Minnan hua* also exist, much like in Switzerland, where one dialect may differ from the other from valley to valley.

The Importance of Local Dialects

The importance of language skills often depends on the job function. Those in sales, for example, who are required to communicate with customers in order to make the sale, should definitely speak Chinese, or more specifically, be able to speak what their customers speak. China, as you are being told throughout this book, is like Europe in terms of size and diversity in language and culture. Being able to speak Mandarin may not be enough to get past the veils of thought your customer may have. In Shanghai, the main dialect spoken on the street is naturally Shanghainese, which is significantly different from Mandarin, similar to the differences between English and French. Speaking to local distributors, for example, I would often learn that Shanghainese distributors would raise issues or speak their minds only after they were able to speak with another salesperson who could also speak Shanghainese.

Language diversity is one of the aspects that make China a truly unique marketplace. While many books cite China as having eight different languages/dialects, in reality, there are hundreds across China. Just look at Chinese money; you will see five completely different official written languages (see Figure 4.1). Growing up in Canada, at home I spoke the *Taishan hua* (or *Toisan*) dialect from Guangdong province, a subdialect of Cantonese only spoken by a couple of million people – which is small when you compare it to China's 1.3 billion people. Many people assume that everyone in Guangdong, a province of 78 million people, speaks Cantonese, or

Guangdong hua. However, Guangdong actually has at least two other major dialects, Kejia, and Chaozhou. Kejia and Chaozhou dialects are spoken predominantly in the eastern part of Guangdong province and the divisions between what is a Kejia area and what is a Chaozhou area is not clear, similar to the ethnic pockets of Bosnia and Herzegovina. Cantonese will get you nowhere and you are better off speaking Mandarin. Like Bosnia, ingrained mistrust often exists among people with different dialects and ethnic backgrounds (see box on page 32). Back in 1997, I was developing distribution networks in the region and was constantly surprised by why the local wholesalers would not buy their products from the local distributor only a few kilometres away. "Because he's a Chaozhou person," he replied. "I've been cheated by too many Chaozhou people; instead I prefer to deal with this Kejia distributor [even though I need to travel more than 50 km through mountainous terrain]."

Although the Chinese currency has only five official written languages, there are in fact many more. Each of the languages on the currency represents one of the autonomous regions of China. In case you are curious about what the script says, it simply means "The People's Bank of China".

Mandarin will give a person a good communication platform to do business in China, but one must realise that Mandarin is often not enough unless you intend to work only in Beijing. Although Beijingers will claim to also have their own *hua* or language, the differences between Mandarin and *Beijing hua* is really in the accent and colloquialisms. I've met a few Chinese who can speak Mandarin, Cantonese and Shanghainese fluently, but these individuals

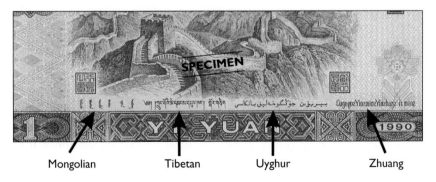

Mongolian   Tibetan   Uyghur   Zhuang

Figure 4.1   Official Languages on Chinese Currency

are rare. If you add in Arabic spoken in the west, Korean in the northeast, Minnan, Kejia, Chaozhou and Dai dialects to the south, for example, it is next to impossible to master them all. Therefore, practicality suggests to be really effective, one must possess more than just language abilities.

Language Barrier Strategies for the Foreign Executive

So if the foreign manager can't speak the local language, then what is the best approach to handling the language barriers? The *China Streetsmart* answer is to surround yourself with trusted people who can. How important language is to your success in China really depends on the job function and what that function needs to do. General Managers and Managing Directors can often get away with no local language skills; however, if you are in a type of business which needs to lobby the government and develop good *guanxi*, and your GM or MD can speak on behalf of the company directly rather than go through a less direct authoritative person like a government relations specialist, things could be a lot easier. The general rule of thumb is the lower down the management hierarchy, the more important it is to have good local language skills, especially when managing local staff and dealing with local customers.

Sales Tip: Beware of Collusion between the Salesperson and the Distributor

A common problem that I have seen arise, given the affinity for people in China to deal with people of their own dialect coupled with the emphasis of personal relationships over company loyalty, is collusion that often results between the salesperson and the distributor. Deals may be worked out that you, as a business manager or executive, may be unaware of. This problem does not only happen in foreign multinational corporations operating in China, but in local companies as well. A Beijing-based local company, which manufactures motor parts, was being cheated by a collusive agreement between their Shanghainese sales force and the local Shanghai distributors to falsify defective parts and sell them off for personal gain. This inability of the local Beijing company to fully communicate on a local level in Shanghai is one of the reasons why there is often a certain level of distrust, disdain and rivalry between Beijingers and Shanghainese.

As with preventing people from building dangerous *guanxi* networks that could endanger your company, what is needed are basic checks and balances and close

---

monitoring and supervision of the sales force. Given the general level of immaturity and inexperience of the sales force in China, I often recommend adopting a tight sales monitoring policy to reduce the temptation for collusion. For example, if a salesman is working with a local distributor of the same dialect, that may be good for developing a good relationship, but to prevent any collusive activities transpiring that could hurt the company, simply continue to make the salesmen accountable for all the basic sales functions, such as rewarding salespeople for sales *only* when payment is received and keeping salesmen on fixed expense accounts.

When extreme sales pressure mounted for companies in China, these basic sales policies were violated time and again. For example, many consumer goods companies in the late 90s, desperate for sales due to an overestimation in market size, relaxed policies on credit and gave away too many incentives to the trade. Companies new to China, not knowing how things were done "locally", would give in to their local salespeople's demands when they were told, "This is how things get done in China." By all means pay attention to your salespeople, since they know what is happening in the field, but any deviation from sales basics such as extending credit needs to be watched carefully. This practice goes back to the basic principle of being *China Streetsmart* – stick to common-sense business practices.

Using professional translators is not the best *China Streetsmart* approach unless that translator is one of your trusted lieutenants. There are plenty of translation services available, but more often than not, full-time translators are young inexperienced graduates who really don't know your products, services or industry. As a result, there is danger of mistranslation leading to misunderstandings. A manager who was setting up a plant with highly technical specifications ran into difficulties once he learned, only half way through his discussions with contractors, that his translator was translating one micron (1/10,000 m) as one millimetre (1/1,000 m). Although I have met many people who have been working successfully in China for a number of years who cannot speak Chinese, what is true about all of them is that they all had trusted senior lieutenants who could speak the local language. Professional translators may be okay as a start, but using them should only be a stopgap service. By the time one is ready to begin serious negotiations, a trusted lieutenant should be in place to act as translator.

5 | The Importance of Listening (Chinese Style)

A Cultural Understanding to Comprehend the Real Meaning of What is Being Communicated

As an avid follower of basic business disciplines, I believe one of the most important skills to develop in business is great listening skills. The problem in China with emphasising this skill, as one of the key action steps for foreign managers to follow, is a cultural understanding issue. The true meaning of the conversation comes often not from what is being said, but rather from what is *not* being said. This cultural quirk is not just common in China, but many other Asian cultures as well. For a foreign manager of non-Asian origin coming to China for the first time, understanding this quirk is frustrating and very difficult to master.

One of the key cultural nuances about Chinese, and often other Asian cultures as well, is that bad news or difficult issues are often not discussed directly. It is not so much that they are purposely hiding things from you, but the Chinese culture in general prefers to avoid conflict and not to deal with problems head-on. My Japanese and Korean friends tell me that this management style also applies to them as well. This nuance is often the cause of huge cultural clashes between Chinese and American managerial styles, since Americans prefer to deal with issues head-on.

The Real Meaning Goes Beyond Basic Listening

In Chinese there is often a difference between saying "yes" or *shi* (pronounced "sher" in Mandarin), and "Yes, I agree with you". A foreign plant manager of a meat packaging plant was explaining to his Chinese counterpart how important it was for the floors to be cleaned several times each day. Throughout the whole conversation, the Chinese manager would be saying "yes, yes, yes" or "*shi,*

shi, shi". After the conversation, the two parted, but the floors never got cleaned. Puzzled, the foreign plant manager confronted the Chinese manager and asked why he never ordered the floors to be cleaned and his reply was simply, "You didn't ask me."

Foreign salespeople often misread the signals of the Chinese. As the salesman goes through his pitch and tries to read his audience, he is encouraged by the fact that they are constantly nodding their heads and saying "yes, yes, yes". However, he becomes incredibly confused and frustrated when it comes to closing the sale and he gets blank stares and the classic words: "Let me think about it. I'll get back to you" – which they often never do.

During the Cultural Revolution those who spoke out got punished, whereas those who were obedient and did exactly or answered correctly what they were asked got rewarded (or were not punished). This lack of freedom of expression or unwillingness to offer more than you are asked is a quirky part of Chinese culture that needs to be understood. It is typical of Chinese managerial styles, relating back to Confucian values of respecting one's position, not to question your superiors, so in a traditional Chinese company if the boss asks you to do something, you do it – no questions asked. Likewise, if the boss likes something and asks the employee for his opinion, the person is highly unlikely to speak out against his boss. This boss or *laoben* (pronounced "lau-ban" in Mandarin) management approach where the *laoben* is meant to solve everything, is one of the biggest challenges foreign managers have with changing the management mentalities of the local staff they hire.

Good "Chinese Listening Skills" Can Save You Millions

While I was working at Foster's in 1998, a rival brewer, which had gained significant market share the year previously, launched a new beer campaign for their best-selling brand of beer in China. Their advertising budget was more than double mine and I was terrified they were going to overwhelm us. Prior to the launch of the summer blitz, a four-month period where 70% of the annual volume is sold, I was beginning to hear rumours of this Great Campaign that was being developed by my rival competitor. I knew some of the account people working in the rival's international advertising agency and naturally tried my best to figure out what this Great Campaign was before the launch. Of course they wouldn't tell me directly, only that their Account Director (a British expatriate) was raving about how good this campaign was going to be and how this new and revolutionary ad campaign was going to take the whole market by storm. Adding to this fear was the rival brewer's Sales Director (also an expatriate) running around, telling the trade they were going to hit the market with a campaign the likes of which China had never seen – "with the effect of an atomic bomb". I was terrified.

When the campaign was finally launched, I could not believe what I saw. They were right; the campaign was a campaign the likes of which Shanghai and the rest of China had never seen. The campaign was completely inappropriate for the local market, but I could understand why it would appeal to expatriate managers. The campaign was a story centred on a young boy growing up with his friends, talking about how important his friends and family are and how they have endured really tough times, such as a big flood that happened during their childhood. Eventually the boy grows up and owns his own home and at the point where they are all happy and celebrating a wonderful housewarming, in comes the beer and everyone is happy. Sounds good you say? Seems like a commercial you would show in the West hitting a lot of emotional hot buttons? You could further back their strategy with research that shows that 80% of beer sold in the mainstream segment is drunk at home; the most important values to local Chinese are family and close friends; and the biggest aspiration of all local Chinese is to own their own homes.

The one critical factor my competitor forgot to ask was *why* people drink beer, which is to relax, and when they relax all they want to do is to escape and forget about their surroundings – which are often harsh and primitive. The commercial instead reminded them of their harsh real life with scenes of flooded alleyways, etc. The campaign in effect "killed the brand" and the brand was never to recover. That summer, the Foster's Shanghai brewery enjoyed record sales; in fact, in July of that year, we set an all-time high sales record for sales in a single month. Sales in Shanghai overall were up 50% year over year. I was ecstatic!

Months later, I had the opportunity to speak with the people of the rival company to learn what had happened. How could they have so missed the mark in reading the needs of the Shanghai consumer?

Affiliation is a common beer strategy in the West. For example, Americans may remember a hot sweaty dirty coal miner coming out of the mine, wiping his brow and saying, "It's Miller Time!" However, in China, affiliative advertising needs to be treated much differently. I eventually got to know the rival marketing director, a local Shanghainese and her staff and when I asked them, they said all the local staff hated the commercial even before it was launched, but no one dared speak up – including herself. The top management was all run by expatriates and they were all convinced that this sophisticated campaign, using sophisticated research modelling techniques and based on a proven method of affiliation in the West, was unlike any campaign that had been seen in China before. They were right, but for the wrong reasons.

I also got the opportunity later to talk with the international advertising agency about the campaign and found the local staff felt the exact same way. They were afraid of voicing their opinions since their British expatriate Account Director was also so enthused over this "revolutionary" campaign. When I spoke with the research agency later, their local staff said the same thing. They asked "exactly" the questions that were asked of them and did "exactly" what they were told. When someone would ask them what they thought, they would just smile, not say a word (or perhaps simply say *shi*) and give a slight ambiguous nod. Later when I thought about these situations, I really couldn't blame the local staff. Here were these senior-level expatriates who ran the brewery, the advertising agency and the research agency, all of them extremely excited about the campaign. I knew their level of excitement for a fact, because I also got to talk with all of them when we were to meet later face to face. Given this excitement and enthusiastic momentum taking place, not only at the brewery, but also at the advertising agency and research agency, who was going to dare speak out? Especially not some local who had only a fraction of the experience compared to these expatriates. Would listening skills have helped prevent this disaster? Most likely not.

The Complicating Factor of Language Limitations

Complicating the issue of developing good listening skills in understanding what is really being said in China is the language obstacle.

Inaccurate translation is an obvious danger, but it is also important to note that if Chinese staff are asked their opinions and they are asked to answer not in their native language, that will complicate the issue even more by deepening the reluctance to speak out, given their fear of their inability to really be able to express themselves – exacerbating the problem. The inexperienced foreign executive may be oblivious to this, thinking, "I asked the question and I didn't hear any problems, so everything must be okay" only to be frustrated in the end at why things didn't work out as planned. Often when I was working with my staff in Shanghai and posed a problem for them to resolve, I made sure they would be comfortable enough in front of me to switch to Shanghainese, knowing it wasn't going to offend me. Actually I would encourage them to debate in Shanghainese, especially when we were discussing important issues such as taglines and campaign slogans. I would let them discuss among themselves and try and listen as best as I could on the sidelines.

For good listening skills to be effective in China, one needs first to be skilled in making people comfortable and relaxed. They need to trust you enough that what they say is not going to be used against them later. While the younger generation in China may know very little about the Cultural Revolution, and admittedly they are easier to train to get them to speak out, it still takes real courage for anyone to say what they really mean in China and even more courage if they are asked to do so *not* in their native tongue. Therefore, I re-emphasise that by following the subsequent six universally applicable *China Streetsmart* action steps, one will be able to exercise the skills needed to make people relaxed and once they are relaxed, they will be able to achieve a greater level of trust and understanding; only then will listening skills be really effective.

6 | *China Streetsmart* Action Step 1

Maintain Management Consistency – Own Up to Mistakes and Manage Expectations

A strong commitment to leadership has significant benefits to companies not only in resolving problems but more importantly in preventing them.

M aintaining management consistency is the first action step I mention because it is often the first mentioned by many of the people I interviewed for the book. Almost everyone will agree that *the* critical success factor in any business is its people. Yet when one examines why some of the biggest and best international companies have failed or are performing below expectations in China, one finds that many of the roots can be traced back to the company's failure to commit to its leadership. Frequent management changes at the top cause disruption and inconsistency in an organisation's ability to operate effectively. While incompetence or inability to work in China may be the reason behind some of the changes, the roots of the problem often lie with those in the head office who craft the original strategy which often contains critical misassumptions, such as inaccurate market size and growth expectations, and the China management team's failure to manage those flawed expectations.

Interestingly, the local Chinese staff also mention strong leadership as the no.1 factor which decides whether they will stay at a company or not. In a study conducted by *The Asian Wall Street Journal* and Hewitt Associates at the end of 2001 on employee motivations, Senior Leadership ranked no. 1 in factors influencing engagement, ahead of Opportunities (no. 2), Work Activities (no. 3) and of course,

Pay (no. 4).[1] Many of these employees were frustrated with their actual experience of frequent management changes causing massive disruptions.

Owning up to Mistakes

Most of the companies not doing well in China today are the result of originally flawed business objectives and plans, which need first to be identified and accepted before a proper resolution can be found. The process requires both the China management team's ability to accurately identify the issues with the original strategy and the head office's willingness to accept the findings. The problem often becomes political when both the local management team and head office begin pointing fingers that either side did not do an adequate job. Strong leadership is required to not lay blame but rather own up to mistakes in order to seek the best resolution. Unfortunately, the reaction for many companies is to simply replace the local China management team, which often is not the root cause of the problem.

For those companies that misread the market and over-invested, for example, a familiar pattern emerged. Once it became apparent that the market was actually much smaller than estimated, dispelling the billion customers myth, companies, in an attempt to justify their return on investment, attempted to appease shareholders by increasing sales and going after market share – since near-term profitability was out of the question given their huge capital investment. "China's a long-term market," they would proclaim. "As long as we are achieving market share, profitability will eventually be achieved through market/sector dominance." But the reality instead was a massive increase in competitive intensity, which highlighted the difficulties in expanding distribution across China, causing costs to spiral upwards. The over-invested companies sank deeper and deeper into the red and began to run out of options in how to justify to shareholders their China strategy. These types of strategies were flawed from the start, but often it was at the head office's insistence that these strategies be carried out, since they were the ones who

---

[1] Hewitt Associates and *The Asian Wall Street Journal,* 6 September 2001, N4.

had shareholders to answer to. The head office could not accept the findings of the local management team, whose recommendations often ran contrary to what CEOs were originally telling shareholders. Such findings included how challenging it was to set up an effective sales and distribution network across China or how uncooperative and obstructive their local partner was being. Whether by Machiavellian design to find a scapegoat or ignorance to the realities of China, China management heads, or entire teams in some cases, were replaced.

The Sad but Common Tale

Parents raising children usually find that they make most of the mistakes with their first child. They make fewer mistakes as they gain more experience, but pity the poor first child. Business leaders operating in China faced a similar scenario. Over the years, head office eventually realised that after repeated changes in management, many of the mistakes were not the fault of local management, but rather the assumptions on which the basic strategy was originally founded. Had they listened to the local management, they could have derived this conclusion much sooner. Many companies that I interviewed followed this common pattern:

1. The CEO visits the market and sees nothing but enormous untapped potential.
2. The company comes rushing into China, invests heavily, and proclaims they will take the market by storm with its "superior products and services".
3. The on-the-ground management, often within its first year, realises the market realities and challenges of working in China, and tries to explain the realities to head office, which either turns a deaf ear, or counters with statements like "I can't believe you can't do such and such; what's wrong with you?"
4. The first generation of management is replaced within one to two years, either from being fired or leaving in frustration.
5. The second generation of management faces the same issues and is also replaced within one to two years, or leaves after it sees that the goals are unachievable.
6. By the third generation of management (if the company is lucky), the company comes around to the reality of challenges of a developing market like China and begins to alter its plans by hunkering down.
7. Hunkering down first involves a heavy slimming-down of the expensive cost structure. Most high-priced expats leave the company and are replaced by locals whether they can adequately do the job or not. They often move offices to much cheaper locations and simply try and survive.
8. The CEO is asked about their China strategy and comments on how the company is committed to China, and views China as a long-term play, and doesn't

---

expect profitability for the next five years or more – the real reason is they have no other choice given their heavy initial investment.

9. Secretly the company looks for a buyer or talks to the local partner about buying back the shares. Local management (including suppliers and distributors) usually finds out about this "secret initiative" and loses interest in supporting the company. The bad news worsens and creates more negative stories on how difficult it is to do business in China.

Managing Expectations

While most of the executives I interviewed in China put the blame squarely on head office and their inability to initially accept the realities of China, the reality must also take into account the local management team's inability or failure to adequately manage expectations. Being on the side of the local management team, I empathise with reports falling on deaf ears and raised eyebrows, but some of the more successful *China Streetsmart* business executives I met were able to convince their head office of the difficult realities and also convince them to buy into a plan which may be different, but would still achieve the company's bottom-line objectives. One such *China Streetsmart* executive was Emil Schlumpf, the General Manager of Siemens Switchgear in Shanghai. When he first started the joint venture, Emil had huge challenges to contend with: a run-down dilapidated factory to renovate, no staff, and pressure from head office to achieve profitability within a set period of time. "The original plan simply was not realistic," he explained, "but as GM, it is my responsibility to not just tell them about the problems, but also provide a plan forward which they can buy into. The timeframe might change, but as long as I deliver on what I commit to then the company should support me." Siemens's head office management did support Emil and his revised plans and he now runs a very successful operation. In fact, Siemens Switchgear was awarded Shanghai's Magnolia Award in 1999 by the government, an award given annually to the best-performing businesses. Not all executives were as successful as Emil though, and the reality was far too frequent management changes. In extreme cases, I spoke with some companies that were on their sixth generation of management in as little as seven years of being in China.

China Streetsmart

Emil Schlumpf meets with then Shanghai Mayor Xu Kuangdi (left) during his receipt of the Magnolia Award for Entrepreneur of the Year in 1999. The Mayor brought out 200 Chinese executives to see what a first-class operation Siemens has set up.

Photograph by Emil Schlumpf

The Right Team at the Start

The importance of consistency in management has other benefits than just trying to resolve past mistakes. Ensuring the right team is in place right at the start of your China investment and is the same group of people who will eventually run the operation will help tremendously. Often corporations send a business development executive in to negotiate and establish the venture and another to actually run the venture itself. **The *China Streetsmart* approach to set up a successful operation is to keep your leadership team intact from the initial stages to the ongoing business operations.** Given the importance of relationships in China and benefits derived from close government relations to help the company navigate the complex and capricious commercial laws and regulations, having a senior leader who knows the history of the company and what was said during negotiations or from the start of its market entry will help tremendously.

Another reason for Siemens Switchgear's success in China can also be pointed to the fact that Emil Schlumpf had been the General Manager from the initial stages to the ongoing running of the operations. Emil initially was meant to stay on for only a three-year period, but at the urging of his Chinese partners, Siemens kept Emil on for an additional two terms for a total of nine years of consistent management right from the beginning. Therefore, Siemens Switchgear's award as Shanghai's Entrepreneur of the Year in 1999 does not come as a complete surprise.

Photograph by John L. Chan

While the exterior may look relatively plain, the inside has been completely refurbished to Siemens's international high standards. Emil Schlumpf, the General Manager of Siemens Switchgear from 1993 to 2002, proudly showed me the history of how the factory has transformed since he first took over. The consistent senior management in place, not only on the foreign side, but also the Chinese side with Mr Xiong, the Deputy General Manager, allowed a strong working relationship to develop between the two sides and is one of the key reasons why Siemens Switchgear is a success.

Anheuser-Busch's China operation is another good example of consistent commitment to its leadership in China right from the start. Top executives August Busch III and IV visit China regularly and their main man at the helm, Phil Davis, has been overseeing China since the beginning. A good test of that commitment was not only in the 170 million USD Anheuser-Busch has invested in China, but in 1999, when Budweiser (Anheuser-Busch's flagship brand) significantly missed their sales target by more than 40% after sales were severely affected by the anti-American goods boycott as a result of the NATO bombing of the Chinese Embassy in Belgrade that year, the core China management team stayed intact. Today, Budweiser is no. 1 in the locally produced premium beer segment in China and has finally achieved profitability – a rarity in China's beer industry.

Furthermore, in 2001 *The Asian Wall Street Journal* ranked them one of the top ten employers in China.[2]

To summarise, there is a strong correlation between a company's success in China and the length of term of its senior management, especially if that core senior management team was present at the start. In a fast-changing market like China, experience counts and those executives with real life Streetsmart on-the-ground experience should be fully utilised. The next time you hear of a company doing poorly or doing well in China, enquire about the length of term of their senior management and if they were involved with the start of the operations.

---

[2] Hewitt Associates and *The Asian Wall Street Journal*, "2001 Best Employer in Asia Awards ranked Anheuser-Busch Asia Inc. No. 7", *Far Eastern Economic Review*, 13 September 2001, p. 38.

7 | *China Streetsmart* Action Step 2

Be Flexible and Adaptable – Develop Based on Local Needs

Be open-minded to the fact that your set paradigms and models may need to adjust to local conditions.

Remaining committed to your bottom-line objectives but flexible in your approach is key to being successful in China. Like Darwinism suggests, only those flexible enough to adapt to their surroundings and local conditions will survive. Throughout the 80s and early 90s, not a lot was understood about what would and would not work in China. Sophisticated business models that were developed for markets very different to China's were imported and applied on a trial and error basis – or as one of the executives commented, "A trial, error, and more errors" basis. Over time and after many blunders, it has become clear that the "tropical bird" model of products and services will not work in an Arctic climate. Many people talk about China being a unique market – they are correct, but the statement needs some clarification. **What is unique about the China market is not so much Mainland China itself, but rather the conditions under which China is changing.** In fact, if we were to look back 100 years at America and Europe we would see fragmented industries, uninformed consumers, limited distribution infrastructure, etc. Now take those hundred years of development and squash it in 20 years and that's what really makes China unique.

Avoid the Temptation to Over-Standardise

Consistent product formulation and maintaining international standards and specifications are always sensitive topics for multinational corporations (MNCs) operating in China. Pressured to uphold international practices, companies investing in China are tempted to use a "cookie cutter" approach, that is to say, the same management system and products and services formulation regardless of country. Even the more sophisticated worldly companies will have a mature economy and a developing economy cookie cutter. **The fact remains that standardised cookie cutters have limited effectiveness, given the fact that each country has its own unique challenges ranging from political to geographical to cultural differences.** Companies are always tempted/pressured to stick to the same "square peg" they use at home – even if the "local hole" (in China) is round, in order to keep head office rather than the local customers happy. In the past, I have been told/ordered by foreign head office staff ignorant about China, with their own different set of objectives: "If the square peg does not fit in the round hole, then simply make the square peg smaller." However, this thinking goes against

Photograph by John L. Chan

McDonald's is another very *China Streetsmart* company, in the sense that they are constantly surveying their customers on how their products and services can better meet local needs. Aside from their standard flagship products such as the Big Mac (pronounced "jew woo baa" in Mandarin), new locally tailored products are introduced on a periodic basis. This McDonald's employee in Beijing is soliciting customers by handing out customer feedback forms.

basic marketing fundamentals, which state that the key to success is the company's ability to meet (local) customers' needs.

In a hyper-competitive market like China, customers in any industry or segment will have plenty to choose from, so if your product or service does not meet customers' needs best, others will. If they are looking for a round peg, they won't choose the small square peg, rather one who is willing to produce or provide the round peg. In the end, the customer is still king and companies need to accept the basic fact that companies willing to offer products and services which best meet local needs will fare best. This marketing tenet explains why local brands have been gaining in popularity. Some people have tried to attribute this to a rise in nationalism but in reality, the most common and obvious reason is simply the local products are priced right and meet their needs best. Why would a customer want to pay three times the price for a foreign joint-venture product when a local product meets 80% of his needs?

China's Geographic Challenges

Even if the company agrees to customise its products and services for China, that may not be enough given the regional differences. For example, companies operating in the food and beverage industry will find that tastes vary greatly from one region to the next. In a market as large and varied as China, this has proven a huge challenge for some manufacturers. While I would not advocate Coca-Cola or Pepsi having 30 different flavour formulations to suit each province, soft drink executives have noted that formulations have been adjusted slightly from market to market or from country to country. Beers face the same challenges, since northern China tends to favour heavier-tasting beers, while around Shanghai, they prefer lighter tastes. Almost all of the international beer brands maintain a consistency in taste profile across China, but the overall taste profile is clearly towards the lighter end. This is not surprising since consumers are relatively new to beer and it is also not surprising that Budweiser's lighter, easier-to-drink beer dominates the premium beer segment. Anheuser-Busch was clever enough to give consumers a wider taste selection by introducing another premium beer with the introduction of Bud Ice.

The people at Lion Nathan, the brewers of Steinlager Beer, winner of the "Best Beer in the World" award for four years in a row,[1] had much to be proud of with their taste formulation, but when they came to China, they were flexible and adaptable enough to adjust the taste profile of Steinlager to suit local tastes. Original Steinlager from New Zealand is a more bitter-tasting beer than Chinese Steinlager. When I was at Lion Nathan I had the honour of launching this beer in the China market and sales grew rapidly. In fact in 1999, Steinlager was the fastest-growing premium beer in the Yangtze River Delta and Budweiser, the market leader, perceived us as their no. 1 threat. On the other hand, the brewers at Foster's were staunchly opposed to changing the formulation of Foster's. It was their "scared cow", as one advertising executive put it. Foster's, known as the "Amber Nectar" in the UK, is one of the best-selling lagers in the UK, but unfortunately not in China. Research showed that the darker colour and heavier taste were not preferred by local consumers. A rigorous debate ensued over what to do. In the end, Foster's did not change the formula and Foster's sales languished.

Understanding China's Stage of Development

Being flexible and adaptable enough to not impose inappropriate measures on your China operation is important to operating effectively. In addition, being committed to your goals of developing the best people is and should remain a key goal for any operation. However, the approach one takes in China more often than not needs to be adjusted. Having interviewed human resource (HR) directors in China and also having come from one of the best HR-managed companies in the world, namely Exxon Mobil, I certainly appreciate the importance of having a strong HR system in place. However, for China, given the lack of strong Western management experience, cultural nuances of not feeling comfortable speaking out or saying what you really mean, and not wanting to criticise your superiors, make implementing the same type of HR development system difficult.

---

[1] Steinlager was voted "Best Beer in the World" from 1978 to 1981 by Les Amis Du Vin, the international wine society. Then in 1985, from a field of 800, it won "Best in the World for International Bottled Lager" at the Brewex competition in England. Source: http://www.realbeer.co.nz/library/authors/holloway-b/19991202steinlager. html

Photographs by John L. Chan

Greenwich USA – Train Station
Commuter Parking Lot

Shanghai PRC – Train Station
Commuter Parking Lot

China Streetsmart stresses the need to focus on the bottom line and not be too distracted by what seems to be a very different picture. While these pictures may seem quite different, the end result is the same – people commuting to work every day. The importance then shifts to understanding what is best for local conditions. In this case, implementing a carpool would not be right for China.

I was working for a company in China that had a "one on one" monthly counselling session that was required of all managers with direct reports. This HR management system was incredibly sophisticated and followed the international goal of becoming one of the leading HR practitioners in the world, modelled after some of the best global companies. Issues arose in the implementation (imposition) of the system. Only a few of us in the company had formal training on how to conduct these review sessions. The system may have been excellent (arguably the best) but the execution or appropriateness for the Chinese staff was questionable. What happened was we were all under pressure to ensure we had our "one on one" reports completed each month and had very little support and training to back up how it was being implemented. I remember a huge fight which broke out between one of my brand managers and her brand assistant because the brand manager felt it was in her right to "criticise" the assistant's mistakes during these sessions and the younger, less experienced assistant was hurt by these formal criticisms, fearing these sessions were a formal documented way of dismissing her rather than a means of cooperative feedback and exchange between manager and subordinate.

The approach and systems foreign companies bring to China may be right in principle, but as you will read throughout this book, **the *China Streetsmart* approach is not necessarily about doing**

what is best – which suggests a superior/inferior relationship, but rather what is more appropriate for any given situation. For Western managers who have worked in a culture of conducting, at a minimum, employee annual review sessions, these HR systems are perhaps easier to adopt and accept, but trying to impose a sophisticated system on a business culture that is unfamiliar with the basics of how the review process works can cause huge shocks in the personal development of staff and can have results opposite to what was originally intended.

Another great example of a successful company that has resisted the imposition of foreign systems inappropriate for local market conditions is Anheuser-Busch. I was speaking with Phil Davis, the Managing Director for Anheuser-Busch Asia, about the principles of developing the best distribution networks in China. He remarked, "When I was working with St. Louis [Anheuser-Busch's head office] to adopt a similar distribution strategy we use in the States where we offer distributors territorial exclusivity, my question to the management was to ask why we did this for the States. In the States we have a very successful method of getting the best distributors by offering a territory to protect their profit and encouraging them to invest their own money behind the brand. In China, we agree with the strategy of developing strong distributor support, but to offer territorial exclusivity in markets where most distributors do not have the funds or sophistication and know-how to invest behind the brand, is the wrong strategy for China. Rather, adhering to the goal of developing strong distributor support by protecting their margin through policies such as consistent uniform pricing, coupled with rebates based on sales performance, is far more appropriate. Now that our China distributors have been working with us for several years now, we are able to see who the good distributors are, like the ones we have in the States. On a limited and selective basis we are starting to implement a similar system to the States, but it would still be inappropriate to do this across the board."

For Coca-Cola, their new worldwide CEO, Douglas Daft, was perhaps a godsend for Coca-Cola China, since he has managed China before and has seen firsthand the complexities each local market presents. He has been a strong advocate of allowing individual markets around the world to develop their own marketing strategies appropriate to local needs. In November 2001, Coca-Cola announced a commitment to inject another 150 million USD into the China market. As a result, it is not surprising to note that according to many surveys, Coca-Cola remains the strongest brand in China.[2]

Photograph by John L. Chan

The impact Coca-Cola has on China is impressive. Since re-entering China in 1979, the Coca-Cola bottling system has injected about a billion USD into the Chinese economy and annually engages over 400,000 jobs (direct and indirect) in Coca-Cola production and distribution.[3]

[2] Douglas Daft, Coca-Cola's CEO, announced in November 2001 that they would build another six plants over the next five years with a total investment of 150 million USD. Source: http://www.ctiin.com.cn/english/inves/inves1112-1.htm

[3] Universities of Peking, Tsinghua and South Carolina, "Economic Impact of the Coca-Cola System on China – Executive Summary", August 2000, pp. 4–5.

China Streetsmart

8 | *China Streetsmart* Action Step 3

Be Patient and Thorough –
Wait for the Right Moment to Strike

Do not rush into making a deal; understand the issues thoroughly before investing.

In China we jokingly say the three keys to success are patience, patience and patience, and if these keys do not work, please be patient. Having discussed this concept with many successful business leaders in China, I quickly found that patience did not mean sitting quietly in your hotel room while your approvals were being processed or contracts were waiting to be signed; rather, patience for them meant not rushing into things before they were ready, and waiting for the right moment to strike. Sitting idle in a hotel room is the last thing an executive should be doing since there is so much to learn, understand and absorb about the unique challenges of the China market. There is plenty of homework and market due diligence that needs to be conducted before the decision to invest is made.

Recently, I was asked by a business delegation visiting China what I thought was the single biggest reason why a lot of companies you read about in the press were not making money in China. I replied, "Most companies came rushing into China with a 'gold rush' mentality, eager to be the first to market and stake their claim. Companies were guided by the basic business principle that states that the first one in the market will be the one likely to capture the biggest share and secure the most defensible position. 'First mover advantage' was the catchword of the day. As a result of the over-eagerness to be the 'first mover', many shortcuts were taken, compromises made, and many of the basic business principles of developing a proper market, such as understanding the market to set realistic sales targets, having the right team in place to manage the operations, taking the time to carefully choose the right joint-venture (JV) partner, and developing sales and human resource systems with the appropriate checks and balances, were not followed."

If you were to look back at the original plans of some of the largest multinational corporations today, many of which are not making money in China today, you would likely find plans built more on broad assumptions rather than a clear detailed understanding of the market. To be fair to those executives though, much was not understood about the market at that time and in some cases almost impossible to predict. For example, who could have predicted that the consumer price index would begin falling for eight straight quarters, beginning in 1998, when only four years earlier in 1994, inflation was more than 24%?[1]

Where First Movers Fail

The principle of first mover advantage was developed in mature Western markets. While this principle is easy enough to understand, many of these principles need to be refined when talking about a rapidly developing immature market like China. Brand loyalty in China, for example, can easily challenge this principle. First mover advantage suggests that those companies that enter into a market first and build market share quickly will be better able to defend their brand loyalty position. In a developing immature market like China, many precious bullets in the war for the customer are wasted just to educate the customer and the trade why their products are better and how the trade needs to handle its products and/or services. Often what happened was the "first mover" foreign competitor did build up significant market share against local competitors and enjoyed comfortable margins in the beginning. These high margins, however, were not enjoyed for long, since the next major foreign competitor, claiming no. 1 status in their home markets (be it Japan, Germany, Australia, etc.), would come along with an aggressive marketing strategy. The incumbent, having fired most of its bullets, would prefer to cut back on marketing spending to reap back

---

[1] China's National Bureau of Statistics.

China Streetsmart

its original heavy investment in marketing and distribution; instead, the new onslaught of competitors forced them to spend heavily to defend their market positions again and again.

A phenomenon known as brand promiscuity often prevents first movers from achieving the benefits suggested especially for services and products with little differentiation such as fast-moving consumer goods (FMCG). Customers, new to these products and/or services, were naturally curious: "So what's the no. 1 widget in Japan like? US? Germany? How about Australia?" Western marketing theory would suggest the need to establish defensible positions by continually reinforcing the brand with product innovation to outclass or outshine "the contenders to the crown". Great in theory, but in sympathy to my fellow marketing directors across China, defending against not one or two worthy contenders, but as many as ten or more within a year or two, makes for a challenging, if not impossible, task.

Where First Movers Succeed

For companies with products that are based on proprietary technology platforms or standards, and companies with products having long life cycles such as elevators, first mover advantages are more likely to abound. Alcatel, Nortel, Lucent, Siemens and Fujitsu, for example, have spent billions already trying to ensure their technological platforms are the models the Chinese telecommunications industry bases its future standards on. Furthermore, it is no wonder that Otis, Schindler and Mitsubishi all set up elevator manufacturing facilities in China early on as well. For FMCG products in maturing markets like Shanghai, the first mover advantages are likely not to come from customer preferences, but rather in the company's ability to control the distribution and trade. In the beer industry, for example, brewers in certain markets which have a strong dominance in the trade will not hesitate to cut off supply to a distributor if the distributor takes up a competitor's product. While this practice is clearly in violation of the anti-competitive legislation China already has in place, the reality is few distributors will challenge the larger company. Distributors and agents are after one thing: to make money, and if there is a danger their livelihood is to be cut off, they had better be guaranteed they would make up their loss in profits by the new challenger – a very high price to pay for a new market entrant.

Be Thorough – Do Your Market Due Diligence

In China, the general level of market immaturity and phenomenon of hyper-competition will continue to exist for many sectors. The distribution networks are not developed enough to completely "lock out" competitors, so it is best to be patient, take the time to fully understand the market and not rush in. Arguably, one of the best strategic moves made by a foreign brewer during the 90s was Miller Brewing Co. (now owned by South African Breweries). They came in and invested in only a small JV in China, but spent most of the time trying to understand the markets and dynamics. During the height of the "China Beer Wars", they decided that it was too high a price to pay (which it was at the time) and decided to pull out. Miller made the right strategic decision to not invest heavily during the 90s, but now could be an opportune time to re-enter the market. The fact that Miller has been patient has its advantages. So much is now known about the market size by segment, trade and consumer habits and tastes. Furthermore, foreign brewers wanting an answer on how to better utilise their excess capacity are willing to toll-brew, so Miller would not need to carry the capital expense. If they wanted to invest for the long term they could buy a state-of-the-art brewery quite cheaply as some of the breweries have sold out at as little as a quarter of the original price that was paid. Even companies who are only beginning to think about entering the market, attracted by China's market size and compliance to international commercial norms following its entry into the World Trade Organisation, should begin doing their market due diligence early. Even with adherence to international commercial standards, understanding quirks such as the importance of registering your trademarks and patents early, covered later in this book, will protect your investments once you decide to really invest.

9 | *China Streetsmart* Action Step 4

Think Win-Win –
But Develop Respect and Trust First

To negotiate the best deal, do not rely on the rule of law, rather the rule of fairness.

While negotiating contracts with the Chinese is often tough and arduous, enforcing the contract after both sides have signed has often proved to be more of a headache than most foreign companies have anticipated. As business professionals, we are trained to negotiate the best deals for our companies, knowing we can lock in favourable deals with a contract. But in China I quickly discovered that this tactic often didn't work. If some of the Mainland Chinese felt they were given the shorter end of the stick, they would try to equalise things one way or another. One executive interviewed noted, "For the Chinese, contracts are nothing more than a formalised piece of paper to document what we have agreed in the principle of mutual benefit and cooperation. Violate this principle and the contract isn't worth the paper it's been written on." For example, you may negotiate a favourable selling price with a local distributor, but once they find out you have been pricing unevenly and his competitor is getting a better deal with the same conditions, you will not be able to force the distributor to honour his volume commitments. Even in cases where you may feel you have some leverage because you have received a deposit as part of the agreement, trying to collect on your receivables later or getting their cooperation when it is needed can prove to be incredibly difficult.

For many Chinese, if they feel they have been "tricked" into accepting a deal which is not equal or at least fair in their eyes, do not expect the contract to protect you as it would in the West. Loopholes or different interpretations of clauses will suddenly appear and contract or not, the Chinese will try their best to eventually even things out. In some extreme cases, it may simply be if the market conditions change unfavourably on the Chinese side, they may feel less inclined to honour the deal even if a contract exists. Patrick Powers, Director of Operations for the US China Business Council in Beijing, related an incident from his days as a commodity trader in the early 90s: a competitor signed a forward contract for agricultural by-products with a Chinese supplier when the market had hit bottom. The market rapidly changed, the price skyrocketed, and the buyer was looking for a hefty profit. When it came to delivering on the contract, they were told the supplier could not deliver because "the fields were flooded". When the company eventually went to investigate, they discovered an area full of the product they had contracted for, with only a particular area flooded. "That [flooded] area is the product we originally had reserved for you," the supplier said ...

Develop Respect, Trust and Mutual Understanding before Negotiations

Not all cases have been this bad, and when I shared these incidents with other successful businessmen in China, they all agreed they had heard similar stories, but pointed out they rarely came across these problems themselves because in the process of working towards a fair deal by being open about what they thought was mutually beneficial, they had also built up mutual respect and trust in getting to know one another. As with the previous example, commodity traders looking for quick buy-and-sell deals like the agricultural by-products just mentioned may not have the opportunity to build a good relationship or *guanxi*. Don't be surprised if you haven't built up a level of respect and trust first; being open and offering what you think are fair terms may result in the Chinese side simply asking for more.

Following Action Step 3 (Be Patient and Thorough) is critical to negotiating a win-win deal. When you hear of some of the horror stories of why some companies failed when doing business in China, try and enquire how their deals were structured, and you will find they were not structured as win-win nor did the parties have a good understanding of each other's intentions. In the haste to cut a deal, many foreign multinational corporations (MNCs) did not understand the Chinese side's true intentions for entering into a joint venture (JV) until it was too late. The Chinese side of a state-owned enterprise (SOE), for example, often couldn't have cared less about the JV making a profit; rather, they were more concerned with the JV ensuring that their thousands of workers remained employed, and with their ability to utilise the technology for the benefits of their other 100% locally owned enterprises. Furthermore, it is not uncommon for many Chinese companies to be very short-term focused, which often goes contrary to the foreign MNC's long-term view of developing the China market. To strike the right win-win deal, these differences in views and objectives must first be resolved.

"So how long do you need? How do I know when I have built up enough respect and trust to move forward?" asked one frustrated American executive. There is no single answer, but how well both sides understand each other is critical. When I asked others who were successful in building the trust which led to fair deals, they often commented on how the trust was built up only after mutual understanding or in Chinese, *huxiang liaojie* (pronounced "who-shiang leeow jeh" in Mandarin) was established through a gradual process of consistently meeting commitments and delivering on what was promised. Cutting big equitable deals at a first meeting rarely happens in China. Therefore, manage your expectations – you can't just fly over to China and conclude a big contract on your first visit. Often companies start small and build the respect and trust over time, which is why **frequent changes in top management often hurt the process of building *guanxi* or relationships and hence negotiating win-win deals becomes even more difficult.**

Win-Win also Means Knowing When to Walk Away

During the early days of foreign direct investment (FDI) in China, many Chinese negotiators would negotiate extremely tough deals and often, these were not favourable or reasonable to the foreign side at all. Some foreign companies would walk away, and the Chinese side would discover the "threshold" or breaking point of how far they could push negotiations. For the Mainland Chinese side, this was a training ground or way of doing their own market research of discovering the best deal or price. Whether these companies and individuals, during the early 80s, were ever really serious about negotiating a deal was questionable. Many Chinese companies during that time didn't have the ability, the proper import permits, or support or backing by the government to go through with the deal. They simply wanted the negotiation practice and experience. If they were lucky they could get a nice trip to the home country of the company they were dealing with to inspect the company (with side trips to places like Disneyland, Las Vegas and almost certainly Hong Kong).

At times you will encounter difficulties negotiating win-win deals since an inexperienced, overzealous or cautious Chinese negotiator may present demands you find unreasonable, in which case, you must be prepared to walk away from the deal. In the past, inexperienced (with China) foreign companies, eager to "start a relationship" or "get their foot in the door", have instead exacerbated the issue by accepting unreasonable excessive terms, raising the bar of acceptability as to how far Chinese companies could push their foreign counterparts. What many foreign companies have failed to understand is how the Chinese negotiation process works.

How Locals Build up Respect and Trust – The Chinese Way

To structure the right win-win deal, it helps to understand how the Chinese like to negotiate (even among themselves). Don't expect the Chinese side to be completely open until a level of trust and respect is built up. Often the Chinese side will not initially offer a fair deal; rather, it is up to the foreign side to ensure the deal is eventually structured as win-win. I've sat in plush boardrooms, dusty distributor warehouses and muddy local vegetable markets negotiating with locals, and I do see a common trait as to how the negotiating process works in China. Watching a Chinese housewife argue over the price of vegetables with the local farmer, for example, can be very revealing. I've followed my mother-in-law many times to the local vegetable markets and watched her in amusement. The farmer would begin by quoting a price, which often she would reject, claiming she got a better quote in the next stall and the price and bantering would go back and forth until they reached an agreement. Next would come the weighing of the vegetables and once again, my mother-in-law would produce her own handheld weigh-

During the negotiation process with foreigners, you may have heard stories about how the local Chinese like to hold banquets as a means of getting to know each other in a more relaxed setting (helped by copious amounts of alcohol). By all means, show your Chinese counterpart the respect they deserve (if your liver can handle it) but friendly gestures and courtesy aside, you should never be lulled into changing your negotiation stance on principles affecting your bottom line.

ing scale, which would then give rise to an argument over whose was more accurate. In the end, they would come to an agreement and she would be off. I asked her later if she thought it was exhausting to do this over a dollar's worth of vegetables. "Not at all," she replied. "He's new to the market and I haven't seen him before. If I didn't do this, he'd assume I was a fool and the next time it would be even worse. It's important to demonstrate in the beginning you are not going to be taken as a fool so the next time I go back to his stall he'll know enough not to try and pull tricks."

When I reflected on my own negotiation techniques with suppliers of point-of-sale merchandise (POSM) in China I realised that I have also done something similar. Each year I would spend millions on POSM such as beer glasses, ashtrays, lighters, beer fridges, etc. As a result, almost every manufacturer for these goods in the country was knocking on my door. In the beginning, since I did not know the "real" cost of goods, I didn't care about the price suppliers would quote me; at the end, I would almost always baulk at the price and dismiss them out of hand. I certainly didn't use Western pricing as a benchmark, a common mistake for the inexperienced, because you would be surprised how inexpensive things can be made for in

China. However, after trial and error (and I am sure many a supplier left my office frustrated), I got to know the actual price, including freight and shipping costs, etc. Those that were persistent enough to stick to my negotiations and match my expectations eventually got my business because over time we were able to develop respect and trust as we got to know one another better. To structure the ideal supplier relationship, price was only one of the factors I looked for. I wouldn't mind paying a slight premium if he could also guarantee quality and delivery. **Too many companies focus only on price when the real win-win relationship should be built on value and reliability.**

Sales Tip: Beware the Bait and Hook Trap

A common ploy to avoid is the old bait and hook trap, where a distributor comes (often from a remote region in China) and the first payments are made promptly and sometimes even in advance of receipt of goods. The orders at first would be small but gradually increase each time. The manufacturer would get excited as to the opening up of these new markets and newly found distributors. They would often next send the salespeople down and the salesmen would often come back with glowing reports about how big the market potential was and how they really needed to invest in this market, not knowing that often these salespeople were now in the paid pockets and colluding with these distributors. Credit terms would be established and sales would continue, orders getting larger and larger. The distributor would come back to the manufacturer asking for more money to invest or longer credit terms to "help him develop the market". Desperate for sales and pressure from the home office to show signs their China investment strategy was working by a growth in sales and opening up of new markets, the manufacturer, often GM or Sales Director, whose job was on the line to meet ridiculously high sales figures, would acquiesce to the terms and sink deeper into credit.

Slowly over time, credit terms would lengthen and the value of accounts receivable increase. Throughout this whole period, both the salesmen and distributor would be raving about the market potential and how they need "just that little bit more investment" to really make the breakthrough. Eventually, the Finance Director starts shouting about the accounts receivable getting out of hand or someone in the head office looking at the aged receivables raises a flag. The manufacturer starts to slow down investment and starts demanding payment. The distributor comes back with the excuse that he can't pay you because he has no money, since he claims he has already sunk the money in the market and needs to wait for the product to sell before he can pay up. The salesmen sent down after him to collect the money then come back with the report that it is really "tough" down there and the competition is outspending them and they are in fear of losing the market if they don't do anything about it (i.e., spend more money, please).

The manufacturer stops sending money down a seemingly bottomless pit and if he is lucky, finds other distributors to carry on. The company takes a huge hit in its accounts receivable and fires the salesmen (but the salesmen have already made their "cut" from the other side). Sometimes the head office even fires the General Manager or Sales Director. One General Manager I met, running a plant in Guangdong province, cynically said about his former employer, "They wanted me to prostitute myself to anyone who wanted our products, so guess what? We contracted herpes!" This unfortunate tale applies to many industries, companies and executives I have spoken to in China and is why often when I go to these companies to do my research, I am often speaking to the third-generation General Manager or Sales Director the company has had in its short history in China.

The Chinese way of negotiating may be different from the Western way, but once again what should never change is your basic business common sense. Following Action Step 2, which is to be flexible and adaptable to the way the Chinese like to negotiate, and also Action Step 3, which is to be patient and thorough in ensuring your bottom-line business objectives are met and you truly understand the other side's intentions, will allow you to achieve Action Step 4, which is to negotiate a win-win deal. Today, after more than 20 years of exposure to Western business practices, more and more types of Chinese companies are available, such as the burgeoning private sector that often better understands the importance of negotiating win-win deals aimed at the long term. If you don't get the deal you want immediately, then simply look elsewhere. If what you have to offer is truly a win-win deal, then through patience and perseverance you will eventually find the right partner, agent, distributor or customer, and conclude the deal you intended to.

10 | *China Streetsmart* Action Step 5

Be Detailed – Clarity Prevents Problems

Attention to detail prevents misunderstanding, enables win-win deals, and helps better understand and manage risk.

When working in a cross-cultural environment, being extra detailed in how you communicate verbally, and how you look at and use documentation, and never assuming too much, will prevent small misunderstandings from growing into big problems. When I asked both foreign and local managers what the single biggest problem between the two sides was, the overwhelming response boiled down to poor communication. Language and cultural differences between Mainland China and the rest of the world are so big that it is easy for miscommunication resulting in misunderstanding to take place. The simple remedy is to ensure you are clearly understood by being more detailed. Being detailed is more than looking at the fine print of a contract; rather, it is doing that little bit extra to be understood even for the simplest of tasks.

An executive responsible for setting up his representative office in the early 90s told me an amusing story I will never forget. He was explaining that there was this doorknob in his office that kept falling off. He asked his office manager to fix the doorknob, which he did promptly as asked. A few days later, he opened the door and the doorknob fell off again. Again he asked his office manager to fix the doorknob, which he promptly did as asked. A few days later, the executive tried the door and the doorknob fell off again! Annoyed, he looked down and saw that the knob was being held together by a paper clip, which was being loosened over time. He angrily called his office manager over to scold him for doing such a poor job. Later the office manager complained to his other colleagues that he had done nothing wrong – he had done exactly what was asked of him.

Every time the doorknob broke he fixed it. What the executive failed to make clear was his instructions: fix the doorknob so it can't fall off anymore.

This example may seem almost comical or too incredible to believe, and I would not have believed the story myself, if I had not had similar experiences. In China you need to understand the distinction between completing a task and completing a task in the best way; in the above case, fixing the doorknob so it doesn't break down again. A little more clarity in instructions would have prevented a lot of problems. In Chinese, there is the word *cou he* (pronounced "tsou heh" in Mandarin), which simply means make do. One of the by-products of people who grew up in a state-run command economy was the mentality that you did exactly what was asked of you, nothing more, and nothing less. Freethinking and innovation were rarely rewarded or encouraged. Complicating this mentality was an economy used to scarcity of available goods, so people constantly had to make compromises and learn to make do. This mentality often frustrated me no end. For example, when renovating my house, I had to be especially careful when working with building contractors, since when I said, "Fix this crack," if I was not careful, I sometimes would get the hole plugged with this lumpy blob of plaster. Instead I learned to say, "I want the crack fixed by using plaster so I cannot notice there is a crack anymore. If you need to, sand it down and paint it if necessary. If you are unsure what to do, then please ask me."

Focus on Being Effective Communicators

Before you start thinking you will appear condescending if your English conversations make you feel like you are talking as if you were giving instructions to a four-year-old, don't feel bad; the real focus should be on being an effective communicator. **If you are communicating to locals (non-native English speakers), speaking more slowly than you may be used to and using simple words free of slang will go a long way towards preventing misunderstandings.** You really need to be the judge of your audience in terms of their language and cultural comprehension, but the rule of thumb should always be to err on the side of more detail – more is better than less. The younger generation of Mainland Chinese, more savvy to Western colloquialisms and eager to demonstrate freer thinking, may not have the same communication challenges, but inevitably there will be misunderstandings. While I was working at Lion Nathan, Lion was able to attract some of the best and brightest young staff in Shanghai given the fact that their wage levels were often 25–50% higher than what local companies were paying. Most were fluent in English, yet I always ran into instances where even the most fluent local managers would miss something if the conversation were in English only. Being conscious of the fact that you are communicating with people whose mother tongue is not English and whose frame of reference could be quite different from your own, put in the extra effort needed for clarity.

Being detailed, however, does not necessarily mean trying to explain everything down to the minutest detail. As a way of training his staff and encouraging their problem-solving skills, Michael Colozzi, General Manager Asia for Portola Packaging (the detailed case study which you are about to learn in Part II), said whenever speaking to his staff, he would speak slowly and clearly about the challenge or problem he wanted them to solve, but he would then make sure his staff understood the problem by asking them to repeat what he had just said in their own words. Only then would he feel he had communicated his goals clearly. Don't feel you are being condescending to your local staff, since they often are not used to working with foreign managers and often appreciate the clarity; it just takes a little more effort on your part.

The Importance of Taking Detailed Notes – and Sharing Them

One of my favourite examples of a *China Streetsmart* individual is Finnur Gudmundsson from Iceland. Finnur came to Hong Kong back in 1999 on the promise of a job, which didn't turn out to his expectations. Stuck without a job after only six months in Hong Kong, having moved with his wife Angela across the world, he had two options: head back to Europe, or try and open a new business to capitalise on the growing opportunities in China. Through his connections, he managed to establish contact with some European department stores and discovered they were looking for a company to help them with sourcing and procurement in China. Finnur started up a company with his wife called OrKa International. At that time, Finnur knew nothing about China. He didn't understand the language or culture, had no connections in China, and had very little capital to start with. His strategy was simple. He went to the Hong Kong Trade Development Council (HKTDC) library and looked up suppliers in China for products requested by his European customers, and then jumped on a train to cross the border into Guangdong province to look for factories willing and capable of meeting his client's needs.

Fortunately, he found some Chinese companies who did have some experience in dealing with Western trading companies and could speak English on a limited basis. As I listened to his fascinating story, one particular trait struck me as to how he was able to be successful in China without knowing the language or culture. Whenever he got into a meeting with the Chinese, he would profusely take detailed notes and after each meeting, apologising that this was his habit of doing business. He then proceeded to make a photocopy of his meeting notes to make sure both he and his supplier had a

Photograph by John L. Chan

Finnur Gudmundsson proudly hold up their portable hot water showerhead they designed and manufactured in China and are now shipping to Europe. Asked about his decision to invest in China, he says, "I love it. It's the best decision I have ever made!"

copy of what he thought was discussed. Time after time, Finnur reflected to me, his notes would prove critical to resolving any misunderstanding or differences in perceptions of what was expected by both sides: "Was it four lights or four lights on each side for that Christmas ornament?" In fact, his Chinese counterpart started keeping a file of all their past meetings and began to make notes himself. I am happy to report today that Finnur has built up his business volume to the point where he is no longer just sourcing, but also introducing new products into Europe from China.

Something so simple as note taking, minuting or documenting meetings seems too basic to need to mention, but it is surprising how often we in the West have gotten lazy. Executives working for some of the largest companies have been guilty of *not* taking detailed notes (let alone sharing them), perhaps thinking this practice as being beyond them. "I seldom took detailed meeting notes until I came to China," Guy Bouchet, Vice President at A.T. Kearney, confesses. "Back in Europe, I remember walking out of client meetings and my boss would ask me, 'Did you get everything – I see you didn't take any notes?' 'Sure!' (he says with a simple wave of his hand). However, after coming to China I got into the habit of taking notes thoroughly at every client meeting. In my first year here, a Chinese client challenged me on a specific point we had cleared in a previous meeting; luckily, I pulled out my notes and showed him what he had said and when. He seemed suitably impressed and we moved on. He became more careful about what he said around me after that ... and I have kept using this simple method to cut through 'circular negotiations' since then."

Having spoken to many executives on this subject, I found that they almost all conclude that the Chinese side appreciates the effort of documenting everything so all points are clearly understood. It is actually when they do not want you to take notes or are suspicious of why you want to take notes, that your own suspicions should arise. Related to this story is another fascinating *China Streetsmart* individual, Gerhard Kutt, son of an Alsatian businessman who went to China at the turn of the century. Gerhard was born in Shanghai during the Chinese Revolution and has never left the region. He now lives in Hong Kong. As I was telling him the story about Finnur and the importance of being clear by being detailed and taking notes, he told me the story when he was the Strategic Planning Manager for The Union Trading Company back in the early 80s. The Union Trading Company, established during the 20s, was at the time one of the largest trading companies in the region and had significant operations in China. At the time, one of their divisions was the exclusive importer of Honda motorcycles in China. Those of you who have travelled in China certainly know the proliferation of motorcycles, especially in Southern China. Annual sales volume of Honda motorcycles alone tops several hundred million USD.

Gerhard also practised the habit of making himself clear by taking detailed notes and passing them onto his Chinese counterpart. As he was working on establishing agreements with all his key importing agents, the largest importer actually took offence to his note taking, saying it insulted the form of trust they were building, and that he didn't believe they needed to document things in this manner. Gerhard insisted and in the end, the importer took his business away from Honda and went to Suzuki. According to Gerhard, Suzuki was later faced with millions of dollars in bad debt from this importer. The importer, as it turned out, was operating only a "quasi-legal" importing licence, built on his close connections with officials in the Guangdong government. The reason he didn't want a record of what was being agreed to was it left a paper trail where he could be personally implicated. Instead, he preferred to hide behind shell companies that issued quasi-legal import documents and receipts.

Never Over-Assume

Making oneself clear, whether by speech or by notes, is only part of what is needed to be effective in China. Another important habit to follow is to never over-assume how things will work in China, especially when preparing contracts or following government regulations. A common negotiation tactic is to ensure that the obligations of the opposite party you are dealing with are as detailed as possible to ensure you are getting what you need from the agreement, while leaving your own obligations and duties vague enough to manoeuvre, claiming a different interpretation if needed. While this may not be fair and could violate the principle of win-win, the Chinese have used this tactic time and again, so do not assume or expect the

Chinese side to be fair and open (in a Western sense) when negotiating a contract.

Many foreign investors coming to China make the mistake of misinterpreting how to "build respect and trust" in China. The previous chapter states that the local Chinese often build respect and trust among themselves through a bantering process of testing each other's limits. Unfortunately, many foreign investors, especially those from English-speaking countries, are not as familiar with this process. "Trust me," the Chinese negotiator would say, knowing this statement was a simple negotiation tactic. "This is how we do things in China." The foreign side, not sticking to the common-sense business principle, would often then acquiesce as a "goodwill gesture". These goodwill gestures, however, have the opposite intended effect, since the Chinese themselves would never have agreed to these conditions when negotiating among themselves and would lose respect for the person who could be so silly to agree to such one-sided terms. **Being detailed during negotiations requires that anything that is important enough to affect your bottom-line objectives *must* be clearly detailed in the contract.** Once respect has been earned, when the Chinese side realises you are not a foolish businessperson, goodwill gestures will then become more meaningful.

Another challenge for many investors in China is how to work within a commercial framework that is constantly evolving. Do not assume that laws set down by the central government in Beijing will be implemented the same across China. Local officials often interpret national laws differently, especially if there are negative local repercussions. Furthermore, do not assume just because a local official says you can do something, the decision will not be reversed later, once Beijing realises that the locality has been operating outside its jurisdiction and cracks down on it. Trying to understand the jurisdiction of federal, provincial and local governments and how Chinese law is implemented and enforced raises many grey areas requiring interpretation. The practice of being detailed, connected to Action Step 3 (Be Patient and Thorough), will help investors better understand where these grey areas are, and the associated risks. For example, foreign investors setting up in small municipal special investment zones should check whether they are sanctioned by the federal government or whether it is the local government acting alone as a way of attracting foreign investment to create local jobs. In the Guanxi Zhuang Autonomous Region in 1998, 143 illegal non-sanctioned investment zones were closed and the original benefits that companies thought they were achieving are now gone.[1] The *China Streetsmart* approach is to use experts to help you understand the specific regulations affecting your investment in a particular area, but before deciding who to use, be detailed in your questioning to ensure they have the proven relevant experience. Once again, do not assume just because they represent a well-known international company that they can meet your needs.

---

[1] The Economist Intelligence Unit, May 2001, "Chapter 5: Investment Locations", *China Hand*, p. 3.

11 | *China Streetsmart* Action Step 6

Maintain a Healthy Attitude – Choose Your Battles Carefully

The point is not to focus on the process of how things get done in China, but rather on your bottom-line goals and how to achieve them.

Frankly speaking, no executive has come out and said directly to me that maintaining a healthy attitude is the key to being effective and successful in China; rather, I came about this view only after being very observant and after getting to know them better. These executives have been in China for years, if not decades, and have a certain resiliency and positive outlook on life. "You've got to be an optimist to work in China," explains James Spears, a 15-year China veteran and Senior Vice President of Chindex, a Nasdaq-listed importing company of medical goods and equipment.

As I was writing *China Streetsmart*, Dell Smith, one of those popular expats who just happens to know everyone in town, helped me

Photograph by Dell Smith

Dell Smith, Business Development Director for Freser Refrigeration, takes time out in a baseball league run by expats in Shanghai. Their championship team, "Shanghai Sally's No. 1 Sons", includes senior executives from a number of leading MNCs in China and the Asia-Pacific region.

do a straw poll among his hundreds of foreign friends he knows are living or have lived in China. We called the straw poll "What Bugs You", to find out the things that annoyed foreigners most about living in China. Through the efficiency of e-mail, he collected dozens of very interesting responses (some of which would have to be censored to be publishable!). There was one common comment that clearly stood out among the other complaints. What drove a lot of foreigners crazy was the fact that **most local Chinese will never admit they are wrong.** Even when the "correct answer" is staring them in the face, they will never admit they are wrong. Actually, the foreigners who feel this way are not acknowledging the cultural sensitivity of "losing face" in China. Furthermore, the local Chinese might genuinely not think they are wrong, given a difference in understandings and viewpoints. Many foreigners find dealing with face issues the most frustrating aspect of working in China, but for the long-term China hands, this issue rarely fazes them – if anything, they are able to use it to their advantage. When I raised these stories, many of the old China hands often empathised with the locals, saying that in situations like these, often the foreigner is the

Photograph by Phil Davis

China can be tough on the foreign executive but *China Streetsmart* executives will always find the time to relax and enjoy themselves as Phil Davis of Anheuser-Busch is clearly doing.

one who has trouble facing the fact, and the fact is not what is right or wrong, but the fact that they are in China.

There are Advantages and Disadvantages to Everything

It is natural that locals may treat you differently because you seem strange and foreign to them. Be prepared that you will likely encounter double standards in China that may or may not work in your favour. Locals may try and "cheat" foreigners because of the way they look. This treatment happens all around the world. In Italy, I used to get frustrated with being constantly "cheated" just because I was assumed to be a rich travelling Japanese businessman. It helps when you can laugh in situations like that and just take it in your stride.

As noted earlier, China is rife with contradictions, double standards and hypocrisy. I say this not as a criticism of my own culture, but rather to point out the simple fact that it exists. My good friend Brad Holt, the General Manager for StonCor North Asia, an American company that makes high-tech industrial flooring, said to me, "You know, John, I hate this double standard which exists in China. The fact is if you and I were to get in an accident [because I have a white face], I would be treated differently [better] by the police than you would." I replied, "Sure, Brad, but that doesn't bother me one bit because with my [Chinese] face, I can get into local business circles that you could probably never penetrate, even if your Mandarin were better than mine." The point being, there are advantages and disadvantages to any given situation. Our attitude towards how we deal with them is what makes the difference.

Sun Tze and the Art of War

The Art of War written by Sun Tze has been translated into English many times and is a favourite of Western business executives in determining their business strategies. One of the fundamental tenets his writings emphasise is that to win the war, you must attack where the enemy is weak and run where the enemy is strong. The main point is to choose your battles carefully. While it is not healthy to view China as the enemy, foreign executives have often commented that at times they feel like they are in a constant battle of wits. Trying to fight all battles with equal vigour and conviction will be a huge drain (on your wits) and eventually you will lose (your wits). Burnout is a common symptom among foreign executives not used to the challenges and differences China imposes. Some learn to handle the pressures effectively by choosing to fight only those really "important" battles that significantly affect their bottom-line business objectives. By being flexible and adaptable (Action Step 2), these people often learn of advantages about China beyond their original expectations and some will even go so far as to say they now *love* being in China. If anything, their frustration stems from when they have to go back to their home countries and try and read-just to working life there. These are the ones who become real China hands, and executives like Mike Blackburn, the executive responsible for setting up and running Mars (makers of chocolate and pet food) in China, now Chairman of Great Lakes Fruit Juices, says he never plans on leaving. On the other hand, there are those who be-

Photograph by John L. Chan

Mike Blackburn enjoys life in China with his better half Jwee San Tan, with the executive search firm Spencer Stuart based in Beijing. This photo was taken in front of a quaint Italian restaurant called Agrilandia, an authentic Italian restaurant that serves only fresh grown produce just on the outskirts of Beijing. "Places like these are what I love about China," says Mike.

come extremely cynical about China. These people never last and burn out after only a year or two. They go back to their home country spreading stories about what a nightmare it was to work in China.

Be Careful of Who You Send to China

The real danger for a company to be aware of is who it should send to China. This issue raises a dilemma for many companies: do you send the most technically skilled executive from home office or do you focus more on adaptability? Hopefully, companies won't need to compromise at all, for example, by choosing from the many skilled and culturally adaptable overseas Chinese expats available. An executive who does not have the cultural appreciation or flexibility and adaptability to work in China can produce disastrous results. Those who are mistrusting, culturally insensitive and inflexible are the ones who often use too much slang when speaking with local staff, and get angry when things are not fully understood. These misfits cause misunderstandings and failed negotiations, lose opportunities and potentially waste millions. "Not enough emphasis is placed on cultural training for executives," says Vincent Wan, Chairman of China Team (international member of the Cornerstone Group), the first executive recruitment agency to acquire a joint venture partner in China. You often spot these cultural misfits at Western bars frequented mostly by expats, constantly complaining about everything. Some come for the money and perks, others just because their head office told them to. Those executives that tend to hide exclusively among the expat community, outside the office, are really missing out the real joys and excitement of what China has to offer. Some feel they are here to do an assignment that will last one to three years, and then "I'm outta here. I did my time."

Most of the more successful executives I spoke to said they received very little to no screening by their company's head office as to whether they would be truly suitable. However, if you asked them whether their company should adopt this practice, almost all agree. In fact, many companies now have very stringent pre-screening procedures before sending someone abroad to work in China. Others are not so fortunate and have to accept the staff the head office provides and pray they get lucky. I got lucky when Neil Hinton from

Photographs by John L. Chan

Vincent Wan is a true blue Hong Kong entrepreneur running through pure hard work and determination, not one, but several successful China businesses, among which he is the exclusive distributor for Perrier in Shanghai and Hong Kong. He also runs one of the top boutique executive recruitment agencies in China, the first ever to be set up as a joint venture in China.

New Zealand came to China from Lion Nathan's New Zealand operations to manage the licensed Beck's beer brand. Initially Neil came for only a three-month period, before I was meant to find a suitable local manager to fill his shoes. When Neil arrived in China, he was very eager to learn about the market and was absolutely fascinated by everything he saw around him. I was impressed by his openness and ability to work with the local staff. So much so, I decided to keep him on my staff and his original three-month stint turned into a two-and-a-half-year assignment, even outlasting my own time in the company.

Cultural Adaptability Extends to the Whole Family

Related to the business executive's ability to adapt to the cultural changes and daily frustrations China has to offer is also the need for the executive's family to really enjoy being in China. An expat's job is filled with stress at work and if the home environment is not any better, his work, and hence the company, will be affected. Making the transition to China can be a shock if one is not properly prepared. Being in a strange land and not being able to speak the local language can be a frightening experience for some, especially if he or she has never lived in a foreign land, let alone one as different as China. **The *China Streetsmart* advice is when screening and choosing a candidate to work in China to manage your business,**

ensure that both the executive and his or her family are willing and capable of managing the stresses that China offers before sending them over. Good screening and advanced planning will prevent too many management changes and the problems outlined in Action Step 1.

Photograph by Guy Bouchet

Taking time out with the family to explore some of the fascinating sites around China can be a rewarding experience and a great way to relieve stress. Guy Bouchet of A.T. Kearney takes time out to travel with his wife Ceil and two children Marc and Annie.

Photograph by Mark DeCocinis

Mark DeCocinis, the General Manager for the Portman Ritz-Carlton, relaxes by taking his family out for rides on his China-made replica of a 1938 BMW. His wife Margie and his two sons Michael and Marchese all love China.

China Streetsmart

PART II

The Application

In this section you will learn how to set up a profitable company in China, specifically:

- How to understand the market and assess your potential.

- How to assess your different investment options and look for the right joint venture partner if required.

- How to anticipate potential problems in negotiating and managing a business, and possible solutions.

- How to look for new business opportunities beyond the original business scope.

12 | A *China Streetsmart* Case Study

A Real Life Application

In 1995, a group of lawyers wrote a soft-cover book costing more than 150 USD called *Life and Death of a Joint Venture* which was one of the best business books on China written at that time. The somewhat dated book is about a fictitious company that went from contract negotiations and start-up; to the cultural clashes and differences in expectations on how the company should be run to eventual "divorce" and splitting up of assets. Although it was a fictitious company, the situation was realistic and gave those coming to China a good case study on what to watch out for and how things could be handled to arrive at the best resolution.

China Streetsmart actually covers a real life case of a company that went through the life and death of a joint venture (JV). It began as a JV with the best of intentions, ran into management differences between the foreign and local side, and now operates in China as a wholly owned foreign enterprise (WOFE). The company showcased is

http://www.portpack.com

Shanghai Portola Packaging Co., Ltd. and is a great success story of an American firm that came to China and faced problems similar to those faced by other foreign invested enterprises (FIEs) operating in China such as how to access the market, determine the right investment strategy, find a suitable local partner, hire staff, protect its intellectual property rights (IPR), etc. A key point to Portola is that,

unlike a lot of negative press about how difficult it is to make money in China, Portola has always been profitable (beginning with their first month of operation) and has enjoyed benefits not previously anticipated, such as increased company savings world-wide by sourcing more materials from China for their other international operations. The main reason for its profitable stance was because its executives did things right from the very start.

Photograph by John L. Chan

The main executive I refer to is Michael Carl Colozzi. He is one of the best examples of a *China Streetsmart* individual I know. A former Vice President of The Gap Stores in America, he came to China back in 1997 to begin setting up an operation to produce and manufacture packaging and bottling equipment for non-carbonated drinks in China. His company is the world's leader in their highly specialised field of plastic closures for the dairy, bottled water and juice industries, with worldwide sales in the hundreds of millions of USD. With 15 manufacturing plants around the world, Portola is no stranger to the international market. For more information about the company, see their website at www.portpack.com. Their China operation has been operating since 1998 with a total investment of around 10 million USD with international clients such as Nestle, Coca-Cola and A.S. Watson.

A word of caution before proceeding: the opinions and techniques that Portola used might not necessarily be the best strategy for your particular situation; rather, you must be the judge as to what is most appropriate for your specific case. For example, Portola China's operation was a relatively small operation needing only 50 people. The fact that Michael did not use many of the professional services such as executive search firms does not suggest at all that these services are not needed. Michael said he tried some of the professional services but found their results were not up to his expectations. However, this should not imply that the professional services available such as executive search, market research, consulting, and accounting services are not useful. In fact, many companies that tried to cut too many corners by doing everything themselves actually ended up paying more in terms of quality of results, lost time, and lost opportunities. Speaking to companies with on-the-ground experience and contacts in China will always prove useful to the new investor, but like in any market or industry, service levels will vary. To determine which individual or companies are useful to help you, the *China Streetsmart* approach is to get good references and look closely at what they have done *in China*. **Do not assume just because a company is a brand name internationally that their services will be good in China.**

China Team, a regional executive search consultancy firm, is a good case of a smaller company that can easily compete with the largest international firms because of their proven on-the-ground track record. Prior to coming to China, I had never heard of this company, but later learned that they definitely were one of the more reputable companies in their field, having the oldest executive recruitment JV in China, with major clients like Nike and Philips. On the other hand, I can attest to the fact that some of the largest brand name firms in the service field, including management training, research, advertising and management consultancy, have produced results below the level of professionalism I would have expected and not worth the top dollar they were charging. One international research executive who saw the results they produced for me was so shocked with the poor output that she said her company would give me "extra research" free of charge as compensation. In other cases, I was not so lucky.

But it is important to emphasise that the past does not have to equal the future. During the 90s when most companies, including the most reputable ones, were just setting up operations in China, some experienced the same start-up pains as any other company and as a result, their earlier performances may not necessarily be indicative of where they are today. In the early 90s, when ACNielsen took over a smaller company called SRG to establish their foothold in China, they went through all kinds of growing pains and the quality of output in the early days was arguably not what you would expect

Alistair Watts, Managing Director for ACNielsen China, speaks at their annual client day highlighting "the five faces of the Chinese consumer" based on their extensive analysis and market knowledge.

from the research company with the highest billings in the world. However, today ACNielsen, with its rich resource of historical data, offers one of the best market research services to help companies understand the retail consumer field, for example.

As with all companies, quality of service depends on the staff's level of on-the-ground China experience coupled with their expertise in their chosen field. Unfortunately, because these experienced people are in such short supply (but getting a little better), there is a tendency for them to be continually poached by different firms in the marketplace. Do not be afraid to challenge or question a firm, regardless of international reputation, as to exactly who from the company will be working with you and their level of "local" knowledge, expertise and capabilities. In short, despite the stories you may have heard about a particular company, good or bad, it is always advisable to see exactly their present experience and capabilities.

Finally, following each stage of Portola's China investment experience will be an analysis from a *China Streetsmart* perspective that will not only highlight what Portola did well (or could have done better), but also discuss other options and experiences for consideration. Portola's case is only one path a company can take. Other companies I interviewed were successful in areas where Portola failed, such as in finding the right local JV partner. The key is to understand the context and reasoning surrounding the result and see how this could apply to your own given situation. This is the *China Streetsmart* approach.

13 | Preliminary Steps
Getting off to a Good Start

Preliminary Steps | Setting the Strategy | Negotiating the Deal | Running the Joint Venture | Ending the Joint Venture | Beyond the Joint Venture

A Familiar Beginning

Back in 1996, a Chinese state-run company called the Shanghai Aquarius Drinking Water Drinking Co., Ltd., now popularly known simply by their phone number 85818, bought a water drinking system from Portola Packaging, Inc. (USA). The management of Aquarius was so impressed with the advanced American system that they began to talk with Portola's Asia-Pacific sales representative about the possibilities of starting a joint venture (JV) in China. After months of preliminary enquiries and letters exchanged across the Pacific, Jack Watts, a Stanford MBA graduate and former Chairman of Flextronics, Inc. (now a multi-billion dollar company) and now Chairman and CEO of Portola, went to China in January 1996, where he signed a Letter of Intent (LOI) that was drafted in only half a day. The LOI was then used by Aquarius to get pre-approval with their supervising bureau (*zhuguan bumen*), in this case, the Shanghai Light Industry Bureau (today the Shanghai Light Industry Holding Co.), to go ahead with talks. Upon returning to the US, Jack asked Michael Colozzi to go to China to explore what he had started.

Michael arrived in China in February 1997 on a 30-day visa, just two days after China's biggest annual holiday, the Spring Festival (the Chinese or Lunar New Year), had started. He knew he was arriving during the Spring Festival, but was unaware that businesses shut down for up to two weeks as people go home and spend time with their families – much like the Christmas holiday season in the

Shanghai American Center, Portman Ritz-Carlton Hotel

West. He didn't get frustrated; instead, he began reading his books on China he purchased before leaving and spent time roaming the streets. He began amassing a huge amount of literature and documentation on China. "Anything I could find [written in English] during those first 30 days I took and read through it all; everything from magazines and newspapers of what's going on in Shanghai, to government bulletins and briefs. That certainly kept me busy during my first week. In fact, somewhere in my office I still have all the documents I accumulated on my first trip. It fills a whole foot locker."

Michael stayed in Shanghai at the Portman Hotel (now run by the Ritz-Carlton), which is part of the Shanghai American Center, owned by American International Group, Inc. (AIG). The hotel is a favourite place for Americans and is where Presidents Bush and Clinton both stay when they come to Shanghai. The main bar in the hotel is called the Long Bar and is a frequent hangout for expats living and working in Shanghai. There, he met up with Paul Ashman, the manager of a local golf club. Paul was organising a golf outing for 40 of the top general managers in Shanghai during the Spring Festival holiday and invited Michael to come along. An avid golfer, Michael happily went and got to meet with 40 general managers representing some of the largest and most well-known companies operating in China today. Needless to say, he subsequently collected 40 business cards at the event and proceeded to go and meet each one throughout the remainder of his 30-day stay. He learned firsthand, the information this book is passing on – the practical Streetsmart advice of how things are really done and how to set up a profitable business.

China Streetsmart

Understanding the Market

Not satisfied to only hear the foreign executive's view on how to set up and run a successful operation in China, he then proceeded to talk and interview local staff of manufacturing enterprises similar to the one he wanted to set up. What he wanted to learn from these locals who had all worked for foreign enterprises was what were the main reasons why foreign enterprises apparently were not doing well in China. He cited four major reasons:

1. **Poor communication.** "This was clearly the no. 1 problem locals had with their [foreign] boss. Simple habits such as speaking slowly, clearly and using simple words rather than slang or colloquial terms can prevent a lot of headaches and misunderstandings. Furthermore, the fact that locals are generally reluctant to say, 'I do not understand what you are saying' doesn't help either. Every one of the locals complained that their [foreign] boss did not really understand them or their needs. The communication was really just one-way."

2. **Cultural differences.** "Many Americans [and Europeans] come to China believing they know it all and are here to show the locals how things are done, rather than being humble enough to try and learn what is more appropriate for China. A common phrase hated by most locals was, 'The way we do it in the US is like this ...' They really don't try and take advantage of the Chinese minds and their way of thinking, sometimes dismissing them outright. Finally, I see a huge lack of respect some of the [foreign] managers have for China and what China is trying to achieve. This lack of respect is felt by the local staff so I'm not surprised they [the foreign executives] get treated the way they do."

3. **Absolute failure to understand the market.** "Anyone can pay a hundred grand [I purposely omit the name of the company] for a market feasibility study, but what you get are one of these young MBA grads who have never run a business in their life, go pick up a statistics book on China and put the

numbers in a fancy report – anybody can do that. If you really want to know what the market is like, the only way you are going to be successful is to go out into the market yourself. Furthermore, most underestimated the level of competition that was about to hit China. Many figured or planned on being the only [foreign] player in town."

4. **Way too many management changes.** "Most of these [local] guys have seen foreign executives come and go. Each time it's like starting all over again – teaching these executives while trying to let them think they are teaching you. Also there is way too much interference from head office. When things start getting difficult, they all start flying in like seagulls, eat your food, squawk a lot, crap all over the place, and fly away again. You can't run a business effectively with that much interference."

What was really interesting about these comments by the locals is that Michael compared the comments to those of the foreign executives and found the list was pretty much identical, with the exception that the foreigners didn't feel that lack of respect was an issue. This difference in opinion is not too surprising. "I won't tell you the names of the people and companies I visited, but you can easily guess who they are," he says with a big grin on his face.

Michael couldn't speak a word of Chinese when he came to China. And to this day, his Chinese is about as proficient as to help him not get lost in a cab by learning how to say, left, right, and STOP! … oh yes, and of course, how to order a beer [*pijiu xie xie*]. But Michael compensated for his lack of language abilities by having a trusted lieutenant right at the start. John Huang, a local Shanghainese educated in both China and the US, is a Partner with AllBright Law Offices. John spent a lot of time with Michael during those initial days and was critical in helping Michael understand what was real and what was not. "The fact that John was a local and could speak the local language really helped open up a lot of doors for me. Sure, I could have used a foreign lawyer who might have been able to speak some Mandarin, but it's not the same as getting a local's perspective. The [big foreign] law firm [I purposely omit their name] can tell you the law, but they can't tell you how to get it [and make it work for you]."

Photographs by John L. Chan

John Huang, Partner at the Shanghai law firm AllBright, was the trusted lieutenant Michael Colozzi used to help him understand how China worked when he first arrived in Shanghai. They spent many evenings together, like they are doing here, at the Executive Lounge at the Portman Ritz-Carlton.

Understanding the market size and potential for his company's products was another critical effort Michael focused on in his early days in China. To get a good feel for the market, he got himself a directory listing of companies that could be either his partner or potential customer and began to visit each of their factories. He would ask simple questions like "So how many water bottles come off your line per day? And how many days are you open?" From these simple questions he was able to start to gauge the rough market size across China. "China is cheap to travel around," he says. "You can travel around the country and live in hotels that cost no more than 40–70 USD per night. I estimate that all the time I spent flying all across China, I could not have spent more than 15,000–20,000 USD; better than paying 100,000 USD to a consultant for a report you can get from buying a Chinese statistics book.

"I also got to understand better how local companies do their accounting in China; for example, as I travelled around to the different local companies I began to see how they often kept two or more sets of (accounting) books. One was an official one for audit purposes with the government, and the others were for their internal use. I learned the reasons for this was often related to the issue of "invoiced" or "off invoiced" sales or purchase of goods. Those that were "off invoiced", i.e., transactions that were not officially recorded, didn't need to account for value-added tax (VAT), which was up to a 17% savings. I would never have learned this from reading a report."

By May 1997, Portola was excited enough about the packaged water market in China, which was growing at an impressive rate of 10% *month over month,* to know they wanted to be a participant in some form. They decided it was time to register both their patents and trademarks in China. What they discovered upon filing for registration was Chinese companies had already registered the patents for the two key products they planned to launch in China, which Portola already owned in the US. For example, Portola holds the sports cap patent, which is the trendy pull cap on single-serve water bottles; however, four other Chinese companies had already registered the patent design in China. Another company was also holding the design and utility patents for their 5-gallon cap. It was then that Portola learned that in China, **Chinese patent law rights go to the first-to-file, as opposed to the first-to-use, a patent or trademark in China** (it is the opposite in the US).

Sports Cap

5-Gallon
Snap Cap

Photographs courtesy of
Portola Packaging

While Portola's products seem very basic, the staff at Portola likes to highlight the high degree of precision and durability that sets them apart from the competition. All their caps are made with anti-tampering devices to prevent counterfeits. Therefore it is not surprising that their caps are among the highest priced on the market.

Assessing their options on what legal action to take, they were advised that it was extremely difficult, but not impossible, to sue a company for patent infringement, since the slightest modification to Portola's original design could be deemed a "different design" While the margins on the sports cap were negligible, it probably was not worth the legal fees to try and win the case over these four Chinese companies. What they were worried about was the one company in Southern China who owned the patent on the higher margin 5-gallon cap. Ironically, Portola was worried about the possibilities of being sued by the Chinese company for a patent that they already legally owned in the US. Michael flew down to meet with the Chinese company to prove to them Portola had the original patent and agreed to "buy back" their own patent in return for a fee and a licensing right to the Chinese company to continue using Portola's patent design. Initially the Chinese company asked for 250,000 USD to buy back the right, but in the end they settled for 25,000 USD paid in instalments over a year. The situation was not ideal, but allowed the executives at Portola to sleep at night.

14 | Preliminary Steps

A *China Streetsmart* Analysis

Preliminary Steps	Setting the Strategy	Negotiating the Deal	Running the Joint Venture	Ending the Joint Venture	Beyond the Joint Venture

The preliminary steps a company makes when first setting up in China is often the most critical to their success. As noted in Action Step 3 (Be Patient and Thorough), the single biggest mistake companies made when entering China was to rush in not really understanding the challenges. The lack of understanding of the market led to misassumptions, which in turn led to strategically flawed plans that often were doomed from the beginning. For Portola, however, they got off to an excellent start. Here is an analysis why from a *China Streetsmart* perspective.

Letter of Intent

The letter of intent (LOI) is often the first serious step companies make in announcing their intention to do business with China. Whether the two parties sign an LOI, a memorandum of understanding (MOU), a project proposal or a feasibility study, the local side uses this type of document to get pre-approval to inform their supervising bureau that oversees the company of their intentions to begin talks. While the LOI is a non-legally binding document, the wording of the document should be carefully checked following Action Step 5 (Be Detailed). Often what the Chinese side will do is to use this document as if it were a legally binding document to pressure the foreign side to stick to what was originally agreed while trying to keep their own commitments vague and flexible to manoeuvre. Fortunately, Jack Watts, a skilled negotiator, was comfortable enough to draft a document which also left their side open to explore many different options, including the right to go with another Chinese partner other than just Aquarius.

Assorted candies
Assorted drinks
Assorted Chinese snack food
Payphone
Cigarettes
Chewing gum
Toys & novelties
Candy bars
Dishwashing liquid
Toothpaste
Soap
Ice cream
Washing powder
Batteries & film
Stationery & school supplies

Photograph by John L. Chan

As Michael walked around the Portman Ritz-Carlton Hotel during his first month in China, he quickly began to sense that while things looked a little different, deeper analysis revealed a lot of similarities to the West. This typical mom and pop kiosk on the left, which is less than 500 metres from the Portman, houses an impressive array of items (SKU's) for its size that could rival any modern-day convenience store. Furthermore, in terms of true convenience, many of these small shops have a delivery number for local patrons to call, which is often what I do when I need a beer delivery.

In Shanghai alone there are over 30,000 of these types of shops dotting every street corner and alleyway.

Information, Information, Information

Although Michael Colozzi had spent time in Japan and Hong Kong, he had never been to Mainland China and knew very little, other than a few conflicting stories, as to whether or not it was a good idea to invest in China. Not being biased by the negative stories many prominent international companies were telling the press about how difficult it was to make money in China, Michael set off to gather as much information as he could. His voracious appetite to learn got him off to a great start. As I interviewed Michael, I discovered that not only is he a very articulate speaker, but he is also an astute listener. He was open-minded enough to just be a sponge in his early days, not rushing to reach conclusions too early. (For more on information sources about China, refer to Appendix A.)

Get to Know the Local Mindset

In spite of Michael's local language deficiency, he still tried very hard to understand the local mindset. I was most impressed with his initiative in interviewing both the foreign and Chinese side to learn what the management and operational issues of running a China business were. His sympathetic stance towards the views of the local Chinese demonstrated that he really cared about what they were thinking – an important process to practising Action Step 2 (Be Flexible and Adaptable). This sensitive view prepared him well and helped him to avoid mistakes made by other foreign managers. As noted in the beginning of this book, how you manage the stories you hear is very important. By sticking to the process of vetting information outlined in Chapter 1, the information should appear less contradictory and confusing.

Local Expertise and Support

Most of the information Michael received would not have been as well understood had Michael not had a trusted lieutenant by his side who knew the local environment. John Huang, the Shanghainese lawyer who studied and trained in the US (LLM UCLA), was the perfect bridge Michael was looking for. He was not only able to translate Michael's wishes in the professional manner most professional translators could not, but he was also able to give insight into what the local Shanghainese were thinking and how to properly address the issues as they arose. "I would have been completely lost had I not had John by my side. He was able to introduce me to all kinds of people and give me advice I couldn't have gotten elsewhere."

Photograph by John L. Chan

Without giving too much credit to the good work that John has done for Portola, I should mention that there are quite a number of excellent lawyers and consultants who are available to help new companies come into the market. But be warned that an experienced China lawyer could cost up to 400–800 USD per hour. While some local lawyers are often cheaper, if they have not spent extensive time in the West, they may not have the professional insight into or understanding of the foreign side to really act as an effective "bridge". In the early 90s, I used one of Beijing's top local law firms and the results I got back were disappointing. Ed Lehman, another excellent prominent China lawyer and an expert in the field of Chinese intellectual property and patent law, is one of the few foreigners who work for a Chinese law firm. In fact his firm today, Lehman, Lee & Xu, is registered as a local Chinese law firm. He commented that many of the local law firms operate more like a big shopping mall, with many of them working under one roof, but operating more independently. Whether using experienced foreign or local firms to help guide you through China, the vetting process is the same – look at their proven track record.

Determining Your Market Potential

There is no single method which is best for determining your market potential; rather it is a combination of knowing how to read the data that is available, use experienced professionals such as market research and/or consulting services to help you understand local needs, and **always, always, always, go out and see the market firsthand**. Those who choose only to rely on reports to manage the business and let others do the fieldwork will severely limit their experience and understanding. Trying to understand the China market is like online dating: you can only learn so much through exchanges of pictures and e-mails; eventually you will have to physically go out and see the person to know if there is a real fit and potential or not.

The more regionally focused your objectives are, the better your results will be. For example, if you are looking at the total China consumer market and only stay in Shanghai to get a feel for Chinese customers' buying habits, you could easily draw the wrong conclusions, since the rural areas and smaller cities often have very different purchasing and consumption habits. Whatever methods you choose, the more you get involved with the research process, the better. Should you use professional services, attend meetings with local groups (even if you need to bring in a translator), go through the test runs on questionnaires and even follow the consultants when they go out into the field and interview the customers you will be working with. I met several foreign executives who felt it "beneath them" to go out and do the fieldwork, choosing instead to get the "executive report". While I'll protect their anonymity, it wasn't a surprise that the companies they represent are losing money in China today.

Professional Services – Market Research

Market research companies can be incredibly useful in China, but like any tool, it is very important to know how to use them. Portola is in a very specialised industry and as a result, a market research firm may not have been as useful as a good consulting firm that could act as a reference check to Michael's own field research. On the other hand, for companies dealing directly in consumer habits, an experienced market research company could prove invaluable.

Alistair Watts, the China Country Manager for ACNielsen, the largest and one of the best market research firms in China, had the fortunate experience of coming to China from Vietnam and knew of

Photograph courtesy of ACNielsen

the challenges a fast-developing country poses. However, as Alistair explains, "The difference between China and Vietnam is that China is such a large country; doing market research for one area only, such as Shanghai, will often not give the proper market assessment if one is looking to extrapolate up for the whole country. Yet most companies are not willing to spend what is really needed to determine their true market potential across China. Vietnam, on the other hand, is much smaller and easier to extrapolate."

Market Research Quirks about China

Other issues to be aware of when using professional services are translation and interpretation problems. For example, understanding different taste habits such as what a "bitter beer" is proved extremely difficult in China since China was full of inexperienced beer drinkers and didn't really know how to describe, let alone translate, a beer's taste as bitter, strong or heavy. San Miguel, Carlsberg, Tiger and Foster's beer are all relatively full-flavoured beers so when it came to implementing taste preference questionnaires developed in the West, most Chinese respondents had difficulty determining what was a "heavy and strong beer" which we call *nong* in Chinese and what was a "bitter beer" which we call *ku*. It wasn't until Budweiser and Suntory beer were introduced onto the market – two incredibly light-tasting beers – that consumers really had a marked taste difference to choose from. Certainly in the Yangtze River Delta, around Shanghai, we know now consumers generally prefer a light-tasting, light-coloured beer.

Different environmental conditions may also affect how your products are perceived in China. Just because the West may use your product or service in a certain way does not mean the same will be done in China. In the West, lager beer, for example, is ideally drunk at 3–5⁰C (35–40⁰F). Two problems exist which we found were unique to China. The first one was the lack of refrigeration rarely creates the situation to drink beer at its ideal temperature. Often the common method in many places in China is to cool beer using ice cubes and the addition of melting ice cubes greatly affects the flavour. Furthermore, we found out Mainland Chinese often consider cold liquids bad for their health. Instead many Chinese consumers would insist on drinking the beer at room temperature or drinking beer that is only cooled in a shaded storeroom. Finding a good market researcher or consultant who has had previous experience with your product or service, or a close equivalent, is critical.

Finding experienced research firms, or to be more precise, experienced individuals, is a common problem companies face. Even the largest brand name market research firms suffered in the early days from trying to learn the best methodologies for China. Finding a company (or really an individual) that understood consumer habits in China and how they were evolving was a challenge. Companies that tried to bring over their tried and proven sophisticated modelling techniques from the West often ran into difficulties in China. I learned these shortcomings the hard way, as I used to subscribe to some of these very expensive market monitors, but was only able to derive limited use from them. To be fair, part of the issue was not related to the quality of the output, rather the time I had to put in to analyse all the ways of looking at the data. Pareto's 80-20 rule really applied for me, where only 20% of the data supplied me with 80% of what I needed.

Professional Services – Consultants

For companies wanting a more in-depth analysis of the market, a good consulting company may often be the best answer to determining your products' market potential in China. However, don't be surprised that as you enquire around China about the usefulness or effectiveness of using consultants, you will get a mixed bag of responses. Many of the executives I spoke to who had used some of the biggest brand name management consultants back in the 80s and early 90s gave comments like "Okay" and "Not worth the money I paid". Having used some of these large management consulting companies myself and seeing the results, especially the business performance of these multinational corporations (MNCs) today, I can understand why some executives would not be over-enamoured. But once again, like using a market research company, it depends on how you use them and what you ask them to do.

Niche Consultants

You may find smaller niche specialists with proven backgrounds in specific industries the better choice. Alan Reid, a lawyer by training and the former head of AusTrade in China, the Australian Government Trade arm, and a China hand for more than a decade, is one of those niche experts. Having run a major corporation in China, coupled with the high-level government contacts he has established over the years, he now spends his time consulting for companies and passing on his valuable firsthand knowledge of how to run a successful business in China. Some of his clients have included the Mars Company, which he helped to get set up in China. Another example of a small but very effective company is Greater China International Services (GCiS), a small group of seasoned China hands, with influential government partners and a strong focus in information technology, heavy industry and manufacturing. Like the larger management consulting companies today, they also have extensive client lists that include a strong mix of local and international clients.

A test of a good consultant is they should be able to help you better define your research goals based on your bottom-line objectives, rather than blindly carry out requests. Consultants who were asked broad questions such as what they thought the China market

China Streetsmart

was going to do often produced mediocre to wrong results. In the early 80s/90s it was difficult for almost anybody, including the central government, to have predicted what was going to happen to the economy and the market. Therefore, if a company paid a high-priced management consulting firm to produce a market potential strategy, they would have gotten a very clever, well-thought-out "guess". The reality is that accurately predicting the market direction of a fast-changing complex market like China is extremely difficult. For example, who could have predicted in 1994 when inflation was at 24% that in four years the prices would actually start to deflate? Companies who were advised (often by consultants) to aim for a 10–15% growth in price in the early 90s, and structure their business models accordingly, obviously ran into trouble when the prices of retail goods began to actually decline in 1998. This is one of the reasons why I often got the comment, "Not worth the money." Another reason why people thought these consultants "were not worth the money" was the fact that they often had the same limitations to data as everyone else. During the 80s and early 90s, many would buy the same China statistical data available to anyone and "put this data in a fancy report – along with a fancy PowerPoint presentation – and charge me a fortune," complained one executive.

It is understandable that people have these negative views of consulting firms. However, consulting firms with experience of working with both foreign and local firms can now bring tremendous value. It's a good example of a situation that may have had some validity before during their start-up period when they were also just learning, but may not be valid today. Over the years, much has been learned about the market and some of the top management consultants I spoke to really know what they were talking about. Given the fact that for many top-level consulting firms, more than 50% of their client base comes from large Chinese companies shows they now have a much better understanding of the industry issues on both sides. This big picture intimate overview of both Chinese and foreign-invested enterprises could prove invaluable to your strategic planning. **The *China Streetsmart* method of determining who the best consultants are is to choose a company not simply based on its size or international reputation, but rather its proven on-the-ground results and experience.**

Unconventional Methods of Information Gathering

Guy Bouchet at A.T. Kearney was telling me that in Europe a lot of companies, rather than just hire consultants, had a knack of hiring people who are good at getting intimate inside information about competitors and suppliers. He said, "One of the traditional ways for Southern European companies in particular was to feed off an informal network of 'information specialists' for market intelligence. A company would contract with one of these 'industry experts' who would take their competitors or suppliers out for dinner in a relaxed setting and try and extract as much information as possible. One could complain about the ethics of this kind of practice, but European and Asian cultures seem to share a more congenial and practical approach: this is simply how things get done! In China, this practice is also common and strongly backed by a pervasive network of personal contacts, which constitutes the essence of many respectable go-betweens' value added ... more so than their actual content knowledge, by the way. Actually, one of the main challenges facing young Chinese professionals hired by multinationals these days is to quickly learn about – and live by – international corporate standards of ethics, confidentiality and professional codes of conduct. For example, they will be astonished to find out that the often-used tactic of going straight at a competitor's staff for confidential data (everybody does that, no?!) may bring them more trouble than kudos with their Western employer! One thing for sure: in the hyper-competitive and data-poor China market, information is not only power, it is a condition for survival. Now go explain that the end does not [always] justify the means."

Do Your Own Market Research

There is no question that using services will help your understanding of the market, but if this is all you do then you will be making a grave mistake. Perhaps one of the smartest *China Streetsmart* things Michael did early on to understand his company's market potential was to go out and spend three to four months travelling around China to see the market firsthand. The firsthand market tour accomplished several benefits:

1. He got to know his customers early

Since other beverage and food packaging plants across China were going to be his potential customers, travelling around and meeting them early allowed him to start a relationship, the first stages of building good *guanxi* based on respect and trust. It also allowed him to understand his potential customers' needs better, even before he thought of doing business. So how did he know which plants and customers to visit? "Easy," he says. "All you've got to do is go and pick up any basic trade journal to find out who they are." Most embassy or consular trade sections will have this basic information and some will even offer to help with introductions.

2. It opened the possibilities for partnership

By meeting the various major potential customers, Michael was also on the lookout for potential partnerships. While Aquarius was eager to set up a partnership, it always helped to have other options in the works should the negotiations fail. By touring the site facilities, Michael was able to get a good feeling as to the level of management sophistication of each of the companies.

3. He saw the differences across China

Steve Watt, an executive with ACNielsen for more than 20 years and the former head of the Retail Audit division in China for more than five years, commented, "Just because a person goes to Beijing or Shanghai doesn't really mean he understands China. You've got to get out into the countryside where the majority of the population still lives. You've got to get into the secondary and tertiary cities to really understand how products move around China. You'll be surprised how different things operate once you leave the cities. For example, determining distribution and market penetration at the retail level is very difficult, since when you ask a shop owner if they carry a particular product they will invariably say yes, it's in the back, when what they really do is run out the back door to a neighbouring kiosk for the goods in question." I couldn't agree more with Steve's comments. In fact, I would say, Shanghai is a bit misleading if that's the only thing you see of China. Yes, **Shanghai is modern** and impressive, but this is really a showcase of what China aims to become, not what it is like now.

4. He got a feel for local staff

One of the observations Michael commented on when visiting large state-run operations was when something broke down at one of the factories, the first thing the workers would do would be to go reach for a newspaper because fixing the machine was the "other guy's" problem. Very little initiative and willingness to take responsibility was demonstrated. He made a mental note of this, so when it came to hiring his own staff he knew what to avoid. Furthermore, he noticed that most staff working for companies were hired as casual labour (often from the countryside), without having to pay any formal benefits, especially among the smaller enterprises. This savings allowed many local companies to operate on a much lower cost basis giving them a big advantage over foreign competitors.

5. He understood the numbers better

By asking the factory floor managers what their output or efficiency per line was, how many lines they had, how many days they operated, and how many factories like these were in China, he could piece together a fairly accurate picture as to how large the market was in China. It also allowed him to get a better feel for how accurate some of the statistical information being reported in some market monitors was. Some market monitor reports, published by Western companies, charged thousands of USD, yet most of the people responsible for compiling the data had never visited the factory floors they were reporting the output for. Many a company, especially in the early days of investment in China, desperate for numbers, would easily spend this money to get "something". Unfortunately, much of the data was inaccurate or misleading. For example, a high-priced beer monitoring report on China, which Foster's paid thousands of USD for, described Foster's annual sales in our Guangdong brewery as approximately 250,000–300,000 hectolitres (hLs). What they were reporting was the total output of beer being brewed at the Foster's brewery in Guangdong, most of which was the much lower priced low margin local brand called Princess Beer. If Foster's was produc-

ing 250,000–300,000 hL of Foster's branded beer, with its healthy margins, I doubt Foster's would have ever sold the brewery back to its local partner (now run by Tsingtao Breweries). A competitor reading this report, believing in the numbers, would actually believe Foster's was selling that much premium beer, overstating the actual size of the market.

6. He got to see how local companies keep track of their finances

As Michael travelled around China he discovered that many (Chinese) companies often kept two or more sets of books, which alerted him early on to how loose the financial systems are in China. The government is trying its best to ensure a better and more efficient system of tax collection, but in a developing economy like China, where tax rules are constantly changing, the loopholes are plenty and enforcement and interpretation vary from area to area. In more extreme cases, people can have an official set of books; an internal set of books to run the business; an internal set of books to manage their partners; and even one to keep from their spouse, in the case of one business I came across. Foreign MNCs and large enterprises are governed and monitored more strictly than small local companies, partially because there are fewer of them and they generate more taxable income, so it is difficult to try and "cook the books", which is not something I recommend. But it is important to be aware of the fact that this situation exists and smaller companies can utilise these loopholes coupled with the common practice of "hiring under the table" to obtain huge cost advantages. Local companies know how and when to use "cash settlements". With no receipt given, goods charged using "petty cash" reimbursements can potentially save 17% in value-added tax, for example. As I was pressuring my suppliers to give me the lowest price, they would often stop and ask me whether I wanted a receipt. If I didn't, then they could do much better, but if I had to have one, since I had to follow the rules strictly, being a foreign invested enterprise (FIE), that was their best price. This understanding helped me understand why it was sometimes better to let local operators handle some of the cost issues since they were more willing to take the risks of working "off invoice".

Official Receipts

An official *fapiao* usually has an official red seal at the top on watermarked thin paper issued by the tax bureau.

One of the first things one needs to grasp in China is the difference between a non-official receipt called a *shouju* (pronounced "show jew" in Mandarin) and an official receipt called a *fapiao* (pronounced "faa pee ow" in Mandarin). *Fapiaos* are issued to businesses and are used to tabulate the amount of taxes paid to the government. Care should be taken when getting a *fapiao* since fake *fapiaos* have been spotted throughout China in an effort to dodge tax collection.

Consistent Management

Maintaining Management Consistency, Action Step 1, also stresses the importance of getting the right management team in as early as possible. Portola's CEO was prudent to choose the person who would eventually run the operation and have him go through the whole process from preliminary first steps, to negotiations, to eventual day-to-day operations. The unfortunate tale I heard from other companies was after the CEO visited China, a business development team would be sent into China and they would produce an optimistic report to his or her liking. Often they would use reports similar to the beer monitor report I just mentioned, which overstated certain segments, drew the wrong conclusions and came back with a glowing report on how big the China market was – knowing they were not the ones to eventually be responsible for meeting the over-estimated targets. By having Michael do the market research himself and also know he would be the one to take eventual responsibility for meeting the numbers, Michael was forced to see if he could balance the numbers to make the financial outcome look attractive enough. Furthermore, consistent management also allowed Michael to establish a close working relationship and understanding with his Chinese counterparts, most notably with Mr Lu Yong Jie, the General Manager for Aquarius – a relationship that was to prove critical when working through the tough difficulties both sides were to eventually experience.

Understanding Intellectual Property
Patent and Trademark Protection

Intellectual property (IP) patent and trademark protection are hotly debated issues in China. Every day stories surface in China of a foreign company accusing a local company of infringing on their intellectual property rights. It is important to understand, before deciding if any laws have been violated, that IP laws are different in China compared to the US. In the US it is the first to use a product that holds the rights to the patent or trademark, whereas in China it is the first to file.

Edward Lehman, an American lawyer who runs a Chinese registered law firm, Lehman, Lee & Xu, is an expert in the field. His firm is one of the limited registered patent and trademark agents in China and his client roster includes Sony/Tristar, Columbia and major Chinese companies such as Haier, Tsingtao and Hi-Sense. Ed is constantly in demand to speak at conferences internationally and all around China on the do's and don'ts of IP protection. In fact, his firm maintains an excellent list of frequently asked questions (FAQs) on this subject at www.lehman law.com.

The first measure of protection is to file anything and everything you plan on using in China. A simple registration of a trademark costs as little as 425 USD (a great bargain, considering in the US you need to pay 3,900 USD[1]). An ounce of prevention can prevent massive headaches later. Edward is also Director of the Foreign Research Pharmaceutical Industry Association in China and he told me the story of Viagra, owned by Pfizer Pharmaceuticals in China. Apparently the people in charge of registering Viagra only registered the English name in Mainland China. The Chinese name *Wei Ge* was registered in Taiwan, but not Mainland China. As a result, a company in the south of China had registered the name first in China and it took Pfizer a significant court battle and a large undisclosed sum in legal fees just to get their name back – all of which could have been prevented with a simple 425 USD registration fee. Portola fell victim to this as well. Had they had the foresight when they first

---

[1] As of 2001, the filing fee for a trademark in the US was approximately 3,500 USD and the search fee was an additional 400 USD. Source: Lehman, Lee & Xu.

registered their patents in the US to also register them in China, even if they had only a remote notion they may one day come to China, it could have saved them significant costs.

You should hire experts to handle registering your trademarks and patents properly. Failure to do so could result in the same headaches as those experienced by Pfizer and Portola. Many Chinese companies have benefited from this lack of due diligence and as a result have won court cases due to failure by the foreign company to follow proper local registration. **Don't simply rely on your law firm in your home country to know all the details and quirks about Chinese IP law.** "One of the problems," Ed Lehman explains, "is that this one guy responsible for registering a company's product all around the world, [often] treats China with the same importance as Zambia." There are differences in how things are registered and protected in China so it pays to be detailed (Action Step 5). Therefore, the *China Streetsmart* advice would be to seek the services of China-experienced professionals and do it early even before you arrive.

Filing and registering are only part of the first line of defence. Another critical factor to consider in protecting your IP is what kind of local partner you should work with, if any. For companies that are in technologically sensitive sectors, the best strategy is simply to operate as a wholly owned foreign enterprise (WOFE) if permitted by the government. A company that has its products handled by local distributors or import agents must understand that if its local

Photographs by Ed Lehman

Ed Lehman has been working as a lawyer in China since the mid-80s. He now runs his own law firm and his firm was voted "Best China Law Firm" in 2000 by Asian Lawyer Magazine. Ed makes regular appearances on Chinese National TV (left) and Beijing Radio (right).

Chinese partner registers the trademarks, it is the local company that owns trademark rights in China. The option of licensing IP rights to a Chinese company also needs special consideration since the rights will automatically revert back to the Chinese company after a set period of time.

Protection of your IP should also begin at the employee contract level. **One of the biggest ways IP gets "stolen" from a company is through employees.** In some instances where manufacturing processes are so sensitive, some companies have prevented non-clearance employees from disclosing their sensitive technology and equipment by erecting covered areas within buildings requiring special passes. Other methods of employee protection are to make sure your human resource (HR) policies are properly designed for Chinese law. For example, I used to think that some non-disclosure and non-compete clauses were unenforceable in China. However, Ed Lehman informs me that non-compete clauses are enforceable, citing a recent case he had won on behalf of his client. "We have designed HR manuals for clients like Nokia to protect them and their IP. Even for Foreign Enterprise Service Corporation (FESCO) employees used in representative offices, he recommends binding them to separate labour employment contracts especially when dealing with sensitive IP issues. The key to enforcing a non-compete clause in a contract is first there must be an agreed form of compensation to prevent the individual from working for a competitor for a set period of time. To protect your IP properly, the *China Streetsmart* advice is to seek the advice of professionals.

As Portola discovered, the Chinese government already has in place IP laws that comply with World Trade Organisation (WTO) requirements and while enforcement of protection has improved significantly since China first re-opened its doors, infringements continue to occur. No matter how diligent and secure you are in making sure you have filed all the necessary documents, if your product makes money and does not require complex technological processes, chances are you will suffer – someone, somewhere, will try and infringe on your rights so you might as well prepare for this eventuality rather than be shocked when it happens. Small backward factories in remote villages run by people out to make a quick buck will continue to pump out illegal goods. The area around pre-

viously hard-to-reach Wenzhou was notorious for producing counterfeit goods. With a fast-growing, difficult-to-monitor economy like
China, it's hard if not impossible to clamp down on all the backyard
bootlegging. Therefore, **the *China Streetsmart* thing to do is to
watch your markets closely, develop good relations with your
local State Administration for Industry and Commerce (SAIC)
for support when infringements are discovered, but mange your
expectations accordingly because you are unlikely to stop IP
infringements completely** – at least for the foreseeable future.

Crackdown on high-tech printing equipment has helped, but
some cynics with legitimate complaints say the government is only
paying lip service. However, many of the executives I spoke to do
admit that the problem has improved significantly. In fact, some of
the executives I spoke to who have company operations in other
parts of Asia say China is not the worst offender, and can cite examples from many other countries as well. "It's perhaps the high profile China takes in the Asian economy that creates more than its fair
share of noise," claims one executive. What some companies have
done is to band together to set up a private advisory council to act as
a lobby group and watchdog, called the China Anti-Counterfeiting
Coalition (CACC) with 27 members including American Standard,
Anheuser-Busch, BAT, Bestfoods, Coca-Cola, Colgate-Palmolive, Dell
Computer Corporation, Glaxo Wellcome, Gillette, Henkel, Johnson
& Johnson, L'Oreal, Mars, Nike, Philips Electronics, Procter & Gamble, SC Johnson, Reebok and Unilever.[2] Perhaps the critical test of
severity of IP infringement in China came when asking this question: "Would you still invest in China?" Almost all the executives I
interviewed said *yes*, they would still continue to invest.

---

[2] China Anti-Counterfeit Online (January 2000 membership list). Also see Apco's
Weblink for more information: http://www.apcoassoc.com/Intelligence/CACC.html

China Streetsmart

15 | Setting the Strategy
Deciding the Best Plan of Action

| Preliminary Steps | Setting the Strategy | Negotiating the Deal | Running the Joint Venture | Ending the Joint Venture | Beyond the Joint Venture |

N ow that Michael Colozzi had got his feet wet understanding some of the critical management issues in China, and had a rough idea of the market size and the challenges of protecting his intellectual property (IP) in China, the next step was to decide what kind of business venture the operation should be – a joint venture (JV) or a wholly owned foreign enterprise (WOFE)? If a JV, would it be an equity JV (direct correlation between share and capital) or a contractual JV (no direct correlation), or would it be partnered with a state-run company or a private Chinese company? During several of his first visits to China, Michael met quite a few potential JV partners. It was a good strategy to "go shopping" since it let your potential Chinese partner know they were not the only organisation in town (something often not available in the early 80s).

One of the options seriously considered was a privately owned plant in Zhuhai (Guangdong province) in Southern China. The owner, a shrewd and very streetsmart (notice I don't say *China Streetsmart*) operator, was potentially offering Portola a better deal than what was being discussed with Aquarius, but when Portola got a closer look at how the owner could offer such an attractive deal, it became evident that many of the advantages were reliant on the owner's *guanxi* to smooth things with the local officials. Michael says, "This guy was making money hand over fist. We could see this guy was doing well. But there were just too many unanswered questions in how he got his deals done that made us nervous. He would

just smile and say, 'Don't worry about that issue, let me handle that.' In the end, we thought his willingness to cut corners and get around the rules and regulation with his *guanxi* was 'too risky' and thought it safer to go with a company willing to operate 'a little more legally' with a little more transparency. Basically we got cold feet. In the end, after combing the country for the best potential partner, Aquarius still seemed to be the best option."

There were many reasons why Aquarius appeared to be the best choice. When Jack first went to visit Aquarius, it was a medium-sized state-owned enterprise (SOE), and one of Shanghai's largest water companies. With a rich history dating back 200 years as China's oldest canned beverage company, Aquarius delivers drinking water in 5-gallon (19-litre) plastic drums to thousands upon thousands of Shanghai customers and is popularly known in Shanghai simply by their phone number 85818 (an auspicious sounding number formulation in Chinese). Also impressive about Aquarius was their General Manager, Mr Lu, who ran the operations. He was an influential figure in Shanghai business circles, with experience listing a company in one of his previous positions. He also had a lot of *guanxi* and was able to work efficiently with the government to get approvals sped through – not cut corners and get around the rules like the Zhuhai proprietor. During the negotiations with Portola, Aquarius was formally amalgamated with a much larger SOE, the Ma Ling (or *Mei Lin* in Mandarin) food group, a company that specialises in canned food. According to Michael, their size grew from a 20 million dollar company to almost a billion dollar SOE. As an example of Mr Lu's *guanxi* and influence, rather than being swallowed up by the larger company, he was appointed the company's Chairman for the whole Ma Ling group.

As preliminary negotiations with Aquarius began, it became apparent to John Huang, Portola China's legal advisor, that if they were to partner the Aquarius group, the negotiations were going to be long and

Photograph by John L. Chan

arduous. Even though John was a former classmate of Mr Lu, he knew Mr Lu's good intentions would be curtailed by some of the more conservative members of the Chinese negotiating team. One of the senior members (now retired), who was also on a committee that could determine Mr Lu's career direction, said to John in Chinese that he was determined to "teach these companies [American and Japanese especially] a lesson". Michael was also concerned about the impact the JV would have on their target customers. They were going after brand name customers like Nestle and Danone, but were worried what these companies would have thought if their supplier were also a competitor. Aquarius would have all the sales data from Nestle and Danone and had these companies known about this, which they eventually would, he doubted they would want to do business with him. During their negotiations, the laws in China regarding the setting up of a WOFE changed and became an available option for Portola. Both John and Michael were strong advocates of a WOFE and explained their concerns in detail to the international board at Portola, but the board went against their recommendation and voted for an equity JV preferring to share the risk and ease the company's cash requirements, and also because they were impressed by Mr Lu's *guanxi*. The board had heard so much about the importance of *guanxi* in China from other people that they felt Mr Lu could make things easier should problems arise. Originally they wanted a 70/30 split, which would have given them much stronger management control of the JV, but eventually had to settle for a 55/45 split.

Running the financial numbers was another rigorous exercise Portola went through in its early days of setting up operations. Michael says, "What I eventually did was to estimate what I thought the market was and what I thought we could sell, then I halved it to see if I could make the numbers fly. I had countless spreadsheets and ran every type of scenario I could think of. Given my limited experience with China, I tried my best to come up with as much detailed numbers as I could find and I always erred on the conservative side. Every time I would learn more information, from details such as salary bands, to how much it costs to lease a car, I would go back to my spreadsheets to see the impact. Getting into the discipline of really knowing and analysing the numbers was critical for us."

16 | Setting the Strategy

A *China Streetsmart* Analysis

Decisions such as whether to partner up with a local company and if so, how, and how large the original size of the investment should be, are perhaps the most important decisions the foreign company will make that determine its success and profitability timeline. As a result, it is not surprising these are areas where problems arise and are often the root causes of companies complaining about China today. However, careful due diligence and a conservative approach to the market can prevent a lot of these problems.

Local Partner Options

Although Michael Colozzi and John Huang were not advocates of working with this particular state-owned enterprise (SOE), that does not mean future companies coming to invest should not seek a local partner as a serious option. While the granting of wholly owned foreign enterprises (WOFEs) is more prevalent than ever, given China's entry into the World Trade Organisation (WTO), certain industries and sectors still have no choice but to find a suitable local partner. In the executive search industry, for example, the only way foreign executive search firms can operate legally as a local company, beyond representative office status, is to find a local partner. Sensitive industries like telecommunications are even more restrictive as to what they can and cannot do.

Same Bed, Different Dreams

The Chinese idiom "Same Bed, Different Dreams" often best describes the difficulties shared between the foreign and local partner. Rather than saying joint ventures (JVs) with local partners are the problem, the key is to find the right partner that shares the same dreams and aspirations. Where problems have occurred is when a local partner, often in the same industry, was chosen that was more interested in obtaining the foreign partner's technology and management know-how for their own benefit – not the JV's. The result would often be to open up another 100% local factory, in some instances, just down the road, which would compete directly with the JV. Other scenarios were when a local partner, often a local municipal government, in return for granting local market access, would obligate the foreign company to pay for the workers' benefits and social regulatory obligations, such as payments to retired workers, and medical and housing allowances, that the old state-run system allowed. Clashes would arise when the JV management would try and focus on company efficiency and profitability. Any moves to slim down the overburdened JV, saddled with huge employee costs, were met with huge resistance. Chinese employees' wages may be cheap, but when you add thousands of them together, they make a noticeable dent in your bottom line.

There were also differences between short- and long-term views in the business. The foreign partner, interested in the long-term view of developing the market, would often want to re-invest the money made back into the business, while the local side would want their share immediately paid directly to them. Many of the Mainland Chinese I have met and worked with had this short-term bias. Talk of long-term development and future rewards would often fall on deaf ears. This attitude applied to the trade and distribution channels as well. The de-emphasis on the long-term view was understandable, given the fact that many of them never had any money before, so when the opportunity to "get something" arose, they would want it now rather than later. Given how fast things change in China, many may have felt they might not be around by the time the long-term benefits were ready for reaping. Admittedly, if I were in their position, I may act in the same way.

On the foreign side, as illustrated in Action Step 3 (Be Patient and Thorough) and Action Step 4 (Think Win-Win), many companies did not do the proper due diligence on their partner to really take the time to understand their needs and motivations. Many, in a rush to enter the China market, hopefully before their competitors entered, took too many shortcuts, rushed to conclusions and/or made assumptions based on vague or general concepts, such as the "one billion customers myth". An equally poor strategy was thinking they could accept "uneven" terms or excessive demands by the local side to "get their foot in the door". In the end, these companies eventually suffered the consequences of their poor strategies.

Finally, there was the classic difference of culture clashes and misunderstandings often due to simple miscommunication. If the six universally applicable *China Streetsmart* action steps were followed, many of the often needless clashes might have been avoided. For this, both sides were often to blame, but the foreign side had the ability to control the situation. Frequent management changes on the foreign side, coupled with bringing in foreign managers not culturally adaptable to China, were a major source of problems that arose between the two sides. The Western bars in Shanghai and Beijing were filled with foreign managers huddled together, complaining about how the Chinese side never did anything right, when if all these managers did was make a few minor adjustments in their approach, such as what is being suggested by the successful foreign executives in China using Action Steps, 4, 5 and 6, for example, they could have prevented a lot of problems without compromising their companies' positions.

Finding the Right Partner

I came across many companies that had great working relationships with their local partners. Rather than choose partners who would be direct competitors, many of the more successful partnerships came from companies from complementary industries. IBM, for example, has many JV partners, one of which is the Ministry of Railways, which not only helps move their product around China more efficiently, but is also laying fibre-optic cabling along their railway trunk lines, helping to bring China into the information age. Another great *China Streetsmart* success story in China is McDonald's.

I spoke extensively with Tim Lai, the Managing Director for McDonald's in North China. Tim is a fantastic *China Streetsmart* individual – passionate not only about McDonald's, but China as well, Tim worked his way up the ranks of the McDonald's empire, proving his skills in Taiwan when he broke company records for the most birthday parties and the fastest customer drive-through servicing at the locations he worked. He was one of the key executives who established the flagship McDonald's in Beijing's Wangfujing Street just off Tiananmen Square. With 20 JV partners in China, McDonald's grew from their first China location in Shenzhen, back in 1990, to more than 500 (as of 2002) across China and the number is growing by more than 100 sites per year. Their first local JV partner was with the General Corporation of Beijing Agriculture, Industry and Commerce (BAIC). Although other potential partners offered McDonald's more money than BAIC, McDonald's was more concerned with finding the "right partner" who shared the same goals and aspirations.

Photograph by John L. Chan

Hong Kong-born Tim Lai, Managing Director for McDonald's in North China, has been working in China since 1991, when he helped open up the first JV McDonald's on Wangfujing Street in Beijing very close to Tiananmen Square, which remains their flagship restaurant.

The McDonald's management was very careful in doing their due diligence before choosing a partner. Often they would ask potential partners to send their senior management to go work in the restaurants, starting with the basic "crew level" which began by mopping floors. BAIC sent two of their senior Deputy General Managers down for this training. The purpose of this exercise was to give the partner a good feel for what it was like to work with McDonald's and what McDonald's was trying to accomplish. Another key aspect in establishing a solid relationship with your local partner is the direct relationship that transpires between the two leading executives of both sides. As long as there is mutual respect and a trusted bond between the two leaders, many of the impending difficulties can be resolved amicably. Mr Xing, then President of BAIC, and Tim Lai developed a strong bond of mutual respect and trust when the first Beijing restaurant opened in 1992 and the relationship has continued to flourish to this day. Even though Mr Xing is now officially retired, he still works with McDonald's on a few "projects" and remains a trusted friend and ally to be counted on. This type of close relationship also proved critical in Portola's case. Had they continually replaced the top management, a failure to follow Action Step 1 (Maintain Management Consistency), this would likely never have been possible.

Managing the local partner's expectations is another factor McDonald's does very well. "Although McDonald's is a 'big name' and can attract a lot of interested investors, we made sure the investors were realistic enough and understood the numbers well enough to realise that they were going to have to work hard to make their returns on investment. Nothing is guaranteed and it would be wrong to think after signing an agreement with McDonald's that they were going to be instantly profitable. It takes a lot of work and we want to make sure our JV partners are really prepared for this."

The WOFE Option

As China's economy continues to become more transparent and WTO rules come into effect, the need for local JV partnerships will diminish. Many of the lawyers I spoke to who are responsible for helping bring clients into China are recommending, more than ever, the option to operate as a WOFE if the option is available. However, it is

China Streetsmart

fair to point out that many of these lawyers have also gone through some of the nastiest "divorce settlements" on behalf of their clients. It is like asking a divorce or family lawyer if I should get married and have kids. There are many benefits a good local partner can bring to the table to help the foreign company operate effectively. Taking the time to understand your local partner's needs and managing expectations, as in the case with McDonald's, combined with a well-structured agreement, can lower the risks of investment, provide financial incentives such as tax breaks, and provide the foreign company with good local understanding and support with local officials. One hundred per cent localisation may be the target for many companies, but despite the fact that China's entry into the WTO should bring about better conditions to doing business in China, we certainly are not at an ideal situation yet, so JV partnerships may still be needed.

Since each company's case is different, it would be dangerous to say one option is better than the other. However, in circumstances that involve companies with sensitive technologies and proprietary manufacturing processes to protect, the *China Streetsmart* option is definitely more towards a WOFE. However, as Bing Ho, partner for Baker McKenzie's China practice said, "It is difficult and misleading to make general comments since each case is unique." As a result, keeping these points in mind, the *China Streetsmart* thing to do is you should then consult with an experienced China lawyer. He should be able to provide you with all the detailed pros and cons specific to your case.

There's *Guanxi* and Then There's *Guanxi*

During the search for the right partner for Portola, Michael came across two types of individuals who both displayed impressive abilities to exercise *guanxi* with their network of contacts to get things done in China. The first type is represented by the private owner in Zhuhai. He exercised a type of *guanxi* that is not *guanxi* in the traditional sense at all; rather he was buying short-term favours, which may or may not always work. In Southern China, such as Guangdong, Jiangxi and Fujian provinces, far away from the bureaucratic controls of the central government, business can operate at a different pace and in methods very different from what you see in Shanghai and Beijing. Businessmen and in some cases local officials in these parts of China are very streetsmart (note again, I do not say *China Streetsmart*). They figure out how to use their connections and influence to make a quick buck. Often these bucks are not little either and could involve millions, if not billions, of dollars. Yet this "back door" way of doing things changes frequently and involves a higher degree of risk.

Many Taiwanese and Hong Kong businessmen get around the risk elements by letting the local Chinese side take all the risks, such as the responsibility for the importation and handling of goods. Billions of USD of goods has been smuggled through China's ports. China has more than 300 ports of entry of which half are in Guangdong province alone. With so many ports and so many officials involved, it is not surprising that an enterprising entrepreneur would be able to use his "influence" to be able to clear customs easily and often at a favourable rate. However, this form of business does involve risk. The government is cracking down on corrupt practices more and more. High-level government officials are being prosecuted on corruption charges. One of the most highly publicised cases in recent years was the execution of the former Vice Governor of Jiangxi province, Hu Changqing, who took 87 bribes from more than 18 people – most of whom were private businessmen.[1] Even the Chinese government would not claim that it has been completely successful at cracking down on corruption and tightening the measures by which business is conducted in the country. As a result, the wheeling and dealing will continue, and evasion of the rules and regulations will go on, with many people profiting from the process. However, playing these "games" is not something I would recommend for the inexperienced China investor, and certainly *not* what I would call *China Streetsmart*. Portola, an established international company with a reputation to protect, probably made the right decision to pass on this potential partnership.

The second type of individual is represented by Mr Lu. Mr Lu's *guanxi* appears to be different. One of the things that impressed

---

[1] Huang Weiding, 2001, "Fighting Corruption Amidst Economic Reform". In Laurence Brahm (ed.), *China's Century*, pp. 44–45, John Wiley & Sons.

both Jack and Michael when coming to China was the professional business acumen demonstrated by Mr Lu. Having travelled the world, businessmen like Mr Lu are becoming more commonplace in China. He has enough business sense about him to know how to work his audience. "You could tell he acted very differently when he was in the room with his subordinates present and when we were alone," said Michael. "The conversation and his tone, depending on who was around, were very different. He knew China, but he also had a good understanding of what we wanted as well." I'm sure it wasn't only Jack and Michael who were impressed, since the promotion from being the General Manager of a smaller medium-sized enterprise to being the head of a large SOE like the Ma Ling Group involved not only a proven track record, but extensive *guanxi* as well. Other successful and internationally astute Chinese business leaders like Liu Chuanzhi, the CEO of Legend, or Zhang Ruimin, the CEO of Haier, China's leading computer and appliance manufacturers respectively, represent China's future.

"Better to Be a Live Dog Than a Dead Lion" – Be Conservative When Making Estimates

Fast-developing economies like China represent a lot of uncertainties. Inflation, competition and government policies change rapidly, and accurately predicting how they change is almost anyone's guess. On the other hand, **good business plans need to be built on solid predictions of the market and when this is not possible, the *China Streetsmart* approach is to be conservative.** China is littered with many dead lions. Companies today that complain how difficult it is to make money were often too aggressive in their approach to the China market before they really understood the challenges such as a massive increase in competition. Those executives in the early days who were conservative were dismissed as being "negative". A Managing Director in charge of a manufacturing operation worth several hundred million USD in China confided to me that before deciding on how much to invest in China, the company made five broad assumptions:

1. Demand would continue to exceed supply.
2. Double-digit market growth would continue.
3. Pricing would be sustained ahead of inflation.

4. Costs would be held below inflation.
5. Competitive landscape would be largely unaltered.

In the end, all five assumptions turned out to be wrong. How could such a huge professional company, supported by one of the leading management consulting companies in the world, have so misjudged the China market? During the period when the strategy was being formulated, manufacturers could not produce enough products. Wholesalers and distributors were actually bidding for goods coming out of the factory doors. During the early 90s, inflation was rising, almost uncontrollably, and peaked in 1994 at more than 24%; and when they looked around to find foreign competitors, few were to be seen. They didn't notice the dozens of other foreign competitors, all leaders in their respective home markets, who were hidden away locked behind closed meeting rooms literally thinking the same thing, "I've got the whole market to myself and I know I can beat the key players already in China."

Whether it was a gross oversight in the looming overcompetitive landscape which was guaranteed to produce an oversupply of product, driving prices down, or simply arrogance that they were better than the competition, given their superior market positions in their respective home markets, many of the companies who are complaining about how difficult it is to make money in China today misread the market conditions. **The problem is not that they made the decision to invest in the China market, but simply their decision on how and how much**.

Hearing this sobering tale being repeated from the 40 senior managers of foreign enterprises Michael met during his first 30 days in China encouraged Michael to be conservative in his approach to estimating the market size. "I would rather get things wrong and have the market chase me," Michael told me. "I don't want to be one of those guys caught with my pants down, scratching my head on how I am going to fill the plant." Furthermore, his conservative strategy also avoided the trap most multinational corporations (MNCs) unknowingly fell victim to, which was positioning for rising prices when prices were set to fall. Back in 1997, a 5-gallon or 19-litre drum of water was selling for 28–35 RMB with healthy margins. Since then, the increase in competition has been staggering. Both foreign and domestic producers increased capacity and the surplus drove down price – which today hovers between 10 and 14 RMB (Aquarius charges 14 RMB). The significance of this drop to a packaging supplier like Portola was that costs suddenly grew in importance to water bottlers as margins were continually eroded out of the business. No longer could many of the bottlers afford Portola's higher grade, but also higher costing, cap.

Know Your Numbers – Controlling Costs

Forcing the discipline of making sure you can make a conservative sales plan work requires the company to be very conscious of market conditions. The one factor Portola did have some control over was costs. Once again, during the 90s, many of the companies complaining about how difficult it was to make money were often victims of their own spending zeal. The way some of these large multinational manufacturers were spending money in the early days of investment in China was very similar to how a lot of the dot-coms were burning through investor's money. Having been a recent Director at Asia Online, I got to witness the industry craze firsthand and the parallels between the two periods were frightening. Companies in the early days of their China investment would rent prime office space in Hong Kong and house their executives in some of the best properties, paying rental prices of 10,000–20,000 USD per month per family.

Lavish Spending

During one of my earlier consulting projects, I recall spending time with the Director of Sales for one of the large pharmaceutical operations in Tianjin in 1995. He was staying at the Sheraton in Tianjin and, as per his contract, was supposed to live in a certain sized house. However, because there were no Western equivalent housing available in Tianjin at the time, the Sheraton modified three adjoining rooms as a substitute. Charging 300 USD per night per room the monthly cost should have been 27,000 USD per month, but since he was a long-staying resident, the hotel gave the company a "discount" charging only 18,000 USD per month – and to think he wasn't even General Manager of the operation!

Many of the companies, to get operations "running smoothly", would bring over an army of expats each costing hundreds of thousands of USD each. Often a single expat's monthly cost would be the equivalent to the entire local Chinese side's department they were representing and in the early days, rarely were there only one expat working in a given department, rather as many as five or six. When it came to the manufacturing/operations side, you could expect small communities of expats with their families and children's school tuition running between 18,000–25,000 USD per child per year. Given the fact that most of these multinationals expected to make a loss in the first year of operations didn't cause many of them to worry about the heavy spending. It is when the sales numbers, given their misread in the market, started to come in well below expectations that the red flag was raised and eventual panic button pressed.

Mike Blackburn, the former General Manager of Mars in China for more than six years, confided to me what he would do differently if he were to restart his China investment strategy: "I'd definitely have brought in less expats. Great Lakes Fruit Juices (of which he is now the Chairman) is essentially run by three key locals with only one expat who is the General Manager. Furthermore, expats need time to understand the local conditions so they are not as fully effective in this environment as one would hope. Finally, too many expats creates the perception of a glass ceiling for some of the promising locals, which is an incentive for them to leave."

As an expat myself, rather than focus on how much we cost, the key is to focus on being cost effective. A seasoned executive with the right knowledge of how things are done in China can actually save a company many times the salary he or she commands. The more relevant question is whether or not you need second- and third-tier layers of management made up of expats. Working around conservative sales numbers will force you to control your costs at the outset and prevent an over-exuberance in spending – of which expats are only one factor. As long as there are management skill gaps, especially at the senior level, expats will still be needed in China.

Office space is another area where there is an opportunity to control costs. Many of the well-known companies I visited are now housed in relatively modest office spaces. However, during the early days of investment they had rented lavish Grade A office spaces costing between 30,000 and 40,000 USD per 100 sq m or 1,000 sq ft per month. Now that many of them are in "hunker down" mode, lavish offices have been one of the first cuts made. As Sam Crispin, a specialist in the field and the Shanghai General Manager for FPD Savills, suggests, **the *China Streetsmart* thing to do when first setting up an office in China is to consider a business centre.** Alan Seigrist, one of the main business directors for The Executive Centre, which runs business centres all over the Asia Pacific and has operations in one of the prime buildings in downtown Shanghai, commented, "Many companies were renting huge amounts of office space in anticipation of their growth. What happened was approvals took longer than expected and as they discovered the market was smaller than they anticipated, much of the office space remained empty [wasting thousands of USD per month]."

Inexperienced China investors should really benefit from working with a qualified property consultant. Experts like Winnie Yip, the General Manager for DTZ Debenham Tie Leung, one of the largest and best property consultants in China, explained the confusion over what Grade ABC buildings really mean or do not mean. "Technically, according to international standards, in Beijing [at the end of 2001] only two buildings, the China World Trade Centre Tower Two and the Kerry Centre, fit International Grade A classification." Nevertheless, Beijing building owners wanting to charge Grade A

Photographs by Kevin Crowe

The Executive Centre is one of the business centres FPD Savills recommends to their clients and is a good example of how to manage costs effectively by not over-committing your investment. The Centre's unique shape offers 12 corner offices like that pictured above in a centralised location, with flexible leasing periods. The professional staff run by long-time China hand Kevin Crowe can answer your calls and meet your other basic needs, freeing one's time to concentrate on the market opportunities, rather than get bogged down with administrative hassles.

rental prices would assign their building a Grade A anyway– a "Chinese Grade A". It pays to hire experienced property consultants like Sam and Winnie since they are able to guide your company through the confusion and also warn you of potential pitfalls you may not be aware of, such as which buildings do not provide air conditioning 24 hours a day, seven days a week for critical areas such as computer rooms which could cause computer servers to overheat over the weekend when the air conditioning is shut off. Knowing and preventing these pitfalls is part of Action Step 5 (Be Detailed).

17 | Negotiating the Deal

Issues to Expect

| Preliminary Steps | Setting the Strategy | Negotiating the Deal | Running the Joint Venture | Ending the Joint Venture | Beyond the Joint Venture |

As a state-owned enterprise (SOE), Aquarius was not the only party that needed to be at the negotiation table; the Shanghai Light Industry Bureau, now called the Shanghai Light Industry Holding Co., Ltd., which oversees the Aquarius operations, among many other SOEs, is also very much involved with the decision. The Shanghai Light Industry Bureau had a lot of experience negotiating with foreign investors and was a tough negotiator. "The negotiations were exhausting," Michael points out. "Often they would try and exhaust you by having ten people on their side versus only myself. We would be arguing and negotiating for hours over a single issue and minute details and just when I thought we would have an agreement, we would go home and the next day all the previous agreements and concessions would have been 'forgotten' and we would start over again. I knew what these guys were doing; they often wanted to see where you would make concessions to see how far they could push you. At times, I really didn't think they were negotiating in good faith. Had it not been for Mr Lu and the respect and trust I had for him, I probably would have walked away from the deal."

Now to give the story of Portola's China experience the proper perspective, it helps to understand Michael Colozzi a bit better. When you first meet Michael, he is soft-spoken, articulate, and the kindest, most polite gentleman you will ever meet. However, when you get him excited over an issue he comes alive and is as animated as any Egyptian rug trader working the local bazaar. "Hey, I'm Italian!" he quips jovially. "Don't mess with me." The son of an American military career officer, Michael grew up in military bases around the world, and eventually attended the prestigious Virginia Military Institute and specialised in military intelligence. It helps to understand this because although Michael's strong personality and military training was what helped him survive the exhaustive negotiations, they also proved to be the source of cultural clashes with some of the local management he eventually had to work with.

The total investment to get the joint venture (JV) off the ground was less than 10 million USD, small relative to the hundred million USD deals I have discussed with other executives in China, but the principles in forming the JV were essentially the same. The JV was to be a 55/45 split with Portola taking the majority share. Initially, the Chinese side wanted a significant portion of their investment to be the contribution in the value of the land and factory space they were offering to Portola. Michael spent extensive efforts visiting plots of land the Chinese side was offering but rejected them on a number of accounts. For example, one site was located in Pudong's eastern industrial zone in the remote suburbs of Shanghai, and was so far away from the city it would have been difficult to find people willing to work that far away or access a ready pool of local talent. Another site discussed was in Kunshan, in the administrative region of Suzhou, which borders Shanghai. But since a percentage of goods for the JV was going to be made for export, the extra cost of shipping them overland to the nearest port could have made the goods uncompetitive. Portola insisted on the right to approve the site and they had made it very clear that they were prepared to walk away from the deal if this condition was not met. Aquarius and the Shanghai Light Industry people also knew that Michael was having discussions with other potential partners in China, such as the private entrepreneur in Zhuhai. Finally, both sides agreed that each side was to contribute the amount needed in cash, based on the exhaustive spreadsheet modelling Michael had done, to be held in a joint bank account to be used to purchase or lease the land, set up the factory, buy the equipment and supplies, and pay the staff.

Another critical negotiation point for the JV was who was going to own which title. The Chinese side insisted that they retain the title of General Manager and gave Michael the title of Executive Vice General Manager, to be in charge of daily operations; after one

Photographs by John L. Chan

Although Michael Colozzi did most of the face-to-face negotiations with Aquarius and the Shanghai Light Industry Bureau, he would confer regularly (nightly at some points) with John Huang, his lawyer, over how to proceed. Often his Chinese partners would insist on certain clauses using the pretext that it was according to Chinese law. Sometimes they were right, sometimes they were wrong, and sometimes clauses were open to interpretation. Therefore, enough cannot be said about having the advice of an experienced China lawyer who really understands local law and how it is really enforced.

year the title of General Manager would be transferred to Michael. Aside from this, the Chinese side also insisted on two other key posts: they wanted the right to appoint the deputy assistant for Michael and also a person who worked in the finance department who would control the chop – the company seal required to approve payments. In return, Michael was granted the authority to approve purchases on behalf of the JV up to 100,000 USD.

Since it was a common practice between foreign and state-owned companies for the clause "equal pay for equal work" to be applied, meaning Mr Lu would be paid exactly the same as Michael, Portola aimed to lower the cost burden of the JV by limiting the initial salaries for the two top executives to 36,000 USD per year. Portola would pay the difference in Michael's salary back in the US, under a separate contract, but the JV would cover Michael's expatriate expenses such as housing, cost of living adjustments, etc. Problems arose when setting the wage scale for the Chief Finance Officer (CFO). The Chinese side was willing to only pay the same rate as CFOs of other SOEs; as a result, the best they could hire was a middle manager from one of the big accounting firms. Unfortunately, her inexperience and unfamiliarity with both international and Chinese generally accepted accounting principles (GAAP) proved to be a problem for Portola when it came to consolidating the Chinese operation with the rest of Portola's international operations.

Another people issue Aquarius and the Light Industry Bureau wanted to discuss with Portola was the JV taking over its workers and in turn absorbing the social regulatory obligations such as the paying of workers' benefits, medical, housing, pensions, etc. This issue is a common facet of negotiating with SOEs, since one of their primary desires is the need to keep SOE workers employed and guarantee that their benefits will continue. Portola had no intention of absorbing hundreds of unneeded workers. However, the translator had not communicated the positions clearly enough to either side as to each other's true intentions and desires. Since the condition never made it in the contract, Michael did not focus on the issue. However, the Chinese side was under the understanding that this would be considered after the deal was completed – a condition that would come back to haunt Michael later.

Michael's main translator during the negotiations was a local Shanghainese woman, introduced through one of Michael's work colleagues, who had previously worked for the Shanghai Rubber Institute. Although she had no professional translation experience, she knew how to do technical translation. As noted in the section on language earlier in this book, **rather than use professional translators, the *China Streetsmart* preferred option is to have it done through a trusted lieutenant.** Problems arose when Michael later suspected that the work colleague who had introduced this particular translator secretly hoped Michael would fail in his negotiations with the Chinese, since she allegedly wanted Michael's job for her husband. Both she and her husband were of Chinese descent and her husband was an engineer based in the US. Coming back to China working for a good American company on an expat package was supposedly their real goal, a goal Michael was not going to learn till later.

Deciding the product lines they were going to produce was another point of extensive discussion. Given Michael's extensive market research, he knew that the two most promising products for the China market were the 5-gallon or 19-litre drum cap and the trendy small water bottle sports cap which was Portola's invention (through a subsidiary they owned in the US). Mr Lu wanted the operation to also produce a special 4-litre "large jug" (1 gallon) cap, but to do so would require additional investment in machinery that went beyond

the economic scope of investment. Portola didn't want to invest in a machine that was going to be only operating at 10% capacity given their market projections. As negotiations dragged on, time became a factor since the "cap business" is seasonal in nature and if they were to find and build a suitable location, bring in supplies and manufacture the first batch of caps in time to meet the coming season, they had to conclude negotiations soon. In the end, to expedite the deal, Portola agreed to supply the equipment if the Chinese agreed to finance (carry the risk) for the purchase of the additional machinery locally 100% from their side, which Mr Lu agreed to. In the end, however, the Shanghai Light Industry Group, upon seeing the deal, insisted that the financing be held 55/45 in accordance with the shareholding split. The machines to make the 4-litre caps never reached the production floor.

Technology and pricing transfers were also discussed, but both sides could not agree on a suitable price. Since timing was getting tight to meet the impending season, both sides agreed to leave the price out of the deal and re-address the issue after the deal was signed. In reality, Michael purposely aimed to not discuss these issues with his Chinese counterparts because he knew they would not be in the long-term interest of the JV. The Chinese side could use the technology against the JV and the Chinese side would almost certainly insist on a pricing transfer agreement below market cost, otherwise why would you go into a JV in the first place? However, Michael only would have agreed to these terms if the price for their technology was at international rates and the JV plant had excess capacity – something that he wasn't planning on.

Portola was careful to outline in the agreement all the standard protection clauses such as what to do in case of partner or business insolvency, etc. The contract was also negotiated with a finite term of 15 years and should either party want to sell their shares, the other party had the first right of refusal. Portola was reasonably confident they were protected, since they retained the control over the patents so there was not much another party could do if they wanted to break away. The contract was drafted in both languages and it was decided that both translations would be of equal value. Should arbitration be needed, the Chinese side said they wanted the arbitration to be done in Austria rather than in Hong Kong. The contract was certainly comprehensive – containing a total of 60 sections. After more than 20 drafts ("We must have killed a few trees," said Michael), the articles of association were finally ready for signing.

In November 1997, both Portola and Aquarius signed the contract. However, a quirk about deals made in China is that the deal is not truly finished until it has been examined and approved by all the relevant government authorities, in this case, the Ministry of Foreign Trade and Economic Corporation (MOFTEC) – the central government body in charge of examining and approving foreign JVs. Aquarius was responsible for getting the deal pushed through MOFTEC. However, they apparently did not work with MOFTEC closely enough because the first submission was rejected on the grounds that MOFTEC felt that the wording in the export requirement was too weak. John Huang knew the local Vice President of MOFTEC for Shanghai, and stepped in using his *guanxi* to help smooth the deal through. Portola and Aquarius were forced back to the negotiation table and agreed to hastily redraw the agreement and change the export requirements to suit MOFTEC. The deal was finally passed in February 1998, just over two-and-a-half months after the first submission. The agreement between Portola Packaging, Inc. (USA) and the Shanghai Aquarius Drinking Water Co., Ltd. officially created the Shanghai Portola Packaging Co., Ltd.

18 | Negotiating the Deal
A *China Streetsmart* Analysis

Preliminary Steps	Setting the Strategy	Negotiating the Deal	Running the Joint Venture	Ending the Joint Venture	Beyond the Joint Venture

M uch has been said and written on how to negotiate with the Chinese. A great story came from my good friend Seamus Cornelius, a prominent lawyer in Shanghai and the Chief Representative of Allens Arthur Robinson, the largest law firm in Australia. Aside from law, if you enjoy golf, Seamus is the man to meet when you come to Shanghai. Coincidentally, Seamus and Michael Colozzi are regular golf partners. Seamus's job is to negotiate on his client's behalf so when he came to China he began to read prolifically on all the negotiation tactics one could expect. "The one

Whether you need help negotiating with the local Chinese or help with your golf swing during the weekend, you will find ten-year-old China veteran Seamus impressing clients with his skill at one of Shanghai's golf courses.

Photograph by Seamus Cornelius

Seamus Cornelius, Partner, China Chief Representative Allens Arthur Robinson

story that always stuck in my mind was about a tactic the Chinese side had of turning on the air conditioners or opening the windows in the dead of winter during negotiations to put the foreign side off – 'Wear long underwear' was the sagely advice. I'll always remember that story," he laughs. "I also laugh when somebody whispers in my ear as to the secret of how to negotiate successfully with the Chinese."

Negotiation Tactics

As mentioned throughout this book, the biggest secret about doing business in China is that there simply is no secret; it is simple common business sense. When it comes to negotiating, common business sense also applies. "Contrary to some of the mythology surrounding the China trade, don't ignore fundamental business principles when doing business in the People's Republic of China (PRC), even if someone says, 'That's not how we do it in China,' " says Patrick Powers, the Director of the US China Business Council in Beijing. "Do your partner due diligence, don't do anything you wouldn't do at home, and above all, make sure you know how you will be paid. Although the results can be hard to quantify, hiring an expert consultant (not a *guanxi* peddler) can save companies hundreds of thousands of dollars by helping them avoid costly mistakes upfront. Company representatives should also try to learn a bit about the local negotiating style in advance, which frequently involves misdirection or outrageous demands just to see if the foreign company will bite, when in reality all the PRC is doing is testing your resolve." However, when the foreign side replies to the outrageous demands with a polite, "Oh! ... ah, oh well ... let's see what we can do...", what this does is to set a precedent as to how far a company will go to get their foot in the door; and back in the early 90s when companies were beset with "gold rush fever", that tolerance to accept the excessive demands by the Chinese was pretty high. Going back to *China Streetsmart* Action Step 4 (Think Win-Win) remember that there are times when you have to be prepared to walk away from the deal.

Negotiation tactics and tricks such as delays and playing the "He said this, but I didn't say I agreed" are common in every country. As Michael was explaining to me the roles Mr Lu of Aquarius and the Shanghai Light Industry negotiators played, it struck me they seemed to be playing the tactic of "good cop, bad cop". Just when negotiations seem to be at an impasse with the Shanghai Light Industry people, Mr Lu would step in and smooth things over. A lot has been written about negotiating in China, some of it good and some of it bad, but in deciding which is the best strategy, it is best simply to use your common-sense business instincts. In addition, it helps to follow the guidelines in Action Step 4 that suggests the best way to achieve a win-win deal is to establish respect first, which then leads to trust, which then leads to better understanding, and which will finally lead to a fair deal. Establishing trust often takes time and once again goes back to Action Step 3 (Be Patient and Thorough), waiting for the right moment to strike. Showing overeagerness and overwillingness to cut a deal is a classic negotiation mistake, which is applicable in any business culture.

Coping with Different Negotiation Styles and Focusing on the Bottom Line

Because people's frames of references and experiences impact the negotiating process, culture should be taken into consideration. A way of describing some of the potential differences between Western and Chinese negotiating styles is to look at a linear versus a holistic approach. As Guy Bouchet of A.T. Kearny explained, "In the West, we like to negotiate in a linear fashion. We line out all the points and issues on the table and begin by resolving them one by one until we reach the end; then we know we have an agreement. The Chinese, on the other hand, take a more holistic approach to resolving the issues. The deal is not done until all the main conditions have been agreed. If one of the main clauses is not satisfied, all the others may be affected and as a result, everything is still open for discussion and modification."

Regardless of negotiating styles adopted, what should not change is your need to focus on the bottom line. As long as you know where that line is, your company's objectives are less likely to be compromised. Follow Action Step 5 (Be Detailed), and do not assume that the Chinese side understands and agrees to vague obligations. Working out all the critical details that affect your bottom line may take more time than expected, but buffer for this time, since the more time and understanding you have of each other's intentions, the more likely you are to cut a fair and lasting deal. In reality, time is actually often on the foreign side, since as time goes on and the economy opens up even further, more and more local partners will become available and if the deal or offer you have on the table is truly fair, eventually by following Action Steps 3 (Be Patient and Thorough) and Action Step 4 (Think Win-Win), you will find the right local partner that will accept your conditions. Those who are interested in learning more about Chinese negotiating styles should read the works of Sinologist Professor Lucian Pye of MIT, such as *Chinese Negotiating Styles: Commercial Approaches and Cultural Principles.*

What's on the Table?

As China was opening up to the West during the 80s, many Chinese companies, which were almost all state-owned at the time, had no cash to put on the table. Instead, their bargaining chips were simple: cheap labour, market access, buildings and land. Buildings and land were perhaps one of the most controversial points during negotiations with state-owned enterprises, since most of the land and factories being offered were shoddy dilapidated buildings built during the Soviet era of the 50s and 60s. In many cases, it appeared that the price and value of the buildings and land would fluctuate with what was needed to complete the deal. "Oh, you need us to put up 20 million USD? Well guess what? It just so happens our building and land are valued at 20 million USD too." Throughout the 80s and even early 90s, many foreign companies were in a "take it or leave it" situation. However, as Chinese companies began to earn more cash, and property valuations became more sophisticated, the argument over what a building and a piece of land were "really worth" intensified. In cases where a "divorce" was taking place between the Chinese and foreign side and the splitting up of assets became an issue, this issue often grew downright ugly. This is no different from a marriage without a prenuptial agreement.

Portola made a smart move to insist that the Chinese side put up cash instead of land and to decide on the building and land purchase or lease after the funds were held in a joint bank account. Furthermore, they protected the funds by insisting that they had the right to approve the buildings and land lease. The situation in China today is far more favourable for the foreign investor. International third-party property consultants such as FPD Savills and DTZ Debenham Tie Leung are available to not only help companies find suitable locations, but also to give a more accurate assessment as to their true market value. Sam Crispin explained that the differences between local and foreign evaluation methods often come down to methodology used. For example, the local side may focus on material and physical costs, while the foreign side concentrates on intangibles such as earning potential and opportunity costs. Regardless of these differences, many Chinese companies now have cash, so the need to resolve valuation disputes has diminished – which is backed up by anecdotal evidence.

While the foreign companies may baulk at the price or valuation placed on Chinese buildings and land, the Chinese side was equally shocked with the valuations placed on goodwill and trademarks. "How could an intangible asset, such as a trademark or brand, have any value in China if no one in China even knows of the company or the brand?" the Chinese would argue. While this is a valid point, foreign companies, having spent millions, if not billions, developing the value of their trademarks and brands at home and abroad, were reluctant to concede. Companies like Lion Nathan even have a specific valuation for their brands that is updated yearly and that they include in their financial statements. As the Chinese side familiarises itself with Western business practices, the situation will only improve, but at the same time, Western companies need to understand they are working in a new and developing market; therefore the valuations in goodwill and trademark need to be accounted for in that light.

What's in a Title?

Titles and rank have always been important in China. Even during the so-called egalitarian period of the Soviet era, titles and rank afforded people varying degrees of respect and privilege. Whether you were the party secretary of a local township or the party secretary of the nation, titles had significance. In Portola and Aquarius's case, the title was more a question of face than one of control. Examining the structure that was negotiated indicates that the Chinese were concerned with who "really" controlled the purse strings. While

Portola had the majority voting rights and the right to approve purchases up to 100,000 USD without needing board approval, the Chinese side had control over the all-important "chop". Anything the Joint Venture (JV) was to purchase needed this "chop" and the Chinese side often withheld the chop or approvals to not only demonstrate real control over the business, but also, as Michael believes, in protest where he tried to force issues through. To a certain degree, Michael was "boxed in" with the Chinese side controlling the management layers above and below, further strengthened by the control over the "chop". Sure, Portola had management voting rights with the board, but to invoke a board decision over issues such as which phone system or air-conditioning system to put in place, even though they shouldn't have to according to Michael's approval limit, would seem ridiculous. As Michael was to later demonstrate, he had no intention of being sidelined by the management structure, and his insistence on "getting his way" with the authority granted to him by sidelining his locally appointed deputy created many flashpoints of discontent between the two sides.

Photograph by John L. Chan

When negotiating with a local partner, it is important to know "who will hold the chop", since the person who holds this innocent block of wood is the key person in any company in China. The chop is usually required to get anything officially approved by the government or paid. Foreign executives new to China are often baffled by the legalities concerning the significance of what it means to have, or consequences of not having, a document with the appropriate chop by the right authorities.

Another common complaint by the Chinese side, especially when they had a strong equity stake, such as Aquarius's 45%, was the heavy cost burden expats had on the JV. Mr Lu probably would have been happier had they also included Michael's full salary in the JV, since that would also mean a huge pay increase for Mr Lu as well, but Portola saved themselves the need to pay over 100,000 USD extra to Mr Lu, who planned to be more of a figurehead General Manager

China Streetsmart

than a true operational manager, by paying Michael separately outside the JV. Michael said he discovered this clause early on when he attended American Chamber of Commerce (Amcham) meetings and heard other executives complain about this topic. The mitigating factor for Portola was that they required or wanted only one expat. Other JVs that have brought in dozens of costly expats was a good reason for the Chinese side to be unhappy, or very happy if you were local beneficiary of the "equal pay for equal work" method.

The financial controller of the JV is a key position. Ideally the controller should take an active role in the finances, as any Chief Financial Officer (CFO) should. But to work effectively in a JV, the controller should clearly understand the differences between International and Chinese generally accepted accounting principles (GAAP) and how to resolve issues that arise. Chinese GAAP has evolved progressively since the opening of the doors to the West. However, significant hurdles remain before Chinese GAAP will be eliminated in favour of a unified GAAP. Issues such as the treatment of assets and receivables have political overtones. For example, when examining the books of Chinese enterprises, care must be taken when looking at their accounts receivables. The overall financial picture may appear healthy because Chinese GAAP does not have the same bad write-off provisions for long-term receivables. If international GAAP were applied, the financial situation for many state-run enterprises would change dramatically. Michael was frustrated over the lack of experience of the local CFO (the salary level was capped according to the agreement made between the two parties, resulting in a limited-experienced financial controller). For example, her limited experience proved to be a problem when looking at issues such as the treatment of depreciation over certain equipment. Trying to balance the books in China under China GAAP and reconciling numbers to consolidate internationally using US GAAP proved a bigger challenge than anticipated.

Avoid Staffing Traps

In the interest of creating a "profitable" streamlined organisation, Portola did the right thing to not make any concessions in the contract in taking on unqualified or unnecessary staff. Issues such as nepotism, where the Chinese side would staff key positions with people more because of their *guanxi* than their qualifications, were commonplace. Sometimes the foreign side would turn a blind eye to the son of the chief negotiator becoming "deputy something or another", but occasionally there would be management conflicts as unqualified staff would make bad decisions, based on inexperience, that would disrupt the business.

In other cases, deals were negotiated where JVs had the right after a few years to downsize the staffing requirements if desired. Clauses like these need to be watched and managed very carefully, since who is ultimately to take care of the displaced workers and to pay them compensation needs to be very clearly outlined and checked with local authorities. Unions and local labour bureaus must all agree, since any measure to create more unemployment will be met with stiff resistance by local government authorities. Action Step 5 (Be Detailed) really applies here. Based on my own experiences, I am not in favour of these clauses, since it only prolongs the anxiety of the workers as to who will stay and who will eventually be let go, which affects productivity. The JV invariably loses. In some cases, I have seen workers occupy the management offices of a JV in protest, blaming not the Chinese side for agreeing to the clause, but the foreign side for exercising it.

Who's in Charge?

Knowing who has real negotiating authority is another basic negotiating principle, but once again, this is not always clear when negotiating with state-owned companies. During the early stages of the negotiation, the foreign side may believe they are negotiating with the relevant people, but often the real authority to approve agreements may not even be people the foreign side has ever had contact with. This lack of transparency bothers many foreign investors and is why foreign companies often prefer to work with the growing number of local private companies. However, not all the confusion over who's in charge is deliberate. As the economy in China evolves, so have the governing authorities overseeing the state-run industries. For example, in March 1998, the central government's ministries were significantly restructured. During this restructuring, the Ministries of Post and Telecommunications, Electronics, Coal, Chemical and Machine Building were all abolished. The Ministries of Post and Telecommunications, Electronics, and Radio, Film and Television, for example, were all rolled into the new Ministry of Information Industry or MII (which also oversees the Internet sector). Significant changes like these create confusion as to who really is in charge. As China continues to modernise, major changes like these can be expected to continue.

The fact that Mr Lu of Aquarius agreed in writing to finance the cost for the machinery for the 4-litre (1-gallon) cap 100% from the Chinese side and had to later rescind because the Shanghai Light Industry people insisted the financing be shared 55/45, is not uncommon. Luckily, Portola did not take the expense to ship the machine over and then find out. **The best protection a foreign company can take, where financial commitments are involved, is to make sure these conditions are checked and double checked by your lawyers before transferring any funds, equipment or goods.** The government bodies that oversee Chinese companies will continue to evolve so make sure the clauses containing financial commitments are protected and able to supersede any complications stemming from this inevitable fact – an experienced lawyer is really required here. "Step by step" or *yibubu* (pronounced "yee boo boo" in Mandarin) is a commonly used phrase in Chinese; so prepare for the negotiations step by step to be long and arduous – and if they are not, then consider yourself lucky.

MOFTEC Approvals

The examination and approval process of the Ministry of Foreign Trade and Economic Corporation (MOFTEC) is extremely bureaucratic and highly regulated. As a result, it is wise to seek advice of officials in the early stages of negotiation to ensure that the JV's business goals will be permitted in the same fashion desired by the JV. A problem could arise if the JV's business scope is not completely in line with the list of set approved business identities outlined by MOFTEC. **In short, a business cannot simply outline what it wants to do. It must fit a predetermined outline specified by MOFTEC.** While the outlines provided by MOFTEC are extensive and detailed, they do not force businesses to be treated in a similar fashion and where there are discrepancies, MOFTEC is available for discussion. Often what happens is that if a particular business identity has a

90% fit, officials will often let the deal pass. However, be aware that the official certificate will not include the 10% "out of scope" so technically when the business does exercise that part of the business they would technically be operating outside their "legal" scope of business. The good news is that lawyers have told me this is unlikely watched or checked by MOFTEC unless blatant abuse is involved. However, do not count on getting anything in writing from officials saying they can go outside their assigned business scope.

An example where this could prove to be an issue is when a manufacturer sees itself not so much as a manufacturer or seller of goods but as a "solutions provider". The incentive of coupling a strong service component to the charges to his customer could enable the company to potentially save on taxes, since goods are subject to 17% value-added tax while services are subjected to only 5% tax. However, the business scope certificate issued by MOFTEC may not acknowledge the strong service emphasis the JV desires, instead labelling the company as a manufacturer or (re)seller of goods. How they often resolve this service component is to categorise it simply as "after-sales servicing" or "consulting services related to the sale of goods". As long as this condition is not abused, the business is unlikely to be questioned – but once again, you will not get this in writing.

Why not in writing? Government officials when dealing with grey areas will unlikely address it in writing, but could tell you verbally it is okay to "go outside the written boundaries since no one will check or ask". These are the moments when having good Chinese listening skills helps – experience is needed in interpreting what is really being said. However, for those who prefer everything to be in black and white, you could feel dissatisfied – but do not fret. "It's one of the quirks about China," says Tim Lai of McDonald's. "I have had to explain this quirk to our American management when they came over that this is how things are done. If you try and force the issue you won't win, rather what I often do is to send the government officials a letter thanking them for meeting with us and 'giving us the benefit of the doubt' so at least we have something in writing. Often I say if you have any problems with this or that, then please respond within say, one week, which they never do, so everybody is happy."

Fortunately for Portola, they did not run into these issues. Instead, the condition they had to change was simply to increase the amount of production they reserved for export – a condition no longer relevant now that China has entered into the World Trade Organisation (WTO). The Aquarius people should have known about this had they been talking to the Shanghai Foreign Investment Commission, the relevant local department at MOFTEC. According to Michael, the person responsible for getting the approval from the Chinese side was the same person that was going to be appointed his deputy. To protect his anonymity, since it wouldn't be fair to use his name when he is not able to defend any allegations against him, I'll simply refer to him as Mr Deputy. This oversight was the first of many major mistakes Michael claimed Mr Deputy was to make. Fortunately, John Huang's *guanxi* with the Vice President of MOFTEC helped. The rejection in submission caused about a 3–4 week delay. It is possible that John could have tried to use his *guanxi* harder, but he didn't, because the slight delay did not significantly affect the business. Calling on your *guanxi* needs to be exercised appropriately for when you really need it, which is exactly what John did.

MOFTEC approvals are also relevant if the JV wishes to change their future status such as selling their assets to another party such as a local company. For example, just because the local company you are negotiating an exit strategy with may have all the direct parties agreeing to the sale or transfer, does not mean that the deal is consummated. It will be consummated only after the final blessing is given by MOFTEC. Failure to acknowledge this could have grave consequences. During the bloodshed of the late 90s when many foreign multinational corporations (MNCs) were bleeding profusely and looking for an exit strategy, many had put their assets up for

sale, prepared to take a "one-time" loss by selling off their assets and stop the bleeding.

In one case, a large well-known state-run company offered to buy the assets of one of these well-known foreign companies. It was rumoured that the "real" strategy by this state-run company was to strike a deal they knew MOFTEC would never approve of, and damage their competitor. What happened to the MNC was, once word leaked out that the company was pulling out of the market, productivity dropped, employees started looking for other jobs, and distributors and other suppliers stopped shipping goods and froze their payables. The total disruption to the business damaged the MNC, allowing the state-run company to gain even larger market share. "The deal's not over until the money's in the bank," claimed one executive who fell victim to this situation. "We had everything signed and chopped, or so we thought; we were all ready to walk away only to find out that we couldn't. Now we are back to square one and in a much worse-off position. We didn't think MOFTEC's approval would have been a problem." **The *China Streetsmart* advice is not only to seek MOFTEC's advice in the early stages of setting up the JV, but also for any potential changes to the JV you are considering such as the selling back of assets to the local partner.**

An Exit Strategy – Prenuptial Agreements

Although Portola had buyout clauses, they did not formally include in the contract a contingency plan in the event of a "divorce" – a prenuptial agreement. The contract had provisions for arbitration, but an exit strategy was not considered, probably for the same reasons two people getting married would feel uncomfortable writing out a prenuptial: "Why should we plan for a divorce when we plan to live together forever?" **Given the amount of "divorces" that have been happening between local and foreign companies, the *China Streetsmart* thing to do is to always ensure there is in place a proper exit strategy and clear demarcation in how the assets will be split up in the event of a divorce.** Some of the horror stories that have contributed to the negative news about investing in China are because no such provisions were made and as a result, the outcomes have been "nasty and messy". Stewart Wong, a senior lawyer at Lovells in Beijing said, "In the early days the Chinese companies were suspicious why Western companies would insist on putting in an exit strategy; but as they were told repeatedly that this was a standard business term and more and more boards were requiring companies to include them as a matter of process, their concen was reduced."

Seamus Cornelius, the Chief Representative and head lawyer for Allens Arthur Robinson, said there are essentially three ways JVs end. The first way is the foreign partner simply walks off, writing everything off. The second case is when a formal procedure is set up for liquidation and bankruptcy proceedings. However, the quirk in Chinese law is that you can only liquidate the company if you can demonstrate you can pay all the creditors, which kind of negates the need for liquidation or bankruptcy in the first place, but this is a sample of the many quirks in Chinese law you will discover. You should also be aware that in China, a foreign invested enterprise (FIE) cannot go bankrupt, since there is no bankruptcy law for FIEs. In these cases, FIEs often try to follow bankruptcy rules stated for local companies, but to do so, the local governing district must first "allow" the company to go bankrupt. Given each governing district often has an unpublished "quota" of the number of enterprises that can declare bankruptcy, most are reluctant to give their quota away to FIEs, instead reserving them for the many local companies who may really need the bankruptcy protection.

The third scenario of an exit strategy is the sale of the foreign side's assets and contributions. If this is to a local company, this could prove difficult since the company will cease to be an FIE; however, it is entirely possible to sell the shares to another foreign party. Often what happens in this case is when the agreement is first drafted, a special-purpose vehicle (SPV) is drafted which is an offshore or, for example, a Hong Kong business entity specifically set up for the purposes of engaging in the JV with the local Chinese partner. In theory, if there is no "change in control" provision in the contract, the foreign side, if looking for an exit strategy, could simply sell their SPV to another foreign entity and just "walk away" without the need for MOFTEC or local partner approval.

Exit strategies can be complex and the information cited is simply to give you an idea of some of the complexities involved. Since each case will be different, make sure that your lawyer has China experience on how proper exit terms should be drafted. Also be aware that the government approving body will look down unfavourably on an agreement which is too one-sided in favour of the foreign company. In some cases, the conditions on which the agreements were drafted and agreed by both sides have been rejected. Once again, Action Step 4 (Think Win-Win) applies. While the Chinese side may not always be counted on to make the agreements equal, it is within the control of the foreign side to ensure they are. To quote the old saying, "Hope for the best and prepare for the worst."

19 | Running the Joint Venture

The Birth of the Joint Venture

| Preliminary Steps | Setting the Strategy | Negotiating the Deal | **Running the Joint Venture** | Ending the Joint Venture | Beyond the Joint Venture |

Completing the deal, valued at less than 10 million USD, took more than six months of solid negotiations and just over a year after the letter of intent (LOI) was first signed. The Ministry of Foreign Trade and Economic Corporation's (MOFTEC) approval of the joint venture (JV) completes the examination and approval process, but the business must then be registered and granted a business licence to operate, which is done with the State Administration for Industry and Commerce (SAIC). Unfortunately, MOFTEC and SAIC are separate government entities, so if MOFTEC approves a complex JV, then the JV may have to go through an explanation process all over again with the SAIC officials. Fortunately, Portola's case was very straightforward.

Once MOFTEC issued its certificate stating that the Portola JV was allowed to exist, Portola then took the MOFTEC certificate to SAIC to get an interim business registration licence, which allowed them to register with various government departments, such as the tax authorities, the customs authorities, the local public security bureau (PSB) and the labour bureau. The interim certificate was also good enough to open bank accounts where one of the first things to be transferred was the agreed capital to get the JV started. A local accounting firm must then audit the JV to ensure all the funds and agreed capital and equipment had been fulfilled according to the terms of the contract, and then issued Portola a capital verification report. This report allowed them to go back to the SAIC officials and get their official business licence. This business licence was equivalent to the certificate of incorporation and Portola was meant to hang the certificate in a public place. The whole process took about three months.

Photograph by John L. Chan

One of the reasons Michael gives for the smooth set-up of Shanghai Portola was the help of Sharon Miao, who began as his Executive Assistant. Her proven track record at Portola allowed her to rise through the ranks and she now holds two positions – as Human Resource Manager for Shanghai Portola and Administration Manager Asia-Pacific Region for Portola Packaging, Inc.

While the approval process was in full swing, the more pressing issue was finalising the site where Portola was to set up the factory. Michael Colozzi hired First Pacific Davies (now known as FPD Savills), even while he was looking at sites being put up by the Chinese side, to keep his options open. The site requirements were very specific for Portola. They wanted a "metal build" which was essentially a building made out of steel girders forming a frame where walls surrounding the frame could easily be moved and new steel girders added to expand the factory as the business grew. Another important consideration was floor load. The foundation on which the machines would eventually lie had to be sturdy enough to support a machine of several tons punching out high precision plastic bottle caps. The slightest movement because of a weak foundation could seriously affect the machines and the quality of the output. Michael knew his sales estimates were on the conservative side, so in case the market took off, he knew he could expand quickly. In the end, FPD did find a site that fitted Portola's needs in Xinzhuang Industrial Zone, only 17 kilometres from the Shanghai city centre (See Figure 19.1). The site was approved in December 1997, before final approval was given by MOFTEC. Mr Lu, understanding that time

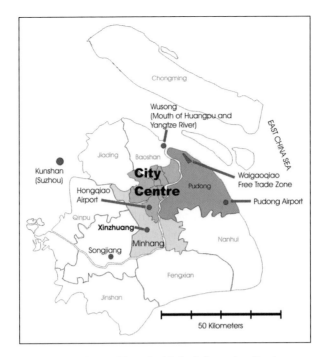

Figure 19.1   Shanghai Administrative Region

Xinzhuang is one of the fastest growing areas in the Shanghai (Puxi) region, attracting investors such as Portola Packaging and Siemens Switchgear. The last stop on the Shanghai no.1 subway/metro line gives convenient access to the city. To accommodate this influx of new investment, the government built this brand new metro station.

was of the essence in getting the building construction started, and confident of approval by MOFTEC, as a matter of good faith, agreed to put up 480,000 RMB in cash as their portion of the land deposit even before any joint bank accounts were set up.

Conflicts between Chinese and Western Expectations

While the negotiations were arduous and the bureaucratic approval process slow, the JV was steadily making progress. Although Michael did not save very many kind words for the Shanghai Light Industry people, given their tough negotiating stance towards him, the first real signs of a cultural conflict that would negatively affect the direction of the JV began to surface with the appointment of Michael's deputy from the Chinese side. As per the agreement, Aquarius appointed Mr Deputy to be Michael's assistant. His job function was to assist Michael, but according to Michael, in reality he was trying to control the day-to-day business functions while reporting back Michael's activities to the Aquarius management. Michael called it spying. Mr Lu, on the other hand, while officially the General Manager, was not there on a daily basis, but would meet with Michael frequently, often during the evenings over dinner.

The first real conflict between the two sides arose over how the factory should be built. Mr Deputy had brought in a number of contractors that Michael claimed appeared to be more his "cronies" than serious contractors. For about five months Portola let Mr Deputy handle this side and with each new contractor he introduced, Michael would question them on their methodology on how they planned to fit out the plant. He quickly discovered their methods were well below the standards Portola was looking for. "Simple things like the need to put epoxy on the floors and the importance of floor load were unfamiliar to them," Michael said. Frustrated over the longer-than-expected time to select a contractor to get the time-critical construction going, Michael took things into his own hands and began to look for contractors himself. Eventually he found a suitable contractor, Porta Asiatica, run by two Canadians. "These guys understood my needs: they were knowledgeable enough about the local market to give me good local alternatives that were cost effective, while not compromising my need to meet the stringent US Food and Drug Administration (FDA) standards our plants demand."

Upon hearing the JV was going to use Porta Asiatica rather than local contractors chosen by Mr Deputy, which were quoting up to 20% less, Mr Deputy was furious and reported back to Aquarius's head office. To help Mr Lu understand why they needed this level of contractor, Michael claims he spent many evenings over dinner carefully explaining to Mr Lu why it was necessary. In the end, Portola did use Porta Asiatica, but only after Mr Lu came back with the ultimatum that if they were prepared to lower their bid by 80,000 RMB they could have the job. The management at Porta Asiatica baulked when they heard the request, claiming they had already lowered the bid down as slim as they could and if they had to lower the bid by another 80,000 RMB, then the deal simply would not be worth pursuing. Michael resolved the issue by getting Porta Asiatica to lower the bid by 80,000 RMB and in turn reimbursed them the 80,000 RMB directly via Portola's US office to a Hong Kong account. "Why 80,000 RMB?" Michael asked himself. "I'll never know how they came up with that number but it was one of the quirky things I experienced from our Chinese partners. They would come up with this figure or request that seemed to be from out of the air, and so we had to follow. I was more concerned with getting the factory built on time than to understand why. We had originally planned to start formal outfitting of the plant in June, but due to the delays caused by Mr Deputy, we didn't get started until September, which was cutting out time to get ready for the coming season extremely tight. I speculate why Mr Deputy was so upset was because he probably had kickbacks lined up. He must have seen this position as his chance to make a lot of money for himself – which I was not about to give to him."

Shanghai Portola Packaging today. Detailed requirements such as floor load were important considerations in finalising where to build their site since their high precision and heavy equipment, such as the 150-ton machine (upper right), needed to be built on an extremely solid foundation.

Building the Team

Building the Portola team was another critical success factor Michael executed well, which has contributed to Portola's success today. "In all my jobs, my success has really been on finding the best people for the job. It's what helped me while I was at The GAP (the American clothing chain) and it's what saved me here too." Core to his staffing needs were 5–6 line directors he wanted to be able to work together like "brothers and sisters". While Mr Deputy was working on finding contractors, Michael concentrated on building up his team. He took out a large wanted ad (written in English only) in Shanghai's main newspaper, the *Xinmin Wanbao* (New Peoples Evening Paper) that advertised his new company with the promise of "training in the US". The response to the ad was overwhelming. During the few weeks the ad was run, Michael claims he received over 1,500 curriculum vitaes (CVs). "Training in the US" apparently was a big factor for the high response. While staying at the Portman Hotel, he says the bellmen would literally wheel in boxes full of mail filled with CVs.

Here is a photocopy of the original employment advertisement that Shanghai Portola placed in the Shanghai *Xinmin Wanbao* newspaper.

Carefully selecting and interviewing each of the potential candidates were really important to Michael. Each of the 50 successful candidates, from line director to factory floor worker, was interviewed no less than five times to ensure they were suitable to their operation. By this point, the issue arose from the Chinese side that they wanted the JV to consider the many people they had in their current operations to fulfil the needed spots – as was discussed during the contract negotiations. Michael, having seen the level of cooperation he was having with Mr Deputy and the productivity of their appointed "watchdog" in the finance department, was ada-

China Streetsmart

mantly against taking in more of Aquarius's people and because it was not in the contract, he refused to budge on this issue. His Chinese partners pressured him and insisted that he give it serious consideration. Having visited his share of state-run enterprises, he wanted to avoid bringing in the type of people whose mentality was if something broke down, the first thing they would do was to go pick up a newspaper until the person responsible fixed the problem. In the three years since the business has been in operation, he claims to have lost only four staff. "I want staff that are willing to accept more responsibility, can think on their feet, and grow themselves as the company grows," he says. "I want people who are after more than just money; I want them to feel they are joining a family." He did interview the various candidates put forth by Aquarius, but rejected all of them. The rift between he and his Chinese partners deepened.

A Successful Launch

Notwithstanding the looming cultural clashes and differences of opinion Michael was having with his Chinese partners, the business was eventually launched in March 1998 with resounding success. Within the first month they were officially opened they had completely sold out their production line, which in turn allowed them to turn in an instant operating profit. Since the opening, Portola has not looked back. Much of the success can be credited to careful preparation of Michael and his new team. The first members of his core staff he brought on board were marketing people and they immediately set out to contact the people and factories Michael had visited on his previous field trips throughout China.

20 | Running the Joint Venture

A *China Streetsmart* Analysis

| Preliminary Steps | Setting the Strategy | Negotiating the Deal | Running the Joint Venture | Ending the Joint Venture | Beyond the Joint Venture |

The business registration process for Portola went relatively smooth but others I interviewed said they experienced problem and delays, especially during the 80s and early 90s. The problem often stems from the fact that the Ministry of Foreign Trade and Economic Corporation (MOFTEC), which approves the investment; the State Administration for Industry and Commerce (SAIC), which issues the business licence; and the Tax Bureau, which issues and collects taxes, are all under different branches of the government. Since China is a developing country, commercial laws are constantly evolving and affect each department differently. The good news is that the process of approving and registering a business is getting much easier. Straightforward business requests in some of the more progressive investment-savvy areas of Shanghai, for example, can obtain approvals within weeks, as opposed to months previously. Furthermore, specific "coordination departments" are now being set up to help businesses deal with the complexities of working with MOFTEC, SAIC and the tax authorities. Some areas in Pudong (Shanghai's eastern area), for example, are now even offering employee recruiting and other employee management services. The *China Streetsmart* approach would definitely be to seek out these areas and services.

Get to Know Your Local Officials

While there is no simple straightforward method of handling all the

issues as they arise, it is important to note that policies set out by the central government are only as useful as the local officials enforcing them and as a result, the *China Streetsmart* thing to do early on is to **get to know your local officials**. *China Streetsmart* companies are able to cultivate good working relationships with all the bureaus they deal with and use their relationships or *guanxi* to help smooth things over when problems arise. They understand getting things in writing is not as important as getting their cooperation to help resolve problems as they arise.

While I worked in the beer industry, we tried very hard to keep good relations with local government officials. A serious issue requiring local official support surfaced in 1998. To lower the incidents of exploding beer bottles, national legislation was passed that required all beer to be bottled only in specially made bottles that had a "B" embossed on the glass bottom. Furthermore, the bottles also had a date embossed on the bottle and no bottle over two years old was meant to be in circulation. Six months after the legislation went into effect, any brewer caught violating this legislation was subject to a heavy fine and penalties. This legislation proved to be a nightmare for brewers. Millions upon millions of bottles had to be hand inspected. There was no way a complete overhaul of the bottle float (between 30 and 50 million bottles) could have been completed within six months. If we had not cultivated a strong relationship with the local officials, we would have been in trouble, since we heard the policy enforcement really varied from district to district – even within the same city. The fact that none of the officials were willing to put anything in writing was not as important as the fact that they did not enforce the rules as long as we were making a concerted effort to abide by the law.

Since Michael had a language barrier, getting to know the local officials was personally difficult. Instead, he appointed his executive assistant, Sharon Miao, to handle government relations. An experienced local, Sharon proved many times her ability to forge a strong relationship with the local officials, helped the company navigate through many complexities and was a critical reason why the registration process went so smoothly. For example in one case, a disgruntled worker claimed more compensation than he received when he was let go and charged the company with various employee violations. He was one of only four employees to have left the company over the past three years. But because Portola maintained such strong relations with the labour bureau and had such an impressive record in retaining its employees, the case never received serious consideration. The labour bureau officials would meet with Portola regularly (over lunch or dinner) and knew Portola was a valuable and fair local employer – certainly probably far more even-handed than many of the other local companies operating in the area.

Finding the Right Property

Whether you are building a plant or opening up a new office, deciding on where you set it up can have a significant impact on the business. Since Portola was setting up a new joint venture (JV) manufacturing operation, the choice was almost certainly in a special investment zone that offered tax breaks and other concessions. But where? The first special economic zones were set up in 1980 in Southern China. Since then, dozens of cities across China have developed their own special economic and technical development zones (ETDZ), high tech development zones, and free trade zones (FTZ). Smaller municipal governments, seeing the benefits of attracting foreign investment, also began to set up their own zones, now numbering in the hundreds. Within Shanghai, Portola had the choice of no less than seven state-level and nine municipal-level investment zones. Each zone had their own specific tax advantages, such as a three-year tax holiday after the first profitable year, plus an additional three to five years at a reduced rate of up to 50% and beyond, a 15% tax rate opposed to the standard 33%.

It is important to note that many of the ETDZ's tax concessions may be phased out by 2004–2005 as part of China's commitment to the World Trade Organisation (WTO) to bring a fair "national treatment" to both foreign and local companies. As a result, one must double-check which incentives still apply to the specific zone you are thinking of investing in and if so, what are the "grandfather" provisions in place. Other details to examine carefully is whether the zone is sponsored or recognised by the central government. As illustrated in Chapter 10, on the importance of being detailed, some of the smaller municipalities set up "illegally" have now been shut down by the state or the tax concessions offered by these smaller municipalities were unable to be honoured, since the local poorer municipal government must still pay the tax revenues to the central tax authorities.

The zones in the Pudong area of Shanghai, for example, are fully legal and have long been used by the central government to pioneer and test economic reforms. As a result, the four state-level zones in Pudong have been the favourite for foreign investors, attracting thousands of companies. Specialised zones such as Pudong's Waigaoqiao's (pronounced "why-gow-chow" in Mandarin) state-sponsored FTZ allow companies within the bonded zone to import, manufacture and export goods duty free, while conducting foreign exchange transactions is easier than in other parts of the country. Local officials within zones like these are among the most sophisticated in China and easiest to deal with. Even when the tax incentives are eventually eliminated, these zones intend to continue attracting foreign investment with the offering of higher end services such as consulting and coordination services, within the different government ministries, and employee services such as recruitment and human resource benefits administration.

Portola chose not to invest in Pudong and instead set up in the Xinzhuang (Minhang district) Municipal Zone – one of the nine local zones set up by the Shanghai government. Although the tax concessions were not as long and favourable as potentially other areas within Shanghai, they got a good lease on the building with an option to buy. Nevertheless, Portola was able to secure at least a three-year tax holiday with a possible extension of another two years if

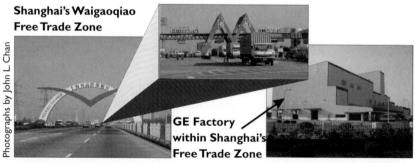

Shanghai's Waigaoqiao Free Trade Zone (see Figure 19.1 for location) located in Pudong was the first and currently most successful export-processing zone in China, complete with its own port facilities. Some of the most famous international companies have set up operations here.

they met or exceeded their export quotas – which appears to be the case given the fact that recent export figures have been up to 90% of total production. Key factors in Portola's decision were timing and a ready source of qualified labour. To set up in Pudong required a greenfield operation that could have delayed the opening by six months or more and caused the business to lose a critical selling season. On the other hand, the building in Xinzhuang was ready to be outfitted and its close proximity to town gave them a ready pool of skilled workers.

As Action Step 5 suggests, being detailed is important when choosing a location. Portola knew what they were after in terms of technical and physical requirements, such as metal frames and floor loads. "We like these kinds of customers," quips Sam Crispin, the General Manager for FPD Savills. Given some of the shoddy construction, which took place during the 50s and 60s, not all buildings were built with the proper concrete foundations in place. Furthermore, the ground around Shanghai has been known to be soft, so Portola was correct to examine these details carefully. Portola also had a clear understanding of how their expansion plans would work. The empty factory next door to Portola's, which was controlled by the same landlord, was a possibility, but they made sure they did not make any firm commitments until they were sure they had the market. If anything, Michael informs me they may have underestimated their expansion requirements, as the business has been so successful and may require the company to move to an entirely new larger location.

Acknowledging and Understanding Corruption and Graft

Being *China Streetsmart* with regards to purchasing and tendering in China unfortunately has really little to do with purchasing and tendering at all, rather more with corruption and graft. The fact is in almost every position I have had in China, I have witnessed corruption, graft, kickbacks, bribes or whatever you want to call it. In any society where deals are worth a huge value and regulations are very loose, the temptation for corruption will always exist. For people who earn 2,500 RMB per month and need to make decisions involving hundreds of thousands of RMB, where a 5-10% kickback could be worth half a year's salary or more, the temptation to give in is enormous. It is important to note that the people offering the bribes are as guilty as those who receive them. **The Chinese culture is not** corrupt; rather, **the loose situation in the way business is conducted is prone to corruption** and this is true no matter which culture, society or country you live in.

It is human nature to be tempted by money, especially when suppliers and other service agents are habitually offering "benefits" or "gifts". A senior executive I know well was extremely disappointed and almost heartbroken when he learned that one of his trusted local employees was taking kickbacks. This employee was well educated and the son of parents who were well-off diplomats. He had spent many years living abroad himself and knew Western culture. He was placed in charge of procurement, which involved millions of RMB, and eventually succumbed to the temptation of bribes suppliers were offering him – almost daily. At first the senior executive refused to listen to the rumours that this was happening, until the evidence grew so great he had to act. His former "trusted" employee eventually went to jail. It is not just locals who take money. In one case, I personally discovered an expat taking kickbacks, or at least the "smoking gun" or circumstantial evidence was so great that the expat eventually left the company.

While it would not be fair to accuse Mr Deputy of attempting to line his pockets with kickbacks from building contractors when he has no chance to defend himself, I would not be the least bit shocked if it were true. On the contrary, I would be more shocked if there weren't an offer on the table since the amount of money involved was so high. In China, this issue can get complicated when you begin mixing cultural customary elements of entertaining and showing of gratitude by giving gifts. What is pure graft (or bribery) and what is "cultural appreciation" is not black and white and rarely will anyone in China come outright and "ask for something" – not like I am told is the blatant and bold practice in Russia these days. Western corporate policy against gift-giving can sometimes go against cultural practice. However, even in the West there are many ways around the issue. While I was at Exxon, I received a beautiful titanium golf club from Pepsi. Since it had a big Pepsi logo embossed on the club, it was considered "advertising and promotional material" so I got to keep it. However, **in any case where a manager is in charge of making financial decisions involving large sums, the best protection is to have more than one person involved with the decision and to make that decision as transparent and open as possible.**

Dealing with Corruption and Graft

As Action Step 6 suggests, maintaining a healthy attitude is key to not letting the issue of bribes and corruption depress you. It is not constructive for the foreign businessperson to look at every local employee with a distrusting eye. Rather it is more useful to focus on putting in place a system to minimise the temptation. There is no simple solution or system to adopt. In one of my previous companies, we stopped having my brand managers make purchase decisions over our point-of-sale and promotion material (worth millions each year) and moved the purchasing decision over to the finance department. Problems then arose over quality and timing of delivery. In another case, I know of a General Manager who became so paranoid about kickbacks happening among his staff he began to approve all purchases, even as small as office stationary. He was overwhelmed with paperwork and the overall productivity in the company suffered while waiting for his approvals. Furthermore, he had to work all the time just to keep up with the paperwork. **The basic strategy to reducing the risk or temptation of corruption and graft is increased transparency.** The more transparent the system, whether purchasing and tendering is made by one or more departments and/or people, the less likely corruption is to take place.

Unfortunately, you will likely never completely stamp out the temptation for corruption and kickbacks – since that would require a change in human nature. People will continue to "pad" their expense reports; office and purchasing managers will continue to receive offers of "gifts, free trips, even brownbag money" in return for the business. The Chinese government has actually legislated a formalised tendering process for both local and foreign companies, which includes mandatory tendering for projects over a certain amount,[1] but critics claim the system is easily by-passed if one wants to by breaking up large bids into smaller projects – which is what

---

[1] Understanding the latest tendering laws in China can be very important and is a good reason for having a very good lawyer who not only understands the law but also knows how it works in practice. As Action Step 5 (Be Detailed) suggests, you really should understand the details, since I have come across companies running into problems with local authorities for not following the correct procedures. As an example of how the tendering process could work take a look at the following link: http://www.tradeport.org/ts/countries/china/mrr/mark0039.html

China Streetsmart

Portola did with Porta Asiatica. It would be easy for me to suggest that the *China Streetsmart* method is to find honest people, but that would be a bit naïve – although there are plenty of truly honest people in China. The *China Streetsmart* action is to accept the fact that temptations exist and to focus on putting in preventative measures, such as increased transparency, which will mitigate significant damages to your company's bottom line.

Building the Right Team at the Start

Ask any executive in China as to *the* critical factor that will determine a business's success in China (or anywhere) and they will all say the same thing – its people. **Getting the right people *right at the onset* of the business is crucial to getting the business off to a good start.** Fortunately Portola did the right things. Portola's commitment to maintaining management consistency right from the start, Action Step 1, was demonstrated time and again and allowed them to avoid many of the pitfalls other JVs experienced. For example, by appointing Michael at the outset, to the negotiation stage, to running the operations, allowed a good working relationship of respect and trust to develop between Mr Lu and Michael. It helped that Michael knew all the dynamics that went into the negotiations so the local side was unable to pressure him into doing things outside the contract. Often what happens when the negotiator and person running the operation are different is that the Chinese will claim "goodwill promises" were made during the negotiations and expect the foreign side to acquiesce. Often if the person from the foreign side is not available to confirm or deny the demands, the local side could use this as an excuse to "withhold other commitments or obligations". This problem was a common occurrence when dealing with distributors. A newly appointed sales director would often be faced with a deluge of demands from the trade based on "promises" made by the previous management, which may or may not have been true, but the trade would often use this tactic as a reason, for example, to withhold payment. These "games" with the trade were common. Had there been consistent leadership and a proper transition of power in place when required, this would not likely happen.

Since Michael knew he was going to inherit what he was starting, he was very careful in writing the business plan and managing expectations accordingly. Had Michael left early after the JV was started, Portola's outcome could have been much different. Other companies I interviewed did not follow the same commitment to their leadership in building up the right team at the start and in most cases suffered as a result.

Recruiting the Right Staff – It's More Than Language Skills

Choosing the right staff at the start is not only a matter of selecting those with experience and skill, but also selecting those who are sensitive to different cultures. Having interviewed and spoken to a lot of people during his early days of understanding the China market, Michael had a clear vision of the type of employee he wanted and given the importance of staffing, he was not going to compromise his standards – even at the risk of upsetting his local partners.

Since English skills were important for Michael's direct reports to have, he made the right decision to place an English-only ad in the newspaper. However, English was not his top criterion. "Job skills and experience far outweighed the need to speak English, that's why I had people go through so many interviews to make sure it wasn't just me that had an opinion," Michael reflected. "Other locals who were helping me in the recruitment process could understand the candidate better because they could get past the language barrier, which helped me get a more well-rounded view of the candidate. In the end, we were able to make the right decision for all of our employees and this is why our employee turnover has been so low."

Choosing language skills over job skills and experience was a crucial mistake a lot of companies made. In the sales field I came across many young local inexperienced sales managers that were promoted to positions of authority quickly not for their sales experience and achievements but because they could speak English well and had good training from a previous well-known multinational corporation (MNC). They may have been able to "talk" a good story to show they understood basic sales management skills, but when it came down to actual execution and working with the trade, their inexperience showed. Street-hardened distributors would "eat them for lunch", as one executive put it. For the sales field, which dealt with tough distributors, often what was needed was a

China Streetsmart

40+ veteran, who often couldn't speak a word of English, but knew all the tricks distributors would try and play. Michael hired about four or five people who became his trusted core directors who could all speak both languages, but beyond that, the English skills needed dropped significantly.

Finding Staff

Although Portola used only a large ad, there are many other methods new businesses should consider when coming to China. Methods such as job recruitment fairs, on-campus recruiting, search agencies and word-of-mouth or referrals are other important venues to consider. The more specific you are with each job requirement, the less chance you have of wasting your time reviewing unwanted resumes, since locals will send out resumes just because the company is foreign and well known.

The Foreign Enterprise Service Corporation (FESCO) is a labour service company that could also be a useful source for companies coming to China. For companies setting up representative offices, they have no choice but to use FESCO or an equivalent government-sponsored employee service company. As China's economy continues to liberalise, this rule should change. Employees who are hired through FESCO (or its equivalent) technically do not work for the company. The company usually does not even pay the employee; instead, all billings including salaries and benefits are charged through FESCO. While using FESCO may appear more expensive than hiring direct, the services available such as a ready pool of experienced employees to choose from, the advantage of not having to worry about how the latest employment rules and regulations surrounding benefits and other compensation are calculated, and the ability to get around the restrictions of transferring employees around China, could make using government-sponsored labour service companies, such as FESCO, a viable choice.

Types of Staff Available

Expatriates

China's local managers are developing rapidly, but the key skills lacking are often still soft skills such as leadership, strategy, vision and problem solving. As a result, experienced expatriates (foreign and Asian) are still very much needed for the top senior positions. The key drawback is costs, as a full expatriate could cost between 300,000 and 600,000 USD per head. I have spoken to some country-level senior executives of major corporations with compensation packages of over a million USD. However, if your investment is in the millions of USD, having a senior experienced executive with a proven track record could be the deciding factor in determining your business's success. Local expats, who are often younger, inexperienced foreigners willing to accept more local-style packages, were once popular in the 80s and early 90s when there was a shortage of qualified staff, but they have all but been replaced with the growing number of qualified local staff. As China continues to modernise, the need for other expats working for MNCs in China will also decrease. This will not be true, however, for the top job(s), especially the General Manager, Finance and Marketing Director positions.

Returnees

Initially I thought Mainland Chinese staff that left China to get an education abroad and are now returning to China, would be a natural target for companies wanting to boost their local presence with Western-savvy local staff. However, after having interviewed a lot of companies, I learned quickly that returnees were not always the preferred choice for companies. One of the major problems is inability to fit back into the Chinese working environment. "As my father used to say, they think their shit don't stink," said one top executive.

Grace Cheng, the Managing Director for Korn Ferry in Beijing and a returnee herself, best explained this discrepancy among returnees. "Returnees can best be categorised into three main types. The first group left China in the 80s and were the cream of the crop China had to offer. They got the opportunity to study and/or work abroad based on their achievements. They often studied at the best schools and/or worked at the best companies and have recently come back to China. (Grace herself studied at Smith College and received her doctorate from Oxford.) I believe this group of people will be the group that will lead China into the future," she claims. "Just look at returnees like Edward Tian, the CEO of China Netcom (one

Photograph by Michael Guo

Michael Guo, the Country General Manager for Gallup China, is an excellent example of a successful returnee. Unlike most returnees who went to the US or UK to study, Michael went to work in Panama for a Chinese trading company for four years from 1990 to 1993 and even managed to secure a Panamanian passport. Seeing better opportunities in China, he returned and gave up his Panamanian passport (as China does not allow for dual passport holders) and went to work for Gallup China. He has been with Gallup since it first set up in China in November 1993. Upon returning, he was acutely aware that local staff would be wary of working for a returnee so he focused hard on not portraying himself as a know-it-all, choosing instead to earn their respect based on his accomplishments.

of China's main telecommunications companies). These people have the understanding of China and ability to work here." Indeed, many of the executives I met such as L.J. Jia, who is the Chief Representative and Country Manager for American Express China, and Michael Guo, the Managing Director for the Gallup Organisation, all fit into this category.

She continued, "The second group of returnees are the ones who went abroad to study but have no real working experience upon returning to China. Typical job experience in the West was nothing more than odd jobs [waitering or washing dishes] to help pay for their education. Finally you have a third group that I call 'sojourners'. For one reason or another they were able to travel abroad, perhaps because they had money or because of the June 4 Tiananmen incident, which allowed them to stay in their respective countries long enough to get a [foreign] passport and are now returning to China because of the greater opportunities here. These groups of people are often not as strong in experience or ability and their background needs to be carefully checked."

However, the effectiveness of a returnee may have nothing to do with the actual persons' abilities and experience, since resentment by local staff towards these returnees was also a factor affecting company performance with some of the companies I interviewed. Whether it was a case of arrogance by the returnee or jealousy by the local staff, often the relationships between the two created more conflicts for the company than anticipated. **I certainly wouldn't dismiss any candidate because he or she was a returnee, but as I would for any foreign expat coming to China, I would screen the candidate carefully to ensure they had the cultural fit to work in today's China *and* the local staff could accept working with that person.** Many of the successful returnees I interviewed, including Grace, were not thrown into their senior executive roles at once; rather, they worked their way up the ladder just like everyone else and were promoted based on achievements.

Experienced Locals

These people are often the hottest staff on the market and quite frankly, the most difficult to keep. Many of these experienced locals have worked for foreign enterprises for years and if you look at some of them, you will see that their stay in one company could be as short as six months to a year. Given the rapid expansion during the 90s, with so many foreign companies coming to China, there was a feeding frenzy for those people with "experience". Often experience was no more than an English degree at a local university with an entry-level marketing or sales position at another MNC. However, because they were working for a well-known MNC, they were highly sought after. The salaries and title inflation grew rapidly, going from Junior Brand Assistant to Senior Brand Manager in as little as two to three years. Many had more than doubled or tripled their salaries in the process. In Shanghai it was not uncommon to see salaries start at about 1,500 RMB per month after these people graduate from university and within three to five years, they would be earning up to 10,000–15,000 RMB per month.

This group of locals does not necessarily make the best staff for a company. Some of these individuals did not have a conscientious career development plan. Many changed jobs because of the name or international reputation of the company, some changed jobs simply for higher salaries and titles. Most did not stay long enough in a company to develop a solid skill base. This was clearly evident in the sales field. Many of the early sales directors were foreign nationals sent over to set up operations and had no choice but to hire (often inexperienced) staff with English skills as opposed to non-English speaking sales managers with real experience. Recruiting local staff from brand name universities has also received some negative feedback recently, as some have felt that students graduating from the top schools were a bit elitist and not willing to roll up their sleeves like everyone else.

When interviewing some of these "hotshot" local candidates, I would almost hold a strike against them if they could speak English well, since they were ripe for poaching and the disruption to the business of re-hiring and re-training was very arduous. The good news is given the slowdown in the economy, poaching and matching-the-competitor's-offer game have been less prominent and local employees are beginning to learn the importance of career development. Many now stress that training and opportunities for advancement within the company are more important than job title and pay. My research is backed up by *The Asian Wall Street Journal* report on the 2001 Best Employers in Asia Survey in factors influencing engagement conducted by Hewitt Associates that indicates local staff ranks pay fourth behind 1) senior leadership, 2) opportunities, and 3) work activities.[2] However, the real test will be after China's economy improves with the influx of foreign companies, as a result of China's entry into the WTO. Companies aggressively entering the market will once again begin poaching these "hotshots" by offering attractive salary packages and promotions for these talented locals and my prediction is that you will once again see huge disruptions in MNC operations.

State-Run Employees

It is easy to dismiss state-run employees as unsuitable to work in a Western-run company because of the baggage they often carry with them, as was cited by Michael. These employees are unlikely to show initiative and are unwilling to take risks and responsibilities because that was the system they were trained to follow. However, **dismiss-**

---

[2] Hewitt Associates and *The Asian Wall Street Journal*, 6 September 2001, N4.

ing all state-run employees out of hand is *not* a *China Streetsmart* thing to do. I have personally experienced, on many occasions, positive results working with former state-run employees. Mr Li Jianyi was my Head Sales Manager in Tianjin, and Mr Li Jie was my Chief Logistics Manager. Both came from the former state-run company Foster's had taken over and had no university education, but they had more than 25 years of experience each in the brewing industry. Together, these two, with a salary of no more than 2,500 RMB (300 USD) per month each, back in 1996, were the critical lynchpins in making the sales function smoothly and efficiently.

I often refer to them as good examples of being open-minded and flexible when it comes to developing local models based on local needs. Their sales and logistics methods were crude, but they had a unique understanding of how the primitive, but often adequate, system worked in China. Forget about computerised logistics, order balancing and just-in-time (JIT) warehouse management; using their management method of pen-and-paper order taking, Tianjin Foster's was able to launch a locally developed beer called Largo and achieve more than 90% distribution and more than 20% market share in Tianjin within six months of launch. If your company happens to be taking over a state-owned enterprise (SOE), take the time to really understand the (primitive) local methods, especially in sales and distribution. These veterans in the trenches will likely prove more valuable than most of the savvy English-speaking inexperienced undergrads. In the distribution game, you need these older street-hardened managers.

Another pleasant surprise I had working with former SOE employees came from hiring displaced workers, which were growing in numbers. Back in 1998, I ran an ad for some part-time help in our customer service department during the busy summer months, since we were understaffed in that area, but I didn't want to take on any full-time staff because of the seasonality effects in the beer industry. I had over 100 applicants applying for this part-time job paying a very low wage. The applicants had all come from a closed-down state-run shoe factory and steel mill – nothing really to do with customer service at all. As I began my interviews, I was immediately impressed by how eager they were to get back to work. Rather than simply look at their backgrounds, I devised a set of test scenarios to see how they would react to customer complaints. There were no clear right or wrong answers; rather, I was looking for people who could "think on their feet". Eventually I found some suitable employees. In fact, I was so impressed with one individual's performance I decided to make him a permanent staff. **Given the uncertain climate with a lot of SOEs, there are people in China who are very hungry for work and will work incredibly hard if given the chance.** You may have to be extra detailed (Action Step 5) to get them to do exactly what you want, but I am sure there are plenty of former SOE employees who will be incredibly valuable and productive. Don't be afraid to look among the rubble to find the diamonds.

Residency Permits and Personnel Files

Hiring staff in China is not as simple as looking at one's resume and making a decision. Before even going to the hiring consideration stage, one must consider the applicant's residency and personnel file status. Everyone in China has a residence permit called a *hukou* (pronounced "who-ko" in Mandarin). This permit allows people to receive local medical benefits, schooling, etc. and is meant to prevent people from flocking to and overcrowding certain cities. For example, residents of Wuhan cannot just pack up and settle down in Beijing. The personnel file or *dang'an* (pronounced "deng ahn" in Mandarin) is the employee file that enables a person to work at a particular company and is a requirement by the labour bureau. Workers who work for SOEs, for example, cannot just freely leave the SOE to go work for a foreign investment enterprise. They must first have the permission to leave or the SOE must be willing to release their *dang'an*.

Officially registered companies can only hire people with these two conditions: they are allowed to live and work where their *hukou* permits and their *dang'an* are free and clear of any other employer. MNCs run into these restrictions all the time. Once I tried to hire this manager of a local Shanghai bar to work for me in the sales promotion department since she knew the nightclub business where premium beers are sold, and she was very keen. Only later did I discover she was from Wuhan, where her *hukou* was registered, not from Shanghai, and was "moonlighting" by working "under the table" for the bar. In the end, I could not hire her. The transfer of personnel files was another complication I ran into. Employees that appeared available to work, officially could not, because they had unresolved issues with their former SOE employer and the SOE would not release their files unless a large fee covering their past benefits and dues were paid. Instead, they would continue to moonlight (for years) illegally. In fact, if you go to many of the small local companies operating in Shanghai and Beijing, for example, many of the lower paying jobs are being paid to staff hired without the proper permits and personnel files transferred. They are simply moonlighting or working under the table. Small local companies often get away with this, as it is difficult for the labour bureau to inspect everyone. As a result, the cheap "illegal" labour local companies hire often gives them a competitive advantage over their foreign counterparts.

Salary Ranges

The salary ranges across China vary significantly from one area to the next and also depend on the employees' background (see Figure 20.1). To illustrate, in 1996, my top sales manager (formerly from a state-run company) in Tianjin was getting paid approximately 1,800 RMB per month base salary with another 400–600 RMB bonus. In Shanghai, an equivalent experienced top-level sales manager (previously hired from an MNC) was receiving up to 15,000 RMB per month and in Guangzhou, a top sales manager (also previously from an MNC) was getting paid up to 20,000 RMB per month. Salaries or more correctly, employee compensation and the rules and regulations surrounding benefits, are changing rapidly and at different paces across China. Employees for the large centres – Beijing, Shanghai, Guangzhou and Shenzhen – are typically the highest paid in the country and the regional variations could be significant. If you are setting up a new operation in China with many different job functions, it pays (pardon the pun) to hire a professional human resource (HR) consulting company, such as Watson Wyatt or Hewitt Associates, to help you understand how to set up a competitive compensation structure for each of the specific markets you intend to operate in. Furthermore, these companies can help you understand the "oncosts" or the obligatory benefits (housing, medical, pensions, etc.) a company must pay according to Chinese employment law that could be as much as an additional 25–30% on top of the employees' base

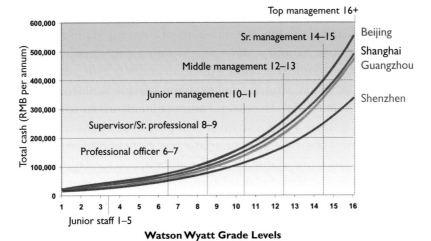

Source: Watson Wyatt Worldwide July 2002

Figure 20.1   Salaries by Cities

Watson Wyatt has highly detailed information on specific job functions by individual markets across China. The graph should act as a rough benchmark only. To understand the details of exactly what each job function means as it pertains to the specific job function(s) you have in mind, you should contact Watson Wyatt directly by checking out their website at www.watsonwyatt.com

pay. There are no provisions to award stock options in China; however, certain companies have successfully worked around the regulations by setting up their own "ghost option" programmes. The rules and regulations surrounding compensation and benefits continue to evolve, so rather than go into specific details here, be prepared that the employee cost structure needs to be examined in detail and the best way is to seek the advice of experienced professionals.

Localisation

Many MNCs today talk about localisation as one of their primary business objectives, but the results from many of the companies I spoke with were mixed. Some companies localised too quickly, often pressured by cost reductions. Promoting someone into a job before he or she was ready often resulted in further disruption to the business and the company having to bring back expats. This problem was common for senior positions in the field of finance and marketing. Sales and HR are often more easily localised and operations were mixed depending on the level of technical support needed.

On the other hand, where localisation happens to be moving very slow is in the top job, the positions of General Manager, Managing Director or Country Manager. As noted earlier, while locals may learn the technical skills of a position quickly, "soft" skills such as leadership, vision, strategy and problem-solving skills need more time for them to master. However, I suspect **localisation would also be sped up if there were a stronger emphasis on mentoring.** The fact is, many of these top foreign managers have confided that they do not want to leave China. With the benefits of tax equalisation, housing, cars and drivers, maids, country club memberships and top schooling all paid for, it is not surprising that many would not want to leave. However, for a company to be truly successful in China, as Mike Blackburn notes, the locals must believe there is no glass ceiling. A key success factor for a General Manager or Managing Director should include the mentoring skills of building up his or her successor. As one HR executive mentioned, "A completion bonus should be included as an added incentive." It would also enforce a time limit and manage the expectations of the expatriate that the passing on of his skills to the local team is a necessary condition for the company's success. Furthermore, a smooth transition of power over a longer period of time prevents negative disruptions to the business.

McDonald's is perhaps one of the best companies demonstrating a solid localisation programme. They actually got off to an early start when most of their Hong Kong and Taiwan operations were localised during the early 90s. By the time McDonald's entered Mainland China, most of the team comprised local to regional (Greater China) executives as McDonald's had a strong policy of promoting from within. Tim Lai summed it up by saying, "It is important for us to let the local executives know the operation will be theirs someday. By knowing this, they are prepared to work much harder to build their own future – which is in line with the company's objectives. Our goal in all of our operations is 100% localisation."

21

Ending the Joint Venture

The Death of the Joint Venture

Preliminary Steps | Setting the Strategy | Negotiating the Deal | Running the Joint Venture | Ending the Joint Venture | Beyond the Joint Venture

Almost overshadowing the successful start of the joint venture (JV) was the deepening rift between Michael Colozzi and his Chinese partners, spearheaded by Mr Deputy. It became increasingly difficult to get things done. "Every day a hundred issues would arise," claims Michael. "Constantly I was at loggerheads with my deputy over even the simplest issues, such as what kind of phone system we would use. He would propose a cheap Chinese phone system, I would want a Western system because it had a 'hold' button; he would want Chinese-made air conditioners, I would want Western-made ones – the fights went on and on. Often what my Chinese partners would do in protest would be to withhold the 'chop' to pay for the purchases – even though I had already approved it. I had to constantly push and prod every step of the way. Three nights a week I had to meet with Mr Lu to get the chop for this or that to explain why we needed to do it this way or that way. Sometimes I won, sometimes I lost. I had to learn to pick my battles carefully. I spent 90% of my time managing my Chinese partners and only 10% managing the business. It was exhausting."

By November 1998, just ten months after the JV was started, Aquarius was amalgamated with the much larger Ma Ling food group and Mr Lu was promoted to run the new larger operation. Also during this time, Mr Lu started to run into health problems. Unable to devote his time to being General Manager of Shanghai Portola and running the larger group at the same time, and beset by health problems, Mr Lu decided to step down from his post in January 1999, and promote Michael to full General Manager – ahead of schedule. During this period, the rift between Michael and Mr Deputy worsened to the point that it was affecting the other key staff. After several serious clashes between Mr Deputy and Shanghai Portola's Human Resources Director and company purchasing manager, a showdown caused Mr Deputy to leave the company. "If he [Mr Deputy] had stayed on, all my people would have left," says Michael. "The Aquarius people didn't even take Mr Deputy back either, which further reinforced my belief that Aquarius was only dumping [second rate] employees on us." Instead, Aquarius appointed Mr New Deputy.

Although Mr New Deputy was not as belligerent as Mr Old Deputy, by this point, Michael already was starting to sense that positive cooperation with his Chinese partners was not going to be possible. "I actually liked Mr New Deputy, but by that point, my patience had run thin and I probably didn't give him the face he deserved." As a result, the clashes continued and the Chinese side was clearly tired of working with Michael too. The insistence on hiring a more expensive foreign contractor did not win any favours from the Chinese side – even though they potentially did a better job. None of their staff they had hoped for and discussed during the negotiations ever made it to the new JV, and some accused Michael of going back on his word. The only Aquarius employees that made it to the JV were ones specifically mentioned in the contract, namely the deputy and the "finance watchdog". Furthermore, Aquarius was not sourcing any product from the JV as they had originally planned for their own bottling plants because the caps Portola was producing were priced too high (with healthy margins) and since the plant was already running at capacity, it didn't need any more business. Michael had refused to lower the price for them because "it didn't make good business sense to the JV. We came here to make a profit and we were doing well. Why would we want to lower our price to anyone when we knew we could get that price on the market?" Technology transfers were a previous hope, but since it was not in the original contract they knew they couldn't just count on the spirit of goodwill and cooperation; rather they would have to begin negotiating all over again to see "what was in the best interest of the JV". By March

1999, just as the products were finally beginning to roll off the production line, the Chinese side decided enough was enough and called Jack Watts directly to demand Michael's removal from the JV.

The month of April was perhaps one of the most difficult times for Michael. As if the enormous stress and pressure from his Chinese partners calling for his resignation weren't enough, Michael's father passed away on 8 April 1999 in the US. Now for those who think an expat's job is overpaid, the enormous stress one carries is certainly commiserate to the pay we receive. While each executive's case is different, China can be an enormous pressure cooker. The JV General Manager receives pressure internally from both the foreign and local sides, and externally from both the competition in the marketplace and capricious and vague government regulations. Often, the General Manager is faced with a no-win situation. When you understand the real pressures and situations faced by many of the General Managers, it's not surprising so many of them never survived.

Michael went back to the US to attend his father's funeral and during the trip, made a stopover to visit Jack. That evening in Menlo Park, Michael had dinner with Jack Watts and Jim Taylor, Portola's Chief Operating Officer. Sympathetic to Michael's predicament, but nervous over the exposure of their China assets, they simply said to Michael, "Your job is your last priority you need to worry about right now; just make sure our assets are protected. I know this is not in your nature, Michael, but when you go back to China, we want you to eat humble pie."

Armed with the renewed confidence that he had the backing of Jack and the rest of Portola behind him, Michael went back to Shanghai and set up a meeting with Mr Lu. His tone with Mr Lu was much different at this point. No longer the feisty Italian American, he wanted to let them know they had won. They had made their point and Portola and himself were now prepared to do anything to save

Photograph by Scott Kippenbrock

Scott Kippenbrock, General Manager of Shanghai Portola.

the business. Michael agreed to step down from his post as GM for China and assumed the new role of General Manager for Asia. For some time, Michael had been contemplating this move and had his eye on a potential successor. He used this reason to hire Scott Kippenbrock, an American engineer with plant management experience in China who could speak fluent Mandarin.

Regardless of the management changes, it was evident that long-term cooperation between the two parties was unlikely. The Chinese side was receiving very little benefits from the JV other than some dividends, given their profit-making position, but was this worth tying up millions of USD? Michael sensed the same feeling and had already made the recommendation to Jack that they "file for divorce" – but how? Either the Chinese side would buy out Portola or vice versa. Eventually Michael managed to get Mr Lu alone in the room with a neutral translator and Mr Lu said, "It looks like you want to buy us out?" Michael flipped the question around and asked, "Do you want to be bought out?" Within five minutes they had concluded the deal and pretty much agreed on the divorce settlement. The settlement was simple: Portola would simply give them their original investment back in cash plus interest. "Done," said Michael and within the week, Fred Janz, Portola's International President, was in China with cheque in hand. Michael speculates that the Ma Ling group at the time was borderline profitable and could have used the cash, so the timing was right. A small hiccup ensued over where the money should be held pending the "divorce papers" being ratified by the Ministry of Foreign Trade and Economic Corporation (MOFTEC). The Chinese side wanted a Chinese bank and Portola wanted an American bank. In the end, they settled for the Bank of America's branch based in China.

While the agreement to divorce and terms of settlement were worked out between the two parties in just five minutes, it took MOFTEC another seven months to approve the divorce/buyout. MOFTEC could not understand why a JV that was making money would want to be dissolved. Careful explanation needed to be made to the concerned government parties that jobs were not going to be lost, for example. Portola was very careful to draft the specific conditions under the terms of releasing of funds. For example, all the transfer of licences, business, export, labour, etc., was to be made

before the funds were to be released. On March 2000, just over a year of being a JV, the Shanghai Portola Packaging Co., Ltd. became a wholly owned foreign enterprise (WOFE) – exactly what Michael wanted from the beginning. Some on Portola's board suspected that Michael had intentionally orchestrated the divorce. When I confronted him with this, his customary Cheshire cat grin grew wider than usual.

22 | Ending the Joint Venture

A *China Streetsmart* Analysis

As I listened to Michael Colozzi's story, I noted how close he came to following the same demise as many other business leaders in China. Had the business not been performing well, Michael probably would not have survived and Portola would likely have been on their third- or fourth-generation General Manager, like so many other businesses I examined, trying to figure out "how to get themselves out of this mess". What saved Michael (and Portola) was a good business plan based on a strategy, which acknowledged their limited understanding of the market. They were conservative in their sales estimates while watching costs carefully. Furthermore, they had not consented to any terms during the negotiations of the joint venture (JV) that could ultimately have hurt the business, such as taking on unnecessary and unqualified staff, transferring technology that could be used against them as a competitor at a later date, and agreeing to a transfer pricing agreement, which would have made them sell products to their Chinese partner below the market price.

Flawed from the Start

The goals of both sides were fundamentally mismatched even before the JV was started. The Chinese idiom "Same Bed Different Dreams" applies in this case. What the Chinese state-owned company really wanted was access to Portola's foreign technology, a place they could train their current staff and possibly move (dump) some

staff to alleviate the excess burden of staff at their existing company, and access to superior packaging materials below market cost. Furthermore, they would have wanted to pay for their investment share with buildings and land they already owned at an inflated valuation. The American side fundamentally wanted market access and a lower cost base plant – which Aquarius really didn't care about. This scenario of mismatched goals was common for many JVs, especially during the 80s and 90s when many companies did not have much of a choice for a JV partner. As a result, most of the JVs that were flawed from the start are often the ones contributing to the negative stories you hear about how difficult it is in doing business in China today.

The interesting point in this case is that this time the Chinese side actually made the mistake of "over-assuming" goodwill, which was a classic mistake made by many foreign companies. What was "talked about" during the negotiations, but never agreed in writing in the contract, the other side assumed (or hoped) goodwill would carry their wishes through eventually. What usually happened was once the contract was signed, that was that, and any further concessions or goodwill would have to be completely renegotiated. In most cases, deceit or trickery was not carried out but rather simple hardnosed business tactics – especially common with state-owned enterprises: "An agreement is an agreement; what is in the contract is what we will do, nothing more and nothing less." Michael said he had learned a lot from negotiating with the Chinese. "I heard many stories about this issue of over-assumptions or 'wishful thinking' by Western companies and it was their mistake. **If a clause is important enough to the business by either side, then they should insist it be in the contract.** In terms of how I negotiated the contract, I was just being Chinese," he says with a slight grin.

Ironically, it was because the JV was doing so well that it hurt Aquarius's chance of getting further concessions as they had hoped. If the JV had not performed well during its launch and had idle capacity due to a misread in market size (as was the case with many other JVs), and thus needed Aquarius's buying power to help take up the slack, this would have given the Aquarius group a much better negotiating stance, and would have enabled them to insist that Portola meet their demands, such as taking in extra staff, transferring technology and selling them products below market cost. However, because the JV did so well during the launch, Shanghai Portola didn't need any of Aquarius's "help" and all their negotiating leverage was lost.

The General Manager's Position – Bullets from all Directions

The Portola/Aquarius JV that began with fundamentally different objectives was precariously flawed – although this didn't seem the case when the contract was signed. The amazing point is that after the contract was signed and both parties really began working together, only to discover that their goals and objectives were indeed different, Michael still survived. The General Manager's job in a JV is one of the hardest jobs to have in China – especially if the goals of both sides are not compatible. What often happens after the JV is signed and the discovery of both sides' true intentions surface is that the General Manager is torn between both sides and invariably gets shot from either direction and in some cases both. The fact that Portola's American management followed Action Step 1 (Maintain Management Consistency) probably saved them the business. Often, if the GM is being shot at from both directions and sees no basis for strong support, he will leave anyway.

The pressure executives face in China is enormous. While the executives complain about the external pressures such as hyper-competitive markets and confusing government legislation, when they really open up to you they will most often say their primary source of stress comes from internal pressures. Office politics is evident in any organisation, but the worse the business performs, the more often people run for cover and begin finger-pointing. Strong leadership is really needed in this case, which Portola was lucky enough to get with Jack Watts. Jack Watts, the Chairman and CEO of Portola, was the original instigator of Portola's China strategy, even though some of the board members were very much against going to China. For example, one of the board members is a key executive with JP Morgan Chase and according to Michael, Chase has over 100 invested projects in China, all of them not making money. However, Jack and Michael had struck an excellent open working relationship right from the beginning, therefore commitment to leadership was easily possible. During the difficult negotiations and running of the operation with their Chinese partner, Michael had the confidence to proceed knowing he had the confidence of Jack and the board backing him, even when the Chinese side was calling for Michael's removal. Listening and trusting your "man on the ground" proved critical.

Face Issues and Cross Cultural Differences

In many ways Michael Colozzi's personality encapsulates the American spirit: highly competitive, aggressive, persistent and direct. Therefore, it wasn't surprising that cultural differences did surface as a mitigating factor to the downfall of the JV, but these issues were really secondary to the fundamental problem that both side's goals and objectives were different from the start. If anything, it was the difference in objectives that acted as the spark that ignited both sides.

Much has been written on the differences between Western and Chinese (or Asian) business cultures. Central among these differences is the treatment of "face" or as we say in Mandarin *mianzi* (pronounced "mee-en-ze" in Mandarin). So what is face? Like *guanxi*, people have varying degrees of understanding and misconceptions. For example, one executive tried to explain face as "giving in to the Chinese to let them think they are better than you". This thinking is wrong and misunderstandings like these only lead to further hostilities and unhappiness on both sides. Face is simply a favourable image in the minds of others derived from tangible evidence such as material possessions, physical age and appearances, and from intangible evidence such as background, status and knowledge. To give someone "face" is simply showing respect (not giving in) according to one's position and can be extremely important when working in Chinese and other Asian cultures that place great emphasis on the importance of relationships and harmony within society. Whether you are dealing with individuals of a different age, social/work status or even between nation states, how one deals with "face issues" or issues that influence the way your counterpart is perceived in a greater light, be it in a family or work setting or the world community, can have a huge impact on whether you achieve your intended results.

Sure, the "Chinese face" is imbued with Confucian values, but the view that one who has not been brought up with these philosophical and cultural teachings cannot practise how to give "face" in China is wrong. *China Streetsmart* is all about being practical and effective. It is not about changing the way you are, rather bringing out what you already have to be effective in China. All of us understand the practice of giving "face". **Face or *mianzi* is different from the Western concept of it in degree but not in kind.** The reverence or respect one places on elders or perhaps colleagues is something we all know. In the West, when we walk through doors, "After you ..." is simply an expression we use to show respect. Face is not a Chinese or Asian domain. However, given the importance Asian cultures place on relationships, it helps to be extra conscious of it. Over the past several decades, Western society and certainly Western corporate culture have tried to eliminate the hierarchical values we were traditionally raised with. When I arrived at Exxon, I went through corporate orientation on my first day and was told it was preferable to call everybody, including our senior executives, by their first name. However, in Europe this corporate culture was quite different, when I worked with Beck Brauerei of Germany, I quickly learned that in Europe, many people still prefered to refer to each other as Mr Chan or Mr Müller, not as John or Michael.

Where the issue of face becomes critical is when problems or differences arise. Americans, Michael Colozzi included, tend to be very direct at tackling a problem, whereas the Chinese often prefer a more indirect route. The American would say, "What's the problem? What's the source of the problem? And how do we fix the problem?" The Chinese would say, "Here are the facts, should my superior wish me to help improve on the facts; I am sure an amicable way can be found." The desire by both sides is the same: "There is room for improvement so let's fix it". However, the approach may be completely different, which is where the source of cultural clashes often stems from. The Western side would consider the Chinese side to be evasive, while the Chinese side would consider the Western side to be rude. The *China Streetsmart* approach to problem solving with your Chinese counterpart is not to decide which method is better or correct, which suggests a superior/inferior relationship, rather which is more appropriate for the given situation. The fact is, the

Western company is invariably working in China, so to not take into account the importance Chinese culture places on "face" is usually not a good idea. The company may be of Western origins, the top management may all be Westerners, but when dealing with the local staff in China, which usually outnumbers the expats, the failure or unwillingness to take into account the issue of face shows a lack of respect for where they are. The willingness to understand and accept other cultures and conditions first, before trying to be understood and impose your own values, will make you a more effective business leader.

To be effective at handling issues of face, I refer to a great teacher – not Confucius, rather Dale Carnegie. In 1936, Dale Carnegie, an American, wrote a book called *How to Win Friends and Influence People* which remains one of the best management and human relations books of all time. Throughout the book, he is constantly dealing with the sensitivities of face and how it impacts people's thinking. Simple basics such as not criticising people directly if you want them to listen to you is not a Chinese habit but one of human nature. Avoiding using the word *you* when describing a problem suggests that using a more passive (indirect) tense may help deflect the embarrassment and make people more willing to help you achieve your objectives. **The point is on being effective, by focusing on the goals you are trying to achieve – not the way you achieve them.**

Another celebrated author, Chin-Ning Chu, wrote books on cross-cultural interaction such as *The Asian Mind Game.* Her best-selling book *Thick Face Black Heart* basically states that successful people (of any culture or background) are ones who are impervious to how others view them (Thick Face) and focuses on getting what needs to be done at whatever the cost (Black Heart). Practising Action Step 6 (Maintain a Healthy Attitude) is critical to being effective when dealing with cross-cultural issues. There may be times when you are absolutely convinced you are right and your way is the better way and instead are "forced" to take a more circuitous route to get the problem resolved. Those who can do this and do this happily, with a thick face, are the ones who not only survive but also succeed in China.

Here are some pointers from Dale Carnegie's *How to Win Friends and Influence People:*[1]

- Make the other person feel important – and do it sincerely.
- The only way to get the best of an argument is to avoid it.
- Show respect for the other person's opinions. Never say, "You're wrong."
- Be sympathetic with the other person's ideas and desires.
- Call attention to people's mistakes indirectly.
- Let the other person save face.

While the book *How to Win Friends and Influence People* may not be directly appropriate in all cases in China, as the book was written for a different culture, clearly Dale Carnegie understood human nature, and I am sure that if Dale Carnegie had ever been asked to be a General Manager of a Sino-Foreign JV, he would have been able to work with his Chinese counterparts quite effectively – regardless of any prior knowledge of Chinese culture or Confucian thinking.

Using Face Effectively – Do What Your Great Grandparents Did

The conservative respectful gestures practised by your great grand-parents, such as addressing people by their title and modifying your tone in relation to whom you are talking to and what position they hold relative to your own, is good practice in China. As youngsters, we can all remember our parents telling us, "Don't talk to me that way, young man ..." Practise simple gestures like letting those superior in age or social stature walk through the door first, or showing a guest out of your home or office by accompanying him to the door or elevator or even to the entrance of the building. These simple gestures will help make a positive impression with your Chinese counterpart and start you on the road of building respect and trust. Don't expect these gestures alone to necessarily get you a better

---

[1] Back in 1987–1988 I took the Dale Carnegie training course, which I found to be excellent. For more info on Dale Carnegie's *How to Win Friends and Influence People*, simply type the title in your web search and dozens of links will appear. Here is the link I used: http://www.westegg.com/unmaintained/carnegie/win-friends.html#one

deal, rather, these are simply a sign of respect to help get things on the right track. When problems arise, not openly criticising or confronting local staff, certainly not in front of others, and giving them the face they desire will allow you to resolve the problem and potentially future ones to come. On the other hand, **if you really insult or embarrass someone in China, and "cross the proverbial line" by making them lose face, winning back their respect and confidence can prove almost impossible.** As many foreigners have experienced, revenge is imbued in Chinese culture and when they are given the chance for retribution, watch out; the revenge may be subtle and indirect, but in the end, they will make you pay.

As I spoke to Michael, I sensed that he was probably a bit mellower and more relaxed than when he first arrived several years ago. "I've learned a lot from being in China," he says. "I've changed and I think I've changed for the better." Although I suspect he still gets frustrated at times with the way things are done in China, he appears less outspoken. Action Step 6 (Maintain a Healthy Attitude) was clearly what saved Michael. He's now able to let things run their course in China, demonstrating his thick face so long as he achieves his objectives, and his black heart (not to be taken literally)!

Photograph by John L. Chan

Being able to maintain one's composure in the face of tremendous pressure will not only enable the executive to function better, but also have a positive influence on his staff. As cited in *The Asian Wall Street Journal* report on employee satisfaction conducted by Hewitt Associates, strong leadership ranked no. 1 in the needs of local employees. In this photo, Michael enjoys a lighter moment with his staff.

Choose Your Battles Carefully

One of the keys to surviving in China is learning to choose your battles carefully (something Michael learned the hard way). Following Action Step 6 (Maintain a Healthy Attitude), you need to realise that you are in someone else's "house"; you alone are not going to change the house rules so you had better learn how to adapt to them. However, if you follow the principle of focusing on bottom-line objectives, you will often come up with many situations where your bottom-line objectives conflict with the "house rules". For example, local Mainlanders may try and tell you the way this (convoluted) method is the way things are done in China. This is when your *China Streetsmart* instincts need to come into play; you've got to choose which (convoluted) methods you will accept and which ones you will object (fight against) based on which ones will have the greatest negative affect on your bottom line. For example, I would strongly oppose extending credit terms too liberally even if the local sales staff was telling me this was the way business operated in China. But remember to keep in mind the cultural face issues just described. The way things are done in China is often so different that if you tried to change "everything" you would simply go crazy, burn out, or at a minimum upset so many people; you will just make things harder for yourself in the end. Think about Sun Tze and the Art of War. Learn to single out the really important issues and fight those battles; for the others, you'll learn to let them pass and what you'll learn by developing a "thick face", as Michael has done, is you will be far more effective than you ever imagined.

The Divorce Settlement

Even during the divorce settlement with the Aquarius/Ma Ling group, one of the major factors I suspect for such a smooth and amicable break-up was the mutual respect that developed between Michael and Mr Lu. "I have always had and continue to have great respect for Mr Lu. Whenever we attended banquets together he always made sure I sat on his right side and even when his side was calling for me to be 'fired' I didn't get angry or upset with him. When my mother came to visit me in China, [during the grand opening of the plant, while the Chinese side was calling for Michael's removal]

Mr Lu went out of his way to make sure my mother knew what a great guy I was and what I did for the business. He definitely gave me face. You could see a marked difference between his behaviour when just he and I were in the room or when other staff was present. When we hammered out our amicable departure in just five minutes it was just he and I with a neutral translator in the room. The respect we had developed for each other was built up over the year of working closely together. I watched him closely, as I am sure he did me, but in the end, it was our mutual trust and understanding which enabled our deal first to go forward, then end peacefully."

Frankly speaking though, Portola got lucky when they went through their divorce settlement. I conferred with Michael and John Huang about the settlement, and in many cases with other companies, the Chinese side almost invariably inflates the settlement value. Especially if the business has been operating for several years, settlement buyouts can be several times the value that was originally invested. The fact that Aquarius didn't try this tactic and attempt to have the issue drag on while the JV suffered was fortunate. Furthermore, although I did not hear Mr Lu's side, I suspect Mr Lu's appointment to the much larger Ma Ling group also played an important factor. The politics of moving into such a large role must have been enormous and I am sure he didn't want a messy divorce soiling his reputation and distracting him from the larger issues at hand. Like every golfer's secret wish, Portola got a little lucky.

23 | Beyond the Joint Venture

Shanghai Portola, A *China Streetsmart* Company

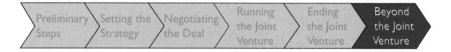

Preliminary Steps · Setting the Strategy · Negotiating the Deal · Running the Joint Venture · Ending the Joint Venture · **Beyond the Joint Venture**

The Shanghai Portola Packaging Co., Ltd. now operates independently as a wholly owned foreign enterprise. I got a chance to visit the plant out in Xinzhuang, the suburbs of Shanghai, and meet with Michael's staff. He took me on a tour of the factory floor and I can claim firsthand the operation is run as well as any operation I have seen in China. As we walked around, wearing hygiene caps, he would constantly point out how certain walls were ready to be knocked down to accommodate his expansion plans using the vacant property beside the present one. It was clear he already knew what the site would look like ten years from when he first chose this particular site. As I looked at his products in his office, which are essentially just plastic bottle caps, I made the mistake of commenting how ordinary and simple they looked. Michael's eyes widened and he exclaimed, "Are you kidding me?" The Egyptian rug trader then went into action and started to explain the technological benefits and superiority of his caps over others. Any guy that can get that excited about a plastic cap is definitely a true company man.

Perhaps most telling of Michael's personality was the way he spoke of his staff. His core executive staff was completely handpicked and Michael went on to describe their backgrounds and contributions that made Shanghai Portola a success in China. "We are like a family here," Michael boasts. Like a proud father introducing his children, he would call each of them into his office and introduce

What is true of all the *China Streetsmart* executives I interviewed for the book is that they all spoke very highly of their staff as *the* key success factor. I got to witness firsthand many of these executives truly enjoying the interaction, saying they often learned more than they taught. In this picture, Tim Lai, Managing Director of McDonald's responsible for North China, catches up with the management of a local McDonald's in Shanghai.

them to me. I couldn't help but notice the similarities Michael had with Tim Lai of McDonald's, another long-term company employee who clearly loved his job and was proud of his staff and company's achievements – much to his credit. "At McDonald's," Tim says, "we have no movie stars, just team players."

Michael has already passed the torch of local operations management to Scott Kippenbrock, as he focuses more on the Asian region rather than just China. However, should a problem arise he is readily available, and he has been very careful to ensure that the spirit and continuity of the operations remain intact. Scott and Michael had a transition of power that took just over a year and this gave them long enough time to iron out any of the transitory issues such as dealing with suppliers, local government officials, etc.

Head office staff from the US visit the plant regularly, but how the head office staff work with the local operations is a sensitive issue for Michael. He has worked hard to ensure that non-interference is the goal. "I am very careful when head office sends people over from the States to help out," he says. "I tell them when they arrive for the first time that if I ever hear them say, 'In the States we do it like this …' I tell them I will be sending them on the next plane home. People need to get used to working in China. We are the guests here so we'd better respect their house."

Initially, Portola's China investment was meant to simply be a "flag" on a map. The joint venture (JV) was not expected to earn a lot of income for the company and they had no plans of trying to repatriate their profits, choosing to simply re-invest the profit over the years and watch the operation grow. However, the success of the venture and the new export markets they have been able to open up all across the Asia–Pacific region, such as in Australia and New Zealand, has caused them to rethink their original strategy. Originally, the JV plan approved by Ministry of Foreign Trade and Economic Corporation required 30% of their production line to be exported, but their exports have now been running as high as 80–90%. Since the China operation is making more money than needed to fund an expansion, Portola has now set up a holding company in Hong Kong, called Portola Asia Holding Co., Ltd. to enable them to repatriate their profits more easily.

A further advantage that was unforeseen in the early stages of setting up their investment was using China to source goods for other parts of their global operation. "China has improved dramatically in terms of quality," claims Michael. "We have been able to help our North American operations achieve better profitability by having China produce parts which were traditionally made in the States. By sourcing in China we were able to lower certain supply costs by more than 50%."

More and more companies are beginning to use China as their export manufacturing hub not only for the Asia-Pacific region, but globally as well, which has contributed to the impressive growth in China's exports over the past 20 years (see Figure 23.1).

Michael was so impressed with the local quality, not only in terms of goods, but also with his staff's sophistication, that he has already started a new Advanced Moulding Division (for high-end packaging, such as cosmetic cases) to complement his China operations, the first of its kind within his company. The cheaper labour and the local market needs offer Portola a chance to experiment with a new division. The machines have just been installed and the new orders

China Streetsmart

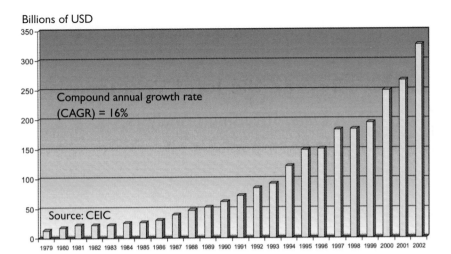

Billions of USD

Compound annual growth rate
(CAGR) = 16%

Source: CEIC

1979 1980 1981 1982 1983 1984 1985 1986 1987 1988 1989 1990 1991 1992 1993 1994 1995 1996 1997 1998 1999 2000 2001 2002

Figure 23.1   China's Export Growth, 1979–2002

from international manufacturers are beginning to roll in. Should the project prove successful in China, the plan is to further expand the Advanced Moulding Division to North America.

"I love China," Michael says enthusiastically. "I am constantly fascinated with what's here in China and how it's developing. The people here are great and you can learn a lot from them if you really listen and pay attention to what they are saying. It takes time for them to trust you, but that's an effort you need to make and practise consistently. You can't ask them to be open and then get angry when they tell you things you don't want to hear. Once you win their trust you'd be surprised with what you really hear and the ideas they can come up with. I am extremely proud of the team we have built and I think our results show. Where we are moving our company now is to really think out of the box – which is what I encourage my managers in China to do. The Advanced Moulding Division is only a start and as China changes we will also continue to evolve but only in a way that makes [profitable] sense."

24 | Beyond the Joint Venture

A *China Streetsmart* Analysis

| Preliminary Steps | Setting the Strategy | Negotiating the Deal | Running the Joint Venture | Ending the Joint Venture | **Beyond the Joint Venture** |

S hanghai Portola is a successful company in every sense of the word. **Their success formula can be broken down to three well-managed executions. First, they did all the right things in the beginning; second, they clearly focused and stuck to their bottom line; and third, the people managing and running the operation were right top down, right from the start.** Now take these three strategies and focus on many of the companies that are complaining about how difficult it is to do business or make money in China and you will invariably see where Portola succeeded and these companies failed. There is no question that a fast-developing complex market like China has significant challenges. Portola certainly faced their own share, such as going through a divorce, but by developing a *China Streetsmart* approach to your investment, as Portola did, you can make money in China and discover further benefits beyond your initial expectations.

Do the Right Things at the Beginning

As noted in Action Step 3 (Be Patient and Thorough), Portola did not commit the single biggest mistake by most foreign companies who are complaining about how difficult it is to make money in China today – they did not rush in till they were ready and had a good understanding of the market. Waiting for the right moment to strike took a lot of patience on behalf of Portola's executives. Knowing the entire packaged water market in China was growing at an astounding rate of 10% month over month, and the price points offering high margins for those companies already operating in the early 90s were great reasons to get excited. Not seeing any foreign competition around gave them the opportunity to gain first mover advantage and was further temptation to push things through quickly. But Portola didn't rush into China. In fact, from the time of signing a letter of intent (LOI) with Aquarius, it took them another year before the deal was finally completed and more than another year after that before they began earning revenues.

During this entire time, Michael Colozzi was watching the market dynamics closely. As he travelled around China, he saw that more and more competitors, domestic and foreign, were entering the market – a natural effect in any profitable segment. He knew the attractive price points could not last and prices would drop. As he explained his analysis to me, he would begin to cross his forearms in front of me. "On one hand we saw the market growth growing like crazy (forearm pointing up); on the other hand we saw the margin being eroded out of the business (forearm pointing down). We knew the honeymoon was not sustainable and that China's packaged water market was going to be in for a tough ride. Hindsight is always 20/20 but upon close analysis, it doesn't take a PhD in Economics to understand that healthy margins will increase the level of competition in any industry, which in turn will eventually erode margins till an equilibrium is reached. Developing markets offer so many unknowns to the market, and **Portola did the right thing by being optimistic towards China, but conservative in their approach**. They did not over-invest; rather, they structured the business to earn smaller revenues and profits in the beginning and as their actual understanding of the market grew (which only comes after you really begin operating in China), they could expand. McDonald's followed a similar strategy. The first McDonald's on the mainland opened in 1990 in Shenzhen and it took another two years before the second McDonald's opened in Mainland China in Beijing. Today, McDonald's is growing by more than 100 sites per year.

Focus and Stick to Your Bottom Line

Regardless of all the excitement happening in China at the time, Portola did not fall into the trap of being overmesmerised by the China market. As good businessmen, they knew what they wanted to achieve and they knew their bottom line. China may be different in terms of its development dynamics and capricious business regulations, but that should not change your bottom-line stance of what you want to achieve in China. Furthermore, many companies misunderstood the cultural aspects of China, overtrusting the Chinese side to carry out aspects of goodwill and not insisting that certain clauses be included in the contract. The fact is, in any business, **if any clause that directly affects your bottom line is important enough to the business, then it should be negotiated in the contract.**

Companies that misunderstood stories about the importance of relationships (*guanxi*) and trust misunderstood how relationships and trust are built up, compromising their fundamental business instincts on getting a fair deal in China. Many of the failing joint ventures (JVs) in China today were flawed from the beginning, as was Portola's. Both sides often had very different objectives and "the smart side" made sure they structured their needs into the contract and tried to leave out clauses that could compromise their bottom-line objectives. This tactic may not be win-win, but if you do not care whether the JV survives, you had better at least be sure your side does. This is exactly what Portola did. Their bottom line included the investing of capital by both sides in cash in a joint bank account and the right to approve the site where the operation was to be set up. They did not transfer technology until there was good reason to, they did not accept unnecessary people into the JV, and they did not agree to any transfer pricing which could have hurt the business.

Action Step 3 (Be Patient and Thorough) and Action Step 4 (Think Win-Win) would have prevented many of the headaches experienced by companies today. They misunderstood what trust means in China. Think about how the Chinese housewife develops trust with the local vegetable farmer (see Chapter 9). Prodding and testing each other's side is how they get to know each other and how respect and eventually trust are built in China. Blind trust takes years, if not decades, to develop, which is why the Chinese place such high regard for "true *guanxi*". Furthermore, when negotiating with the Chinese side, there are so many people and organisations involved, it is difficult to know who really is in charge, so trusting your direct counterpart, as was the case with Mr Lu, may have only limited ben-

China Streetsmart

efits, which once again leads back to knowing your bottom line and not overcompromising your position. Accepting unequal demands in order to "get your foot in the door" violates Action Step 4, and rarely works.

The Right Team in Place Right from the Beginning

As with any business, whether it succeeds or not is determined by its people. Portola had the right team in place from the top down. It all began with Jack Watts, Portola's CEO and Chairman. Jack was and still is very excited about China. His first taste of Asia came from working in Japan, but he had heard enough to know China was different and was willing to take the time to understand how. Fred Janz, Portola's International President, was also a supporter of the China operation, but initially had to be convinced. Like many executives, Fred had to be convinced of the different circumstances China was developing under and initially challenged Michael to explain why things, such as why Portola's traditional management structure, had to be different for China. But Fred was a good listener and by being flexible and adaptable (Action Step 2), he was convinced over time that Michael understood China and trusted him to do things "his way". Finally, the transition and handover of local authority to Scott Kippenbrock had enough time in place to iron out any problems or issues that arose.

Protective of "his people", Michael continually fights hard to isolate his handpicked local team from the politics that rage on around them. He made sure Mr Deputy and other people at Aquarius were kept at arm's length and he made sure it was the same with the American head office. In fact, Fred Janz's role of ensuring head office did not "overmeddle" was instrumental. Michael says, "Before I took the job, I made a list of the American people I did not want coming over interfering with the operation and gave it to Jack and Fred. These guys did not understand China, nor did they have the cultural sensitivities to appreciate how things work here. If they were sent over, I know they would start making recommendations and try to implement things that simply do not work for China. Let me do my job, let me deliver the results, and if I need help, I'll ask." As a result of Michael's efforts, his staff has remained fiercely loyal. Since 1998, Shanghai Portola has lost only four staff.

Michael takes great care in nurturing his people. He understands their insatiable need to continually train and upgrade their skills. "This aspect completely blows me away," he says. "I am so impressed with my local staff and their willingness to improve themselves. I never got this attitude back in the States to the degree I have seen with the people here. They all want to succeed and they are willing to work as hard as it takes to get it." Recognising their efforts, Portola reserves a special fund of several hundred thousand RMB to hand out on a special bonus basis as needed. "I would ask my plant manager to achieve 30% more efficiency and cost savings beyond what anybody else would think possible and if he meets it, I have reserved a special bonus for him. The same could be said about my sales and marketing guy. Yes, our sales targets are a stretch, but if he can reach just this much more, or if I need to clear out excess goods for a particular month, I'll set a special target for him to achieve. You would be amazed with what these guys can do when you set a specific target like this in front of them. It's good for them and great for the business."

Managing Head Office

Managing head office is often a huge headache and constant battle for many of the executives I spoke to. I admire how Michael handled both sides and prevented them from interfering with the operations, but Michael had the luxury of a business that was making money. When things are not going well, everybody wants to come over and give their opinion – whether they really understand the situation or not. This is classic corporate politics. Many of the executives do not realise or want to acknowledge that many of the investments were flawed in their original assumptions and strategies (perhaps directly attributable to their decisions) and the local teams are only trying to "work their way through the mess". When this happens, the first step is to acknowledge that there have been mistakes and the only way to resolve them is to trust the local people on the ground to come up with the best solution – backed up by support from the head office if called upon. The short-term solutions may be hard for head office to swallow, but the alternative is to force the local operation to achieve unrealistic goals, which only creates more turmoil and anxiety. Furthermore, if the local team agrees to the goals, then they must deliver. As one executive confided with me, "The consistent failure to meet your goals completely undermines your position and credibility with head office. If I agreed to them, even reluctantly, it doesn't matter – they are now my goals. As a result, do not commit unless you are sure it will work in China." Once again, the conservative approach is best and the key success indicator is the local executive's ability to manage expectations.

Local visits by head office executives are often good at building a greater understanding throughout the organisation, but short-notice visits often create huge disruptions to the local business. People stop worrying about selling and building the market and instead spend most of their time preparing presentations, not knowing what the head office executives will ask. **The *China Streetsmart* thing to do is to set periodic dates for when head office staff comes over and have a clear agenda on what is to be achieved.** Sudden spot visits can create anxiety – especially if the business is not performing well. I recall in one of my previous jobs that a memo was mistakenly attached to an e-mail message of a short-notice visit by a senior executive. The memo read simply, "9 a.m. [international executive] to talk with [local GM], 10 a.m. [international executive] to address the whole company." No one knew the purpose of the visit or what was going to be discussed; instead, everyone speculated that the GM was going to be fired and for the whole week the whole company was overstressed with anxiety (especially the GM!) – instead, the visit turned out to be a simple stopover.

Additional Benefits from China – A Regional Base

I am not surprised at all that Shanghai Portola has now begun to source parts at better prices for other parts of their global operations. "I kind of see China going a similar route to Japan," says Michael, "I spent many years in Japan and can see a very similar development pattern. Much of the goods coming from Japan were crap in the 70s, but look at where they are today. I see China moving along the same path; only I'll bet they'll achieve it faster. Japan doesn't have a strong resource base of raw materials, which China does; combine this enormous resource base with the type of staff I have working for me and you've got the makings of a real powerhouse." Singaporean Prime Minister Goh Chok Tong also agrees with

Michael's view. In his National Day speech in 2001 he referred to China's economy as "potentially ten times the size of Japan's. Just ask yourself: how does Singapore compete against ten post-war Japans, all industrialising and exporting to the world at the same time?"[1]

Michael comments, "We have only begun to tap into what China is really capable of. The Advanced Moulding Division was not in our original plans because we didn't have a working model in any of our other global operations. But because we are constantly looking at the market, we can see the opportunities here. The capital investment to set up in China is relatively low so we can experiment quietly here to see if it will work for us, whereas if we did it in the States we would have to do it on a much larger scale to make the economics work and if we failed everybody would know."

Cheap labour in China is often what attracts many companies coming to China. Now that China has entered the World Trade Organisation and business transparency continues to improve, China is looking more and more attractive to be the Asia-Pacific manufacturing hub. Portola is a great example of capitalising on this trend. Prior to investing in China, they had an Asia-Pacific sales representative who would tour around the country, but Portola didn't start making serious inroads until they set up direct operations in China. With ready-made export facilities that could produce and ship within a few days' notice, their Asia-Pacific sales representatives, using China as a base, can offer their clients full service while ensuring delivery on a timely basis. Other Southeast Asian economies have already expressed huge concern that an emerging China will continue to erode their business and value. In parts of Southeast Asia, some of the executives I interviewed said that counterfeiting, corruption and difficulties working with local officials are even worse than in China. Added to these issues are the risks of currency, terrorism and political destabilisation. Hence I am not surprised that many companies are moving their manufacturing operations out of Southeast Asia and into China.

---

[1] Singapore Prime Minister Goh Chok Tong's National Day Address at the National University of Singapore, 19 August 2001. See link for the full speech: http://www.gov.sg/singov/announce/NDR.htm

China Streetsmart

Shanghai Portola's Future

The biggest question facing Shanghai Portola's future is now that they have their feet wet and have a much better understanding of the market, how fast do they want to expand? Business is so good that Shanghai Portola runs 24 hours a day and seven days a week. For the whole year they have closed plant operations for only three days. Michael admits he may have underestimated his company's success in China, noting that the expansion plans to take over the factory next door may not be enough. "It's up to the board really," he explains. "If we want to be more aggressive not just by what we see in the local market in China, but what we see opening up all across the (Asia-Pacific) region we will likely have to move to a new greenfield operation out in Pudong (Eastern District of Shanghai). Jim Taylor (Portola's Chief Operating Officer and Group President) just visited our operation in China and he was so impressed with what he saw that the literally hugged me at the Shanghai airport when he left. I know the board will make the right decision and when they do we'll be ready."

PART III

The Outlook

Here you will learn the broader political and economic issues that could affect your investments in China in the long term, specifically:

- How to develop the right perspective of looking at China to give you a better understanding of the government and the facts and figures being reported.

- What the challenges and risks facing China are.

- What the emerging positive trends are and how Streetsmart investors can view risks as opportunities.

- What the Streetsmart investor can do to help ensure that his long-term investments are protected.

25 | Making the Right Long-Term Strategic Decision

Understanding the Macro Issues

The remaining chapters aim to give the Streetsmart investor enough practical knowledge and facts to make better strategic decisions regarding their long-term China investment strategy.

The preceding part on how Streetsmart companies can be profitable in China is focused on the short term, but to continue that success long term requires a deeper understanding of a broader range of economic and political issues. Portola has gotten off to an excellent start, and Michael Colozzi has given his board various strategic options for them to consider. The decision to expand, and if so, how, is the biggest question facing not only Portola's board, but also thousands of other companies operating in China. **Many companies who may not have seriously invested in China yet are now asking themselves, "Now that China has joined the World Trade Organisation (WTO), is now the time to take a bigger role?"**

The implication of WTO, while significant, is just one of the major opportunities and/or challenges the *China Streetsmart* investor needs to consider in balancing his or her long-term risk/reward returns on investment. To set the right expectations, it helps to balance the issues raised by both China's critics and advocates. China's political economy is complex and there are often no single right answers to any given issue, only varying ways of interpreting the facts. The challenges and risks the *China Streetsmart* investor needs to be aware of, such as those major issues outlined in Table 25.1, are too numerous to go in-depth for each topic, since this would be beyond the scope of this book. But a general introduction of the issues will hopefully help the investor to fully understand any specific issue that may affect their investments. This due diligence process is part of

Table 25.1   Major Challenges and Risks Facing China

• WTO – implementation and compliance	• Sino-US relations – friend or foe
• Reform of SOEs – growing labour surplus	• Regional security – North, South and Southeast Asia
• Developing central and western China – infrastructure development	• Human rights – definition and treatment of dissidents
• Counterfeiting and IP compliance – violations and crackdowns	• Taiwan – closer cooperation and reunification vs. independence
• Environment – controlling pollution vs speeding up development	• Tibet and Xinjiang – separatist movements
• Technology adoption – leapfrogging into the 21st century	• Political reform and leadership transition – the Chinese Communist Party's firm grip on power
• Floating the RMB – opening up the currency	• Healthcare reform and the state Medicare system
• Tax reform – collecting sufficient revenues to sustain growth	• Pensions and social security – having an appropriate social safety net
• Banking – debt crises of state-owned banks	• Press censorship – controlling the news and media
• Fighting corruption – in government and the economy	• Religious freedom – tolerance and crackdowns
• Population – One-child policy and the changing demographics and culture	• Legal reform – changing the constitution to be based on more universal principles

Action Step 3 (Be Patient and Thorough). **Do not invest until you have a comfortable grasp of the major issues that may affect your China investments.**

Chapter 26 lays the foundation for understanding China by giving the investor the appropriate perspective. This perspective will also explain some of the motivations of the government, regardless of whether one agrees with its actions. Understanding China's recent history within the past 200 years will help put things in better perspective, but a practical approach suggests we do not need to be political historians to be good investors, which is why I put a selective historical analysis in Appendix B as suggested reading only. Investors go to China to make money, not to become Sinologists. However, a historical understanding will increase one's depth of understanding of China's current issues and how the government may react to impending changes, and will enable the investor to decide whether he or she agrees with China's critics or advocates as to how China will eventually transform.

Chapter 27 looks at the reliability of the data gathered and published on China. Having the proper perspective will also help in understanding how to interpret China's facts and figures by taking into account the difficulties in data gathering and possible biases. This understanding is important before examining the arguments put forth by both the critics and advocates for investing in China. For example, the difficulties in data gathering as a result of moving from an old Soviet-style reporting system and potential political biases all need to be taken into account. Furthermore, basic things such as how unemployment and population figures are reported need to be better understood in the context of urban and rural data to determine the real implications.

Chapters 28 and 29 then examine arguments put forth by the critics and advocates of China. The usefulness of acknowledging these critics or harbingers of doom is so that the investor does not look at China with blind optimism – a mistake made by many during the 90s. Ironically, however, today is arguably the best time ever to invest in China. More information is available to make informed decisions; China's political stability continues to improve as with the commercial laws and business transparency; the local talent base also continues to advance. While it is useful to understand the arguments put forth by China's critics, to create a balanced view, one must also acknowledge the many encouraging trends, which most critics fail to mention since it does not support their argument. **China Streetsmart is not about winning arguments, rather presenting the facts and allowing the investor to make informed choices.** For example, business transparency is improving but corruption still remains a serious problem. Whether one chooses to focus on the good or the bad is often dependent on one's biased interpretation based on one's perspective. The contributors to *China Streetsmart* offer a subjective interpretation of the facts, but ultimately the investor will be the one to make the final judgement as to which views are most relevant to their specific case.

It is also important to understand the fact that with all the simultaneous trends – both good and bad – lie untold opportunities for those investors who can "think out of the box". Within each crisis lie opportunities, such as what to do with excess goods as a result of massive overproduction. Opportunities can also stem from the huge shifts in labour expected to result from the effects of China's entry into the WTO. Retraining workers and supplying new goods and services to satisfy the insatiable appetite of the new generation of Chinese brought up in single-child families also need to be explored.

The final chapter, Chapter 30, explores the role foreign direct investment (FDI) will play in shaping China's future. FDI has had and will continue to have a great affect on the Chinese economy. It will spearhead Western influence, and the continued growth of FDI reacting with this new generation of Chinese that is eager to learn about the rest of the world, yet remains highly nationalistic, will further open up China. This new S-generation, or children of the single-child policy, are materially spoilt, have grown up in times of economic prosperity and have rising expectations both for themselves and the country. This new generation wants all the riches and material comforts of the West, within a proud revitalised China on the world stage.

Fortunately, there is no conflict or zero-sum gain between what this new rising China and the rest of the world want – a vibrant world economy beneficial to all. The World Bank estimates that China's economy will continue to grow to become the second largest economy in the world in less than two decades. China's emergence as a new economic superpower will hopefully benefit the world's economy by acting as a positive spark to keep the world's economic engine from faltering. As a result, the *China Streetsmart* view of China's future is best described as cautiously optimistic.

26 | Developing the Right Perspective of China

Keeping an Open Mind

"Seek first to understand, then to be understood." (Habit 5)

Stephen Covey: *7 Habits of Highly Successful People*

To properly understand China's outlook, one must have the proper perspective in which to judge the information being presented. Throughout the book, I am constantly comparing China to Europe; however, **to fully understand China from a Western perspective, one must view China really as a cross between Europe and the US.** Interestingly, all three areas are roughly the same size. In terms of cultural and language complexities, China is very much like Europe; therefore, determining how you should invest in China is like asking how you should invest in Europe. Rarely do companies try and tackle all of Europe at once; rather investors would go to Germany first, for example, and then expand to France, then Belgium, Spain, etc.

But where China and Europe diverge is in terms of a strong sense of nationality. In this respect China and the US are far more comparable. It doesn't matter if you are in New York, Houston or Los Angeles, but wherever you are in America, you have a strong sense of what America is and what it stands for. Likewise if you are in Beijing, Chongqing or Shanghai, you also have a similar feeling of a strong national identity of China and what it means to be Chinese. When I presented this view to one of my American friends, he said with a smile, "I think I have just been insulted." "I smiled back and replied, "Yes, and if I said this to a Chinese Mainlander, they would probably be equally, if not more, insulted. How dare I compare a country with 5,000 years of history with one barely 200 years old?"

China is more similar to the US than most people realise. Putting aside for a moment the debate or views on human rights, democracy and personal freedoms, let us examine the similarities. Both the US and China were born out of a bloody revolution, where epic military battles were fought and won, and both claim their right to victory because their cause was just and now benefits the people they represent. Furthermore, both use the proof of continual betterment and prosperity of their citizens as justification that their social, political and economic system is the right one for their people.

Sino-American Perspectives

I remember late one night in Shanghai watching an old black and white war movie. The hero in the end gets shot in the chest, but just before he dies, he struggles to pull out a grenade and staggers into the bunker of the enemy and kills all the bad guys. I've seen this movie plot many times as a kid growing up in Canada, only this time what I thought interesting was this was a war movie about the Korean War and the good guys were the Chinese soldiers bravely defending their Korean compatriots and the bad guys were the "invading" Americans. Both cultures have successfully built up over time and enhanced through the use of the media a strong sense of nationalism and what it means to be American or Chinese depending on what side of the globe you were born. Both sides have traditionally had very geocentric views of the world with themselves being at the centre. In fact, for those who don't know what China really means, it literally translates as the Middle Kingdom.

The debate on human rights and personal freedoms very much depends on one's perspective of what is more important – the rights of the individual, or the rights of the group. In countries like the US, individual rights and freedom of expression are paramount, while in countries like China, the rights of the group or society are supreme. This debate goes back to the time of Aristotle and as I like to jokingly point out, the Chinese are simply being good Vulcans (from *Star Trek*), where "the needs of the many outweigh the needs of the few ... or the one". This concept is also supported by former Singaporean Prime Minister turned Elder Statesman and author, Lee Kuan Yew, who writes about the fundamental differences between Western concepts of society and government and East Asian concepts.

Keeping an open mind and not imposing one's original views (developed in another country under different circumstances) as

Prior to 1990, all foreigners in Beijing had no choice but to live in cramped apartment buildings designated for foreigners like those on the left, paying up to 10,000–20,000 USD per month for a family-sized apartment. Today, foreigners (and locals) have the choice to live in Western-style housing just like that of my friend Graham Niven, Managing Director for Crichton & Co., an aircraft leasing company. His house pictured on the right is in the Dragon Villas residential compound located in Beijing's Shunyi county. Rental of houses in the Dragon Villas starts at 2,000 USD.

the only way of looking at an issue is part of the *China Streetsmart* approach of being effective by developing a deeper understanding – Action Step 2 (Be Flexible and Adaptable). Ideally, the best way to develop this perspective is to go to China and see firsthand what is happening. **Visiting Beijing and Shanghai on a group tour or trade mission is not enough to really understand how China is developing.** Almost everyone I know marvels at the economic progress of Shanghai, but realistically Shanghai is more representative of where China wants to go than where it is today. Visiting the countryside and travelling to some of the more rural markets as I have done will give one a better perspective – since about 70% of China is still classified as rural. Even conservative politicians like Newt Gingrich felt better about China after he came over in 1997 to see what was happening himself.[1] Firsthand experience will help dispel many of the negative stereotypes we were brought up to believe.

---

[1] In March 1997, US House Speaker Newt Gingrich went on a three-day visit to China with 11 other members of Congress. American reporters covering the event reported Newt Gingrich as speaking "glowingly about new freedoms that have come to the Chinese as the result of the country's double-digit economic growth". The Michigan Daily Online, 31 March 1997, "Gingrich Concludes 3-day Visit to China; House Speaker Expresses Enthusiasm for China's Future". Web link: http://www.pub.umich.edu/daily/mar/03-31-97/news/news8.html

Growing up in the West, especially North America, we were taught Communism was "evil" – a godless repressive system, where everyone lived in fear of a government that exploited and repressed its people for their own benefit. Visions of George Orwell's *Animal Farm* spring to mind. On the other hand, those growing up in a Communist system were taught capitalists were corrupt exploiters of the middle and lower class. For North Americans like myself, I grew up influenced by people like Ronald Reagan labelling Communism as "the evil empire". To clearly understand China, one of the first things North Americans especially need to discard from our heads is the negative connotation about Socialism and what the Chinese Communist Party (CCP) really represents and wants.

Chinese Communists or Capitalists?

Historically, the Russians never saw the Chinese as true Communists or Socialists, which was a major source of disagreement between the two countries for decades. Stalin used to call Chinese Communism the "radish kind", red on the outside only while white on the inside. When you look at how the Chinese government has adopted Adam Smith's principle of "What the buyer will bear", such as when it came to charging foreign investors exorbitant market prices for scarce office space during the 80s and early 90s, you could never believe there were any Marxist principles involved. But the government, from Deng to Jiang, has consistently said that China's socialist market economy with Chinese characteristics will be much different from any market economy in the West.

The phrase "Chinese characteristics" is commonly used in government speeches. This phrase commonly refers to the unique complexities of a huge population with wide varying cultures and languages over a vast geography developing at varying rates. No other country can claim these complexities; therefore it goes to reason that the Chinese government is right in labelling the uniqueness of their situation. However, **I want to re-emphasise that even with these unique Chinese characteristics, common-sense business principles discussed in the earlier part of this book still apply.**

The Importance of Understanding the Chinese Government

What also helps in gauging one's long-term strategy based on one's

outlook of China is to understand the actions of the Chinese government. Regardless of one's personal views of the CCP's practices of the past or present, or direction they propose for the future, a historical understanding of China especially from 1800 to present day will help strengthen one's perspective. While you do not need to be a China historian to be an effective investor, it helps to understand some critical points in China's history since it does affect the psyche and actions of the government and its citizens today.

While China has arguably *the* richest and longest civilised history on the planet, for the past 200 years, China has been struggling to regain its foothold. The struggle was most pronounced during the 150 years prior to China's re-opening of foreign investment in 1979. During this 150-year period, China suffered from wars, famine, and political unrest that have resulted in an estimated 60–70 million deaths.[2] With such a tumultuous and bloody past, it is understandable that the government's primary objective is to maintain stability. **Stability is the central theme in analysing the Chinese central government's policies.** In America the central theme may be freedom, but in China, it is stability. Chinese officials often point to the huge destabilising economic and social upheavals in Russia when political reform took precedence over economic reform.

The Great Leap Forward [Backward]

The Great Leap Forward was China's attempt to overtake the West in steel production by mobilising China's masses to use primitive production techniques that resulted in poor quality [useless] steel being produced and, more critically, caused massive crop failures due to neglect. No one wanted to report the bad news and as a result, falsification of economic progress was rampant. By the time the economic disaster was truly known, millions of people are purported to have starved to death.

---

[2] The deaths due to famine, wars and political unrest for the 150-year period from 1829 to 1979 is difficult to quantify because records were either not well kept or released to the public. But the 60–70 million deaths estimate is derived from often quoted figures, such as the Taiping Rebellion (1850–1864) causing 20 million deaths, and the Great Leap Forward disaster (1965) causing an estimated 30 million deaths. If one looks at the population anomalies, another 10–20 million deaths can be accounted from the Boxer Rebellion (1900–1901), the Republican and Warlord periods (1912–1949), the Sino-Japanese War (1937–1945), the Chinese Revolution (1945–1949), and the Korean Conflict (1950–1953).

Top government and industry leaders in China were all veterans of the Cultural Revolution of 1967–1977. The Cultural Revolution was an ambitious but disastrous attempt to re-educate the masses with an unrealistic form of socialistic ideology. The political reforms (possibly as a tactic to eliminate Mao's enemies) created massive social unrest and resulted in denying most of China's current generation of leaders the opportunity for any formal education, as schools and universities were shut down. The reality of this generation's re-education was not so much about socialist ideology, rather about how to survive based on whom you knew, not standing out by saying what everyone wanted to hear, and the "back door system" one had to learn to get anything done.

Businesspeople often complain about the slow overly cautious approach the government takes in implementing reforms in China. However, the current leadership knows firsthand from the Great Leap Forward and the Cultural Revolution the disastrous effects of implementing reforms too zealously without careful study. Officials learned the safest method of political survival was not to say too much and to "sit on the fence" until they could see which way consensus was building. This practice of fence sitting can be frustrating as was experienced by many businesspeople in the Internet sector. The dot-com boom caught many governments off-guard and China's government was no different in trying to figure out how to deal with this technological boom. China's Ministry of Information Industry that oversees the telecommunications and Internet sectors at the outset of the boom sat on the fence on major issues, initially issuing vague and ambiguous policies concerning the dissemination of information and the usage of convergent technologies between telecommunications and the Internet. As a guiding principle to predict Chinese government actions, it helps to understand their thinking which typically has been a conservative approach, where they feel the best way to maintain stability is for the CCP to maintain tight control over the economy and Chinese society. In the case of the Internet sector, it was eventually decided that Chinese websites that post news and information must only use government-approved sources.

People in the West often criticise China's leadership for not being democratic and open enough. Some critics will even go so far as to refer to China's leadership as a dictatorship. However, the definition of a dictator is "a leader who rules with absolute power, usually by force". However, this definition is difficult to apply to China currently, because the first question is, "Who is the leader?" People who assume that whoever is the leader at the top is the person with absolute authority is mistaken. Only Mao Zedong from the start of the Cultural Revolution till the time of his death, and possibly Deng Xiaoping in his last few years of life, could have possibly wielded the kind of power to be accurately called a dictatorship – this is certainly not the case today in the modern Jiang Zemin era. Even Jiang while holding all three top seats of China (as President of China, as General Party Secretary of the CCP and as Chairman of the Central Military Commission) could not implement all his policies nor appoint the people he wanted at will. It would be the same type of question as asking who is in charge in America: the President, the Senate or the House of Representatives? In China, their own triumvirate is made up of government institutions, the CCP and the People's Liberation Army. Young promising cadres can "helicopter" their way to the top and fall just as easily as in any political system.

Multi-party vs. Monolithic Governments

History shows multi-party systems are not always necessary to produce a prosperous society. In fact, one could argue that "lame duck" governments and political gridlock hinder social progress. Monolithic systems, such as the British ruling Hong Kong for almost 150 years, the Liberal Democratic Party (LDP) ruling Japan for decades (until recently) and those in many other countries, have similar proven circumstances. The Mainland Chinese love to show comical pictures of Taiwan politicians breaking into literal fistfights and throwing furniture in their legislature meetings. In fact, only since the 90s has Taiwan had a working multi-party system. Prior to that, under the leadership of Chiang Kai Shek and his son Chiang Ching Kuo, Taiwan's government was every bit as authoritarian and restrictive as those on the mainland. As Taiwan eventually moved to a more open political system, and as the people's conditions improved, so could the Mainland – but they will do so on their own time scale, since they are fully aware of the problems experienced by their former Soviet neighbours.

The problem for many in the West is that because the authority and decision-making is not transparent, people may draw the wrong conclusions. It is not correct to say that China is ruled by a dictatorship; a monolithic party may be a better description. While many people worry about the lack of another political party to hold the CCP in check, those who understand the dynamics of Chinese politics would acknowledge that rigorous internal debates often ensue over critical policy issues within their own party. The CCP, which has more than 65 million members, is open to anyone who has the right credentials, such as good references and a university degree. To give a broader voice within their own ranks, recently the CCP has begun to encourage private entrepreneurs to join the party. This admittance of an estimated several hundred thousand private entrepreneurs (capitalists) is a significant first move by the CCP, in a classic, calculated and cautious move by the government, to test new thinking.

Regardless of the political critics, the irrefutable fact is that the lives of ordinary Chinese citizens have improved to unprecedented levels. Several hundred million people have been lifted out of poverty, and the numbers continue to grow. The significance of the rights to basic food, clothing and shelter may be beyond the full comprehension of most people in the West (especially North Americans) because they have never had to worry about it – but not citizens of developing countries like China. Everyone in China now has enough to eat and it is difficult for those who have never had this fear to understand it. My father-in-law was telling me the stories about the famine that happened after the disaster of the Great Leap Forward. He was studying in university then and told me how you could tell who was going to die of starvation. For example, people's heads would noticeably swell from drinking too much water as a way of trying to stave off the pain of hunger. Starvation and famine have plagued China for centuries. These horror stories cannot be imagined in the West, when during the time millions of students and ordinary citizens were starving in China, students in the West were becoming infected not with hunger but with Beatlemania. My personal view is to challenge those political pundits who call for more rapid changes and reform with the caveat of looking at what happened when China tried to implement changes too fast. If one does take the perspective that China's history is 5,000 years, then gradual change over 10, 25, 50, or even 100 years will seem relatively insignificant.

China Streetsmart

As recent as a decade ago, Chinese living in the north of China had only a limited choice of affordable vegetables during the winter. Every fall, Beijing households like the one pictured on the left would stack "winter" Chinese cabbage outside their doorsteps like fire logs, which they would slowly consume over the ensuing months. Today, Beijing citizens (on the right) enjoy affordable fresh fruit and vegetables imported from all over the world, from Philippine mangoes to Florida Sunkist oranges. In the West we take this availability for granted, but in China, it is still one of the marvellous achievements of the Open Door era.

27 | Understanding China's Facts and Figures
Statistical Reliability and Reality

Reliable and thorough understanding of the data is critical to making informed decisions.

Adopting the perspective that China is not one but many markets developing at rapid but varying paces and that the government's primary motivation is maintaining stability is useful when examining China's facts and figures. China's impressive growth over the past two decades has recently come into question by critics who claim that the Chinese government has been distorting the official gross domestic product (GDP) growth figures for political reasons – are they right? The data available must be reliable to the Streetsmart investor to make the correct strategic decisions; therefore it helps to understand the evolution of Chinese statistics and the inherent challenges it has presented and continues to present. Only then will one be able to decide more objectively whether the Chinese government is "deliberately cooking the books".

The Evolution and Challenges of China's Statistics

Prior to the re-opening of China's doors in 1979, certain statistics were considered state secrets and key information was closed to most Chinese researchers and international analysts alike. However, gradually but progressively the State Statistics Bureau, now called the National Bureau of Statistics (NBS), has opened up the books beginning in 1982 with the publication of the first national statistics yearbook. Since then, the national statistics yearbook has been expanded and definitions revised to be more in line with international norms.

However, this evolution has been fraught with challenges, such as those associated with moving from an old Soviet-style method of measuring output to a modern method in line with an open market international economy. As Ken Davies, the former Chief Economist and Bureau Chief for the Economist Intelligence Unit in Asia, now executive with the Organisation for Economic Cooperation and Development (OECD) based out of Paris explained, the old Soviet method of totalling up the number of widgets produced in a given industry and then totalling up all the industries to measure total output for a country is difficult for a country the size of China which has millions of enterprises that must all be trained in how to send in the figures needed. Furthermore, in the old Soviet system where prices, unaffected by open market forces, were relatively constant, valuations were easier to tabulate. But in an open market economy, where prices change rapidly, assessing the correct valuation is extremely difficult. Even now that China has moved to calculating growth based on the three internationally accepted approaches of measuring expenditure, product and income, the totals of each approach in theory should all be equal, but in China they are not highlighting the challenges of data gathering. Consequently, the government is forced to choose which sets of numbers to use, which Ma Jun, Senior Economist for Deutsche Bank, believes is a compromise between the expenditure and product approach to come up with a single official growth figure. As a result, the 22 provinces, five autonomous regions and four special municipalities across China

Photograph by John L. Chan

Ma Jun (surname Ma), another successful returnee, studied at the top schools in Shanghai before doing his PhD in Economics at Georgetown University. He has also written books on China's economy. Currently he and his wife live in Hong Kong.

regularly report data that has to be revised up or down when consolidating at the national level. In the beer industry, for example, the NBS would publish monthly output figures, but a particular month's output would only be really valid a few months later after statisticians had a chance to look at the way actual data was being reported and make revisions accordingly.

Compounding these difficulties is the lack of a fully developed computerized system of information gathering. The massive amounts of technical hardware and training of personnel needed in China is daunting. I would not be the least bit surprised if in some remote office of China abacuses were still used. While much better today, China's statistical gathering still needs time to catch up with the sophisticated levels of the West.

The Reliability of China's Statistics

While economists and analysts both in and outside of China struggled to figure out what was actually happening with China's economy, the issue exploded in a whirl of controversy when China officially published its 1997/1998 GDP growth statistic of 7.8%. The number reported simply did not add up when cross-checked with other data such as energy consumption or trade exports. Harvard educated Professor Thomas Rawski of the University of Pittsburgh published a report called "What's Happening to China's GDP Statistics?" which highlighted the anomalies. The report speculated that the NBS may have run afoul to political pressures in reporting GDP growth. China's critics used this report and many other similar studies published which put the realistic growth estimates at anywhere from half the official figures, to even negative figures, claiming that the government was intentionally distorting the numbers and duping the international community.

To better understand the controversy, around 1997–1998 China was having tremendous difficulty in maintaining output while trying to readjust to the austerity measures of 1995 which tightened credit to slow down the overheated economy of 1994 and the Asian financial crisis in 1997 that was exploding around them. Furthermore, leaders such as former Premier Zhu made the bold edict to provincial leaders and the world that China would achieve 8% GDP growth that year. The result of all these pressures created what some

216

Chinese analysts called a "wind of falsification and embellishment". As Ken Davies described, "Provincial leaders basically had two choices: either I tell my boss [Premier Zhu] the truth and get fired or I can 're-evaluate' the figures [such as is that stock pile of unfinished goods really finished goods?] and take my chances." Based on the data sent in by the provinces, it appeared that provincial leaders adopted the latter tactic. The NBS and Premier Zhu later rejected the numbers being submitted;[1] in fact, Premier Zhu, frustrated by the data being received from the provinces, eventually got on a plane to fly around China to see what was happening firsthand. Yet the 1997–1998 published official number of GDP growth of 7.8% remains unchanged and continues to be adopted and quoted by leading international organisations. The controversy then led to a re-examination of all of China's past reported figures and threw into question whether China's official numbers were accurate or reliable at all.

Ken Davies, Principal Administrator, Investment in China, Director for Financial, Fiscal and Enterprise Affairs for the OECD based out of Paris has been involved with the China market for more than 30 years. A fluent Mandarin speaker, prior to joining the OECD, Ken was the Chief China Economist for the Economist Group and Bureau Chief for the Economist Intelligence Unit (EIU) Asia.

While it appears that political pressures may have distorted the official macro results, it is unlikely there was a mass conspiracy by the central government to deceive the international community; rather the likely scenario was certain provincial leaders trying to "save their jobs" coupled with the previously outlined challenges of gathering data across China. However, in the period around 1998, many in the NBS and central government were particularly worried

---

[1] *China Daily*, 6 March 2000, p. 5, "Nation Moves Boldly Forward", sourced from Professor Thomas Rawski's article "China GDP Statistics – A Case of Caveat Lector?", p. 2. Web link: http://www.pitt.edu/~tgrawski/papers2001/caveat.web.pdf

and self-critical about the possible falsifications and embellishments dating back to the dangers of the Great Leap Forward when false reporting of bumper harvests, while crops actually lay rotting in the fields due to neglect, led to the starvation of millions.[2] Good planning requires reliable data and as a result, the central government no longer puts the same pressure on provincial leaders to achieve unrealistic GDP growth targets.

Deutsche Bank has created its own model of looking at the Chinese economy, which includes power production, freight traffic and retail sales which it claims explains 79% of GDP variation from 1981 to 2001. Ma Jun, Senior China Economist based out of Hong Kong and author of a couple of books on the Chinese economy himself explains, "Using our model, GDP growth rate for 1998 was probably inflated by 4.7 percentage points. **The discrepancy between official and re-based estimates narrowed significantly in 1999–2001, suggesting that the official estimates have become more reliable.**"[3] When asked about the current controversy, he remarked, "Most of the press are referring to a report which Professor Rawski first wrote several years back, but now appears to be much less relevant." Furthermore, with the executives I interviewed, almost no one really cared whether the official growth rate was 5%, 7% or 9%. What really mattered was their specific understanding of their particular industry. Most were happy to leave the question of measuring economic growth to the reporters and analysts to debate among themselves.

If the ultimate objective is to know the *real* growth and health of the economy, **the *China Streetsmart* executive must also acknowledge, not just reports on what different analysts (in and out of China) interpret the statistics to mean, but also the *huge* underground economy that exists in China that is impossible to quantify.** Underground or grey market economies exist in any economy, but in China where the rules and regulations are not as clearly defined as in the West, this situation is particularly pronounced. Working without any formal contract and moonlighting or doing more jobs or earning more income than officially recorded is rampant –

---

[2] Ibid.
[3] Deutsche Bank, *Asia Economics Daily*, 26 March 2002. p. 1.

some analysts cite it could be as big as the official numbers reported. This is one of the reasons why it helps to come over to visit China and see firsthand how things really work. Analysts and statisticians can only work from a base of facts presented to them, which will never take into account the realistic, but unaccountable grey market. For example, an estimated 120–200 million people from rural areas,[4] referred to as "floating population" (*liudong renkou*), flock to cities (illegally) in search of work and often find jobs as construction labourers, deliverymen, housekeepers, waitresses and hairdressers. Most are paid in cash "under the table" and their incomes are not reported. As we saw in Chapter 14, as Michael Colozzi travelled around China, he discovered how locals prefered to do business "off invoice", i.e., cash transactions had no official record and locals often kept several sets of accounting books. This business practice is rampant all throughout the Chinese economy. **Therefore, the best way for the *China Streetsmart* executive to use facts and figures about China is to use them as benchmarks only, coupled with their actual firsthand research and understanding of their specific industry to arrive at the proper conclusions** – which was the exact approach Michael Colozzi took at Portola.

Understanding Unemployment Figures

How China calculates its unemployment figures also needs to be understood better. While the government officially publicised 2001 unemployment at 3.6%, other international organisations placed the figures closer to 15–20%. One of the key discrepancies lies in the calculation of who is counted for employment. The government's definition only calculates the *urban* unemployment rate of the *fully employed* and excludes those workers sent home without pay largely as a result of the reform of the state-owned enterprises, called *xiagang* workers, which numbers 9.4 million (1999 estimate).[5] Furthermore, in order to be counted in official figures, one must officially register with the labour department as being unemployed. Using this expanded definition, analysts claim 9–10% is more real-

---

[4] The Economist Intelligence Unit, January 2001, "Chapter 1: Politics, Economy, and Basic Data", *China Hand*, p. 66.
[5] Ibid, p. 41.

istic of urban unemployment[6] and when you take into account the rural population, you have as much as 20% of China's workforce affected. Determining rural unemployment is difficult as there is no commonly used standard and depends on different interpretations. It is estimated that up to 200 million peasants are unemployed or underemployed.[7] The important point for the Streetsmart investor to acknowledge is that rising unemployment has serious political and social implications that could result in policies affecting his or her business. For example, if unemployment rose to the point where the negative consequences of joining the World Trade Organisation (WTO), such as the expected adverse impact on China's large but inefficient agricultural sector, outweighed its benefits, it is conceivable for China's leaders to rethink their strategy of participation (note that stability is the key driver behind the government's actions). Since it is not possible to measure the full extent of unemployment in China, the official reports and trends of urban unemployment can only act as a warning bell. Estimates for 2002 already predict the official rate to climb to 4–5%.

The Trade Deficit Debate

Trade data is often a contentious political issue as the US and the European Union (EU) often complain about the growing trade deficit with China. While it is clear that a deficit does exist between China and the US and the EU, Asian countries such as Japan and Korea have typically maintained a trade surplus with China. Once again, the source of the trade disputes often revolves around the way trade is calculated and interpreted. For example, according to the US government, the trade deficit in 2000 between China was 83.8 billion USD, but according to China the deficit was only 22.5 billion USD[8] (see Figure 27.1). The biggest discrepancy is explained in the exports to Hong Kong (44.5 billion USD), which often then goes on to the US. The Chinese do not count these figures as US exports, rather simply as exports to Hong Kong, whereas the US method accounts for this intermediary. Therefore, it is not surpris-

---

[6] Ibid.
[7] Ibid.
[8] Ibid, "Chapter 3: Trade", p. 27.

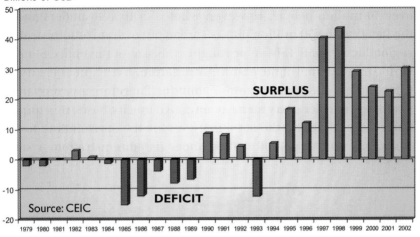

Billions of USD

SURPLUS

DEFICIT

Source: CEIC

1979 1980 1981 1982 1983 1984 1985 1986 1987 1988 1989 1990 1991 1992 1993 1994 1995 1996 1997 1998 1999 2000 2001 2002

Figure 27.1   China's Trade Balance, 1979–2002

ing that according to China, Hong Kong remains China's third larg-est trading partner next to the US and Japan. However, the US also follows the same practice in that American-made goods shipped to Hong Kong that end up in China are only counted as exports to Hong Kong. Further discrepancies are derived from the fact that the US calculates their trade account with China based on the final value of the goods received and do not account for the fact that tranship-ment mark-ups (80% of US imports use this method) placed by third-party intermediaries often have nothing to do with China itself.[9] The simple fact to be aware of is that published trade figures have political overtones and as a result, depending on which country pub-lishes the trade statistics, results could vary quite substantially.

Figure 27.1 shows the trade balance view using Chinese figures. If you analyse the US and EU figures you will see a difference.

Urban and Rural Population Statistics

In China, each major city is actually divided up into administrative regions (prefectures). What people often do not realise is that the population figure reported representing the city actually represents the region in and around the city (see Figure 27.2). The city of

---

[9] Ibid.

Chongqing, for example, has the largest population in China with over 30 million people. However, what is critical to understand is the fact that the 30 million plus is spread out over an administrative region larger than Taiwan or roughly the size of the entire State of Ohio or Austria.[10] The actual population living in the city of Chongqing is no more than 6–7 million. Therefore as companies plan their market entry strategy on a city-by-city basis, it is important to keep in mind the actual city versus the surrounding townships and smaller satellite cities under its administration. A sales

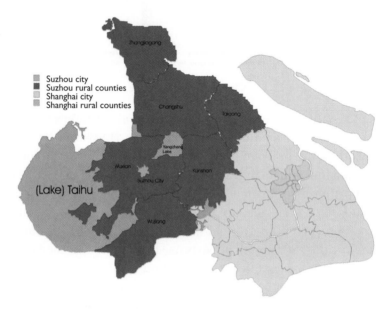

Figure 27.2   Suzhou and Shanghai Administrative Region
When quoting the populations of Shanghai or Suzhou, for example, the population statistics also include the areas surrounding the main city under its administration. The statistical population of Suzhou, for example, is approximately 6 million; however, only about 1 million actually live in the city of Suzhou itself (shown in pink). The other 5 million people or 80% of the population is spread out over the surrounding counties and satellite cities such as in Zhangjiagang, which boasts a relatively large and populated port area.

---

[10] On 14 March 1997, Chongqing became China's fourth municipality directly under the central government, i.e., with provincial-level status. It is now officially the world's largest city, both in terms of population and area. The official population is 30.5 million (not counting illegal migrants probably numbering several more million) and Chongqing covers an area of 82,000 sq kilometres or 31,660 sq miles.

China Streetsmart

representative assigned to cover Chongqing might have to spend as much as a day or two just travelling from one area of Chongqing to the next. Furthermore, population figures do not include the migrant workers from the rural areas of China who wander into the cities in search of work. In Shanghai, for example, this migrant population has been cited to be as high as 3–4 million people (and rising) above the official number. During a recent census, the Chinese government tried to make an effort at trying to count these migrant workers by sending census takers down to train stations and other areas where migrants lived, claiming they were there to do census statistics only, but most people refused to be counted, fearing the government would use the data to send the illegal migrants back to their hometowns.

Quantifying the Impact of China's Entry into the WTO

Surprisingly, the overall aggregate direct impact on China's economy from 2001 to 2005 as a result of WTO entry is estimated to be less than 1% or 0.1–0.8% depending on which analytical source you use.[11] One of the reasons for this negligible impact is due to the fact that China has been preparing for WTO entry for some time and has been dropping its tariff rates over time from an arithmetic weighted average of 53% in 1991 to 23% in 1996 to 15% in 2001. By 2003, the tariff rate will drop to 9%.[12]

It is important to not confuse the different methods of measuring the tariff rates for China. The arithmetic weighted average method is often the most commonly reported number, but also the least accurate. This method is calculated by adding up the roughly 8,000 tariff categories and their average rates, then dividing it by the same number. Using this calculation, 2001 tariff rates were 15%. Nominal weighted average is a more accurate measurement and requires each category and its actual trade volume to be calculated

---

[11] Deutsche Bank estimates 2002–2006 GDP growth impact of WTO to be 0.11 percentage points, down from their original estimate of 0.45 percentage points (*China Economic Outlook*, July 2002, p. 8) while economists at the International Monetary Fund predict 0.8 percentage points (Supachai Panitchpakdi and Mark L. Clifford, 2002, *China and the WTO*, p. 5, Singapore: John Wiley & Sons).

[12] Interview with Jun Ma, Deutsche Bank Senior Economist, July 2002.

based on specific volume-based rates. Each category has its own rate calculation and the nominal tariff for 2001 was 11%. Real tariff rates measure the actual tariffs collected by the customs bureau for each category. Most foreign companies, through investment incentives, have been able to import goods duty-free and as a result, the real tariffs for 2001 was only 3.5%, suggesting that China already is essentially a low-tariff country and also why the WTO has such a small numerical effect in the short term.[13]

These figures, while indicative of general trends, are not useful to the investor concerned with a specific industry since the WTO trade agreement impacts each industry differently and must be examined separately to come up with any real significance. For example, the drop in tariffs will have a slightly negative effect on China's domestic auto industry at less than 5%, while the apparel industry will have a large positive impact of up to 40%.[14] Where the WTO changes will have a significant impact will be in the service sector as China meets its agreed obligations, especially in the areas of financial services, retail and telecommunications. For example, five years after China's WTO entry, foreign banks will finally be able to conduct local currency transactions with local customers anywhere in China.

A *China Streetsmart* Balanced View of Looking at the Numbers

How one interprets or relies on the figures available in China often depends on whether one is a China proponent or critic. Proponents of China trade would selectively choose growth figures and numbers that back their already predetermined decision to invest, and calculate market potential using nothing more than applying a simple arithmetic formula based on population and income growth statistics. Specifics such as detailed market segment dynamics, growing competition and local preferences are seldom accounted for. While it was wrong for investors to look at China with blind optimism and selectively choose numbers which only supported their

---

[13] Ibid.

[14] Deutsche Bank, *China Economic Outlook*, July 2002, p. 10.

plans to invest, as was a common practice during the 90s, it is equally wrong to only back the critics and assume that the government has initiated a huge conspiracy, backed by foreign banks who are also their customers, to fool foreign investors into over-assuming a vibrant economy. It is not in the long-term interest of the government to distort figures and recent indications show they are getting better at data gathering and reporting.

The common-sense business approach to using China's facts and figures is to see the market firsthand by interacting with potential customers and partners. This approach enables investors to get a feel for what is happening in China and that often means going beyond just Beijing and Shanghai. Going to markets where your products or services will be used is the real determinant in assessing how to read the numbers. A good experienced consultant or research company can help. Official numbers are often useful as benchmarks, but understanding the challenges in data collection suggests not taking them at face value. Experienced consultants are able to take the reported numbers, conduct firsthand research such as visiting factories and interviewing industry executives, and then use their experience to reach a conclusion – this is the *China Streetsmart* approach.

28 | The Challenges and Risks of Investing in China
Calculating the Risk

The challenges and risks China faces are numerous and formidable but the potential remains for a positive outcome.

The Streetsmart investor needs a sober understanding of the formidable risks and challenges China faces to ensure investment decisions are treated with the appropriate risk-reward expectation. Critics warn investors of the fact that those companies who were most optimistic and bold in their investments in China are now paying the painful price for their blind optimism. Some will even claim that the government was part conspirator by purposely distorting economic figures to not give investors the true picture of what was happening. Furthermore, the harbingers of doom predict that the impending challenges China faces will ultimately bring down the system, making any China investment strategy incredibly risky.

In response to the issues raised by the critics, possible negative scenarios proffered by the harbingers of doom are examined. The contributors to this book counter these negative opinions by offering an alternative view that supports a plausible positive outcome to each of these issues raised. But in reality, no one, not even those currently in power, can accurately predict what China will eventually become. The optimism held by the contributors to this book is based on having lived and worked throughout China. China, like the US, may have its own internal problems and differences, but **the strong nationalistic spirit that has built America into a superpower also exists within China.** The *China Streetsmart* investor, after having understood the issues and possible outcomes, should then juxtapose those thoughts with the emerging positive trends and opportunities laid out in the subsequent chapter to decide for himself or herself which scenario is more realistic and will determine their long-term investment strategy in China.

Historical Harbingers of Doom

For the past two decades, harbingers of doom have been predicting troubles for China. One of the more recent harbingers is Gordon Chang and his controversial book *The Coming Collapse of China*. Gordon takes a sobering contrarian point of view to many of the China optimists. While I respect Gordon's intellect, *I do not agree with his views*. Since 1979, there have been at least four major periods when "China experts" were predicting the collapse of the Chinese system. The first collapse of the system was predicted shortly after the doors re-opened to the West in 1979. The harbingers of doom were predicting that the hardliners, fearful of the "evil influences" of the capital system and very much in control of the military, would clash with the reformers within the Chinese Communist Party (CCP) and the ensuing chaos would eventually bring the system down. Not only has this *not* happened, but in addition, today the military is more under civilian control than ever, with its first non-military background leader, Jiang Zemin, at the helm of the Central Military Commission (CMC).

The second period was after the June 4 1989 Tiananmen Square crackdown on students. Zhao Ziyang, handpicked by Deng himself to lead China on an aggressive path of modernisation, opened China's door wide and with it came loopholes and subsequent greed and corruption by officials. What is not clearly understood by many of the people in the West is that the student demands at the time were not as clear and cohesive as the Western press would like to claim and the call for "democracy and open elections" was really a call to clean up the corruption happening in society and the government.[1] The crackdown sent shock waves throughout China and the rest of the world and threw the pace of investment back. However, one could argue that the slowdown in investment may have been beneficial to China, as it gave the government a chance to "clean its house" as many of the glaring loopholes encouraging corruption were closed.

---

[1] The Economist Intelligence Unit, January 2001, "Chapter 1: Politics, Economy, and Basic Data", *China Hand*, p. 27.

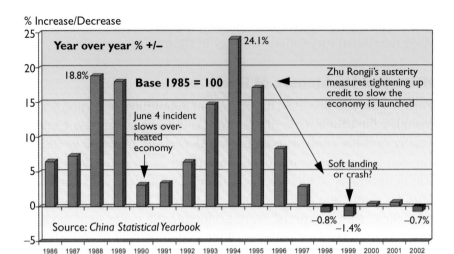

Figure 28.1   China's Consumer Price Index

The third period was in 1994, when inflation, running at a rate of more than 24%, was close to spiralling out of control (see Figure 28.1). Price controls were almost impossible to manage and members in the government had visions of China heading towards Brazil's hyperinflation experience. Thankfully, due in large part to former Prime Minister Zhu Rongji, then Governor of the People's Bank of China, policies of tightening credit slowed the economy down to a "soft landing". If anything, critics are worried that the "soft landing" may have turned into a crash, as China has experienced basically flat to declining price levels since 1998. Only recently have prices begun to rise slightly.

The Risks and Challenges of Today

The fourth period is now. Indeed, the risks and challenges that China faces now that it has entered into the World Trade Organisation (WTO) are significant and need to be seriously understood. Furthermore, not all the challenges have clear solutions and it will be determined as much by how foreign investors deal with the challenges as risks or opportunities that will ultimately determine its outcome – i.e., foreign investors will have the ability to help shape the ultimate path China takes. The following are just a few of the risks and challenges that lie ahead for China.

Growing Unemployment

Now that China has entered the WTO, the fear is that international forces will overwhelm sagging state-owned enterprises (SOEs), forcing many SOEs into bankruptcy. Out of the current workforce of 85 million working for SOEs, an estimated 25 million are expected to lose their jobs as part of the restructuring process.[2] How the economy is able to absorb this huge labour surplus represents a clear risk. The optimistic viewpoint is to note that these millions of displaced workers are reasonably literate and hungry for work. **Over half of China's workforce has had some secondary education with literacy levels more than 80%, as opposed to India which hovers only around 50%.[3]** In fact, the biggest loser of China's accession to WTO will be India.[4]

Photograph by John L. Chan

The literacy rate in China remains one of the highest, if not the highest, of all developing countries, giving new investors a high-quality but low-cost base of workers to choose from.

For enterprising entrepreneurs, this surplus in reasonably educated and semi-skilled labour could present new opportunities. While the agricultural sector will be negatively affected, the textile sector is expected to boom. China's current production of the world's apparel market is about 26% (2001 estimate) and as the West's quota restrictions of the Multi-Fibre Agreement are eliminated between now and 2005, China's market share of the apparel production is

[2] Supachai Panitchpakdi and Mark L. Clifford, 2002, *China and the WTO*, p. 5, Singapore: John Wiley & Sons.
[3] The Economist Intelligence Unit, July 2000, "Chapter 7: Human Resources", *China Hand*, p. 2.
[4] Deutsche Bank, *China Economic Outlook*, July 2002, p. 9.

expected to climb to 41%.[5] Eventually, half of the world's clothing will be supplied from China and this will create many jobs. Moreover, the government is counting on more than the textile/apparel market to create jobs. The service industry is also expected to boom. In Shanghai today, many of the people driving taxis once worked in now closed obsolete state-owned steel mills. Many in the retail distribution chain, for example, prefer not to buy an expensive delivery truck, since they can employ hundreds of workers peddling three-wheeled trolleys for less cost and be more effective in reaching the small neighbourhood mom and pop kiosks that still number in the millions.

Photograph by hn L. Chan

Now that China has joined the WTO, textile factories like this leather garment factory in southern China will begin speeding up production to meet the increasing demand from American and European customers as the Multi-Fibre Agreement quota restrictions are lifted. The macro strategy for joining the WTO is that new export opportunities will create even more jobs for its citizens.

Rising Crime Rates

With many SOE workers out of work, the negative social impact is a rising crime rate, which the harbingers of doom predict will continue to worsen. It is important for people to know that general crime levels (especially violent crime) are far less in China compared to the West. In Shanghai, for example, the police still generally do not carry firearms; rather, they are likely to be armed with a "fine book". In Shenzhen and other parts of southern China where triads are rampant, I have seen the local police carry firearms. However, the sad truth is that burglaries, for example, are rising. Many foreign executives working in China agree that while China may be criticised for its harsh laws and penalties, it still is one of the safest places

---

[5] Ibid.

China Streetsmart

to live in the world. I can walk the streets at any hour in Shanghai without the fear of being mugged. However, based on reports coming from Beijing, for example, illegal migrants coming from the poorer areas of the northeast, with nothing to lose, are becoming more desperate and reports of crime are rising, which once again emphasises the point that **to maintain social stability, the government's main task is to ensure basic living standards for all.**

Growing Urbanisation and the Mounting Income Gap between Urban and Rural People

Related to rising unemployment and crime are the effects of increased urbanisation and the growing income gap between urban and rural areas of China. Roughly two-thirds of China's population is still classified as rural, earning roughly half of what people make in urban centres. As market economies develop, the shift should be towards urbanisation and hopefully higher living standards for all. However, the negative scenario predicts huge upheavals as poor farmers flood the cities seeking a better life, exacerbated by the negative affects WTO will have on the domestic agricultural sector. Major cities, unprepared for this explosive influx, will fall into chaos as its services (e.g. healthcare and sanitation) and infrastructure are overwhelmed. Visions of Chinese cities transforming into dozens of Calcuttas with mass slums of impoverished peasants spring to mind.

The central government has been well aware of this migration risk for decades, which is why the government has implemented

Photograph by John L. Chan

Migrant workers continue to leave the countryside for the cities in search of work and hopefully a better life. While difficult to gather reliable figures, this floating population known as *liudong renkou* has been estimated at well over 100 million and is likely to continue to grow.

the *hukou* system (described on page 167) to restrict free movement of workers. Furthermore, the government's "Go West" initiative is specifically aimed at reducing the growing income gap between urban and rural areas by attracting foreign investment with attractive incentives and creating large infrastructure projects aimed at building better links, such as better transportation, with the more prosperous coastal regions.

Another solution to alleviating the burden on cities is through the growth of satellite towns and "new cities" surrounding the major centres, which are growing rapidly, absorbing a significant percentage of people leaving the strictly rural areas. The city of Suzhou, for example, is not necessarily the major economic centre in the administrative region of Suzhou (see Figure 27.2 on page 222). Less than 20% of the population of Suzhou live in the city itself. Satellite cities such as Kunshan and Zhangjiagang, under the governance of Suzhou, attract a large number of migrants looking for work. Kunshan, for example, has grown significantly because of the new influx of Taiwanese investment. Rural incomes in these new centres may not be as high as that recorded in major cities, but nevertheless still represent significant value. As a result, business development executives looking for new markets should not ignore these growing satellite markets.

Adjusting to China's WTO Entry

Adjusting to an emerging China, as one executive described, is like having an elephant sit up in a glass shop – it doesn't matter what you do, something is bound to get damaged. There is no question that the world will need to go through a significant adjustment as China's entry into the WTO takes full effect (see Figure 28.2). Some of China's critics, if not warning of massive unemployment in China, predict massive upheavals in other countries. Protectionists warn that China's WTO entry will hurt American and European companies by stealing their jobs. However, it is untrue that China is stealing jobs from the West. In reality, China's low-cost manufacturing base has not stolen American jobs, for example; rather, over the past decade they have been taking jobs from other Asian countries as their incomes and cost of living standards continued to rise. The sports shoe industry is a great example. Americans lost the low-skilled, low-wage jobs to the Japanese when Nike moved their sourcing of shoes from the US to Japan in the 70s, and in the 80s moved their sourcing to Taiwan when Japanese wages got too high. In the late 80s, they moved their sourcing to Korea and in the mid- to late 90s, they moved most of their sourcing to China. Today, other cheaper countries, such as Vietnam, are beginning to benefit. West- ern countries benefit from this natural economic migration by en- suring the goods they enjoy and consume will be increasingly af- fordable, while maintaining their high standard of living.

Countries reliant on a low-cost manufacturing base, such as those in Southeast Asia, Mexico and other Latin American countries, are worried of losing foreign direct investment (FDI), hence jobs. The movement and shifting of world resources to those most efficient is an inevitable effect of globalisation, as economists point out. Thai- land's Supachai Panitchpakdi, the new Director-General of the WTO, writes in his book with Mark Clifford, *China and the WTO*, that Chi- na's WTO entry could have positive effects on accelerating needed reforms in other countries and will "spur countries around the re-

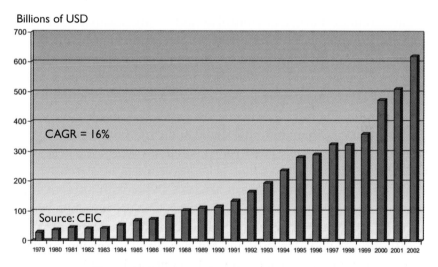

Figure 28.2   China's Trade Growth, 1979–2002
By the year 2020, the World Bank estimates that China's share of the world trade will triple to 10%, making it the second largest trading nation in the world next to the US.[6]

[6] Supachai Panitchpakdi and Mark L. Clifford, 2002, *China and the WTO*, pp. 33–34, Singapore: John Wiley & Sons.

gion to do everything from cleaning up financial systems and making them more market-oriented to cracking down on corruption as a way of improving their economic and social attractiveness in the face of competition from a large, fast-growing China".[7] Furthermore, he cites that Japan and Korea, which China already has a trade deficit with, will be big benefactors, but the oil and gas-producing countries such as Indonesia and Malaysia will also benefit as China's energy needs increase. Mexico and other Latin American countries have a natural geographical advantage of closeness to the huge American market and it will be up to them to capitalise on or defend this advantage.

WTO Compliance

While what China must do to comply with WTO rules is clear, it is expected that compliance and possible different interpretations will vary from region to region. Protectionism exists in every country; just look at US steel producers. To expect China's compliance to be smooth is frankly unrealistic – but not necessarily the fault or design of the central government. Local townships and municipalities in more remote, harder-to-control areas that are negatively affected by WTO compliance should put up tough resistance by using delay tactics or different interpretation of the rules. On the other hand, Shanghai's experience with foreign investment is expected to be where WTO compliance is smoothest and as a result, Shanghai will be one of the major recipients of increased FDI. For the inexperienced investor, Shanghai and Hong Kong (if your business is in manufacturing for trade and export) will likely still be the best staging ground for entry into China. The government is currently promoting the central and western areas of China with attractive incentives, but the *China Streetsmart* approach before investing would be to do a thorough market due diligence study to ensure not only that there are financial incentives, but also other needed factors such as an experienced pool of labour and the right distribution links to your targeted markets. The general rule of thumb is the further you

---

[7] Supachai Panitchpakdi and Mark L. Clifford, 2002, *China and the WTO*, p. 102, Singapore: John Wiley & Sons.

are away from a major city and the more you threaten local jobs, the more resistance you can expect. Knowing and preparing for this likelihood is the first line of defence and following Action Step 4 (Think Win-Win) will enable you to prepare the appropriate entry strategy.

Suppression and Control of the Media

Fundamental to the development of an open democratic market system is the freedom of the press to act independently. Critics point to the censorship that still exists in the Chinese media and claim this will continue to hamper China's development. The government still controls the media, and areas such as publishing largely remain "restricted" to foreign investment. The key point is to focus on where the media and press have come from in China and the direction it continues to evolve to. While in Shanghai during December 2001, I recall reading reports of bombs exploding in Xian and Qingdao. The fact that these types of incidents made the news shows the government is slowly relaxing its grip – just ten years earlier this would not have been possible. New Oprah Winfrey-like talk shows in China are more popular than ever before. I make no illusions that the Chinese press will be completely open and independent in the near future, but it is encouraging to see them extending the boundaries for the press. It's arguable that the government's control of the media mitigated the potential backlash against American interests during the US spy plane clash over Hainan Island in 2001 by not oversensationalising the story and keeping the story off the front pages when the incident first broke out. The debate continues even in the West as to how far the media should go. Many of the Western executives I interviewed, especially the Europeans, feel that in the West, sensationalised Jerry Springer-like shows may have gone too far in expressing freedom of speech. Sensational media, such as the O. J. Simpson trial and the Monica Lewinsky scandal, which does generate public curiosity, distracts society from more relevant issues, such as improving education and reducing crime.

Willy Lam of CNN also adds an important comment: "Apart from politics, control of info has contributed to the screwed-up state of the stock market, with *gumin* [stockholders] being gouged by 'big sharks' [because] only the sharks have the info. *Gumin* [have] been misled by propaganda by the big companies/brokerages, sometimes even misled by government propaganda." While censorship and control of information in China may hurt ordinary Chinese investors, unfortunately this phenomenon is not new to the West either, given the spate of recent accounting scandals such as those regarding Worldcom and the collapse of Enron and Arthur Andersen.

Advertising in the Subway/Metro

Just a decade ago simple advertising like this would have been banned by the censors as being too risqué. While censorship and control of the media remain tight, it is also important to acknowledge the gradual opening up over the years.

The Fiscal Burden of Financing Non-Performing Loans and Pension Reform

Another doomsday scenario is the government's inability to meet its financial obligations to bail out the Chinese banks and the massive amounts of debt they have incurred while also meeting its obligation to finance the pension requirements of China's aging population. Many SOEs, which are required to contribute to pension schemes, are unable to because many are technically bankrupt. As a result, the government must step in to act on behalf of the SOEs and meet the pension needs of its workers. The harbingers of doom predict this massive and growing financial burden will cause the government to collapse as a result of not being able to meet the needs of its citizens causing havoc and civil unrest. They point to the civil unrest already beginning to happen throughout China, such as in China's industrial Northeast, where workers have staged sit-ins and marched on local government offices demanding back pay and compensation, but local municipal governments have been unable to meet their demands.

Ma Jun at Deutsche Bank acknowledges "the problem of the fiscal costs of banking and pension reform to be significant but manageable". A key point to note is that the financial burden on the government is to be spread out over time, since not all workers are at pension-collecting age, thus allowing the government to spread its obligations over the next 50 years to pay down the unfounded liabilities while the new self-determined pension schemes as part of the new pension reforms take effect. The fiscal costs to the banking sector will also be spread out over a period of about ten years. During this period, Deutsche Bank estimates the government will need approximately 300 billion USD to cover the write-off of bad debts held by asset management companies (AMCs) and also to recapitalise the existing banks.[8]

The key warning indicator to watch is the debt to gross domestic product (GDP) ratio, which suggests the government's ability to meet its obligations. At the end of 2001, the official debt to GDP ratio was 18%, which appears healthy when compared to other countries such as Indonesia at 96% or Malaysia at 74%, but when the real costs and contingent liabilities are taken into account, such as those non-performing assets held by AMCs, the debt to GDP ratio in China soars much higher. Deutsche Bank estimates that in the next 50 years the fiscal costs of reforms could be as much as 66% of GDP.[9] The key measure to watch whether the government can handle this critical issue will be its ability to increase its revenue intake and curb expenditure. Already the government has announced new measures to cut tax incentives to foreign investment as part of its national treatment in line with WTO rules, and also curb the fiscal spending surrounding large infrastructure projects.

Lacklustre Domestic Consumption

China's recent economic growth has been largely due to heavy fiscal spending by the government on large infrastructure projects to drive growth – not consumer spending. The negative scenario is that as the government slows its spending, the economy will also

---

[8] Interview with Ma Jun, Deutsche Bank Senior Economist, July 2002.
[9] Deutsche Bank, *China Economic Outlook*, July 2002, p. 11.

slow and as the economy slows so will the government's revenue stream, crippling its ability to meet its pressing financial obligations of banking and pension reforms. Ironically, however, the Chinese have money, with a savings rate estimated at 37-40%, making it one of the highest in the world, more than twice as high as the world average of 15%, but local consumers appear reluctant to spend. Ken Davies, while he was Chief China Economist for the Economist group based out of London, was explaining that this precautionary savings phenomenon was not so much a cultural issue of being Chinese, but rather in line with Milton Friedman's Permanent Income Hypothesis. As uncertainty lessens and incomes rise, so will people's willingness to spend as we witness in the US, whose current savings rate is –3%, meaning Americans are so confident of their future that they live on credit.

The government has been working hard to stimulate domestic consumption with new measures, such as the implementation of new housing loan policies and the implementation of longer holidays to spur spending (see Figure 28.3). A key problem to resolve is

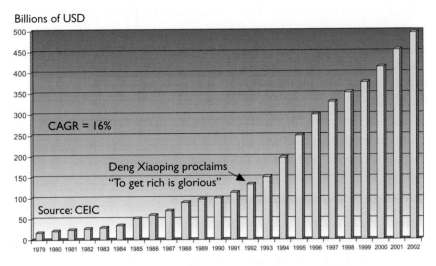

Figure 28.3   China's Retail Sales Growth, 1979–2002

Although retail sales continue to grow at an impressive rate, more needs to be done to ensure that China's economic engine does not slow down. As a warning signal on the health of the economy, slower retail sales could result in lower revenue collection by the government. A serious problem could develop if the government is unable to meet its financial obligations, such as financing the non-performing loans of the state-run banks and asset management companies.

China Streetsmart

credit. A specific point in the Bilateral US-China WTO agreement is the right for auto manufacturers, such as General Motors, to be able to offer financing to assist private citizens to purchase cars. L.J. Jia, the Vice President and China Country Manager for American Express, informs me that currently there are 300 million credit cards issued in China, but most perform the function of debit cards rather than being able to offer real credit, but as China's financial system advances, as it must, as part of its WTO commitments, the eventual availability of credit to ordinary consumers will encourage citizens to spend, unleashing huge amounts of pent-up savings, creating an upward spiral of benefits.

Photograph by L.J. Jia

L.J. Jia, Vice President and China Country Manager for American Express, speaks at a ceremony being held at the Summer Palace in Beijing. L.J. grew up in the Chinese northeast city of Harbin before moving to Beijing and eventually the US to continue his post-graduate studies at the famous Fletcher School at Tufts University in Boston before joining American Express. In spite of the enormous size and clout of American Express, they have focused on developing the China market in a step-by-step approach. L.J. does not rely on a large contingent of foreign expats, having all his China-based offices manned by experienced and capable locals.

Pervasive Corruption

The dangerous fuel that remains spilt on China's floor, which could be ignited by all the sparks generated as a result of China's rapidly growing economy, is corruption. Corruption may have improved somewhat after the 1989 Tiananmen Square incident, but it certainly has not gone away. Huang Weiding, the Executive Director and Senior Economist with the Red Flag Publishing House, wrote an interesting article in Laurence Brahm's book *China's Century*. He argues that power and privilege in any system invite corruption and one of the main causes of corruption within China today is the loose and evolving system as a result of the socialist market economy's unfinished development, opening up the possibility for corruption to exist. He finishes the article with the call that "democracy is a weapon that can kill corruption".[10] While he does not go so far as to call for Western-style democratic elections, he does point out that a more open democratic and transparent system in selecting officials and business leaders of key state-owned industries will eliminate or mitigate the "officialdom" that exists throughout China, where ranking government officials and factory executives are chosen for their connections or *guanxi* with the existing leadership, as opposed to their merits and achievements.

These corrective reforms are under way in China now. Willy Wo-Lap Lam, CNN's senior political China analyst, has written many books on China and its leaders. Willy and I were discussing his views on where China is headed. He told me the reforms suggested by Huang Weiding are happening in China now. Willy refers to this process as administrative reform. Within the civil service, there are far fewer political appointees within the system. Recruitment is now being carried out more often through examination, especially among the large SOEs. Although I have not met Mr Lu who worked with Portola Packaging, those who know him, such as John Huang (they were former schoolmates), tell me he is the new type of business leader to lead some of China's largest SOEs, such as the Ma Ling food group – competent and capable with a proven track record.

---

[10] Huang Weiding, 2001, "Fighting Corruption Amidst Economic Reform". In Laurence Brahm, *China's Century*, p. 53, John Wiley & Sons.

China Streetsmart

The CCP fully realises that corruption is one of the biggest threats to stable social development and its mandate to govern. They continue to implement measures to curb "influence peddling", such as the implementation of formal tendering systems and limiting benefits government officials and key SOE executives are allowed to receive in gifts and entertainment. The critics may cry that these measures are full of loopholes and do not work, but to be fair, the stricter measures need time to be fully understood by all, and show that the government is serious about enforcement. A small indication can be seen in the sudden cutback in lavish entertainment spending involving government officials, which caused a huge crisis in the sale of cognac and other high-end spirits in China, where sales fell almost 50% and literally caused a world glut. In more serious cases, the government has begun to dismiss officials (e.g. former Beijing Mayor Chen Xitong) and in some cases, execute high-profiled officials; the most high-profiled case involved Cheng Kejie, the Vice Chairman of the National Peoples' Congress (NPC) Standing Committee (China's highest governing body) and Governor of Guanxi province.

Decentralisation of Power between Provincial and National Governments

Another steady trend over the years, as a market economy dictates, is the decentralised control over the economy. Once again, it is incorrect to assume that only a handful of people in Beijing control all the influences over the whole country. As certain regions become more powerful and prosperous, such as in Guangdong province, so will be their influence to direct or ignore policies set down by Beijing. Tax collection and the sharing of wealth between the provinces and national governments are already growing issues. Central policies from Beijing will increasingly be subjected to local interpretation and implementation. The harbingers of doom predict that these trends will only increase till the central government finally loses its mandate to function effectively and disintegrates, or at best needs to flex its military muscle to restore order. One thing these harbingers fail to acknowledge is the growing amount of nationalism that exists in China. One of Jiang Zemin's aims is to reinvigorate the "spiritual thought" or "ideological education" within his party. Tying in the spirit of nationalism with traditional Chinese and socialist principles of sharing wealth is what underlies such policies as his "Go West" initiative to reinvigorate the central and western regions of China through investment. It remains to be seen whether the policy will succeed, but regardless, nationalism is very much alive and growing stronger every day.

A Remilitarised China as a Threat to Regional Stability

Another harbinger of doom argument suggests that this rising nationalism will create a dangerous military superpower. Incidents like the spy plane incident on Hainan Island allow the hawks in the Pentagon to point to the fact that China's military spending has been increasing over the years and if it continues unabated, within 50 years or less, this new superpower will challenge the US for global supremacy. To these Cold War advocates, I suggest looking at the facts. While the military budget has been increasing, it still remains just a fraction of the US military budget, and China has been playing catch-up to replace its antiquated equipment from the cutbacks it suffered during the 80s, as more money was channelled into economic reforms. Official figures place its 2002 defence budget at approximately 20 billion USD, around 5% of the US. However, even the more hawkish experts can place it only as high as 15% of America's whopping 379 billion USD defence budget,[11] and that trend or balance of power is not going to change. China's main source of spending will continue to be on its economy, such as that outlined to finance its banking and pension reforms. China's financial resources are also needed to transform its healthcare system and fight pollution. Technologically, even with the acquisition of relatively sophisticated Russian aircraft, overall China's military is still relatively backward, more than a decade or two behind the West.

---

[11] The size of the US defence budget compared to those of other nations is staggering. In the post-Cold War era, Americans face threats from Muslim terrorist groups and the so-called "Axis of Evil" (Iran, Iraq and North Korea). The proposed 48 billion USD increase from 2001 is equivalent to the entire defence spending of the next biggest military spender, Russia. In 2001, the US spent twice as much on defence as all the other NATO members combined. Source: The Globalist. Web link: http://www.theglobalist.com/nor/factsheets/2002/02-25-02.shtml

To gauge the military threat from China, it is important to look back at history. China has never been a hegemonistic power like the Western countries and the Soviet Union have demonstrated to be in the past – even when they had the maritime and military capabilities to do so over 500 years ago.[12] In fact, the People's Liberation Army (PLA) today has stated publicly in writing in a White Paper on Defence under what conditions it would use military force and nuclear weapons. The White Paper states specifically that it would never use nuclear weapons first, and certainly not against non-nuclear states, and it would never pursue military expansionism abroad. Where military intervention has been a flashpoint is usually over China's borders. I recall an article written by anti-China hawks who believed that setting up a reconnaissance station in the mid-90s in the disputed and largely unpopulated islands called the Spratlys (or what the Chinese claim as their Nansha Islands) was akin to the Nazi's annexing of the Sudetenland. While this fearmongering may make for a great Tom Clancy novel, this type of thinking is simply that – fiction. Solving border disputes is best achieved through diplomatic dialogue, which over the past several decades China has consistently adhered to.

Military Clash over Taiwan's Independence

The classic doomsday scenario *China Streetsmart* investors need to be aware of is the issue of reunification with Taiwan, which China claims as a renegade province and on which it has declared to use military force should Taiwan ever declare independence. As much as China would like to keep the "Taiwan issue" an internal affair between the Mainland and Taiwan, the reality is that Mainland China, Taiwan and the US do form a delicate triangle, where the wrong move by any of the three countries could dangerously upset the balance. Taiwan's current government is the Democratic Progressive Party (DPP) led by Chen Shuibian, and is known for his pro-inde-

---

[12] The Chinese ocean navigator Admiral Zheng He (also known as Cheng Ho, 1371–1435) is not well known in the West, but he sailed a fleet of ships from China throughout the Asia Pacific to Africa and back in several expeditions in a fleet of ships far larger in number and size than those of Christopher Columbus. What is more remarkable is that he did this up to 87 years earlier than Columbus's journey to the Americas.

pendence stance. In August 2002, Chen showed his true colours by calling for a referendum on Taiwan independence and shocked everyone in China, Taiwan and the US. In Taiwan, after his statement, the stock market plummeted and his personal approval ratings dropped to an all-time low. According to some political analysts, Chen's strategy of calling for a referendum was more a move to bolster his sagging position within his own party. Since 1949, all three parties have understood the sensitivities involved and the fact that, at the very least, maintaining the status quo was in everyone's best interest. Political experts like Willy Lam of CNN believes that, in spite of Chen's remarks, the Taiwan issue will not be a flashpoint for the foreseeable future.

The one catalyst that hopefully could point to a peaceful resolution is the growing prosperity and economic benefit of all those involved. Taiwan is becoming more closely integrated with the Mainland than ever before. 2–3% of Taiwan's total population now live in and around the city of Shanghai with a potentially greater number in neighbouring Fujian province. Investment and cross-strait links continue to grow. Provided that politicians do not upset the peaceful balance which exists today, mutual economic prosperity can flourish, which will naturally lead to even closer integration. By maintaining peace, over time, economic dynamics will act as the catalyst to a peaceful resolution. Interestingly, the one leader that both the Mainland and Taiwan acknowledge as the "Father of Modern China" is Dr Sun Yat-sen, who declared China a Republic after 4,000 years of dynastic rule. A huge portrait of Dr Sun is often displayed in Tiananmen Square at the opposite end from where the famous portrait of Mao permanently resides, the two great leaders facing each other.

Changes in Leadership

As of 2002, more than half of the members in China's Politburo, including the Standing Committee, have been replaced. The biggest question the Western press has been asking from these changes in leadership is what kind of leadership will China's new President Hu Jintao (pronounced "Who Gin Taow" in Mandarin), Jiang Zemin's handpicked successor, bring to China. The answer is that it is too early to tell, since the country's influence is and will continue to be under Jiang for some time to come. Although Jiang has stepped down from the Presidency, as outlined by the Chinese Constitution, he still retains his important seat as Chairman of the CMC – a post formerly held by Deng. Do not expect Jiang to slip into the twilight. Deng was not at the height of his powers until he "officially" retired in the early 90s. Like Deng and other senior retired party elders during the 80s and 90s, the current leadership that is stepping down can be expected to continue, "pulling the strings" for some time to come. Much remains to be seen as to what kind of leadership Hu will bring to China, but it will likely be years, as was the case with Jiang, before any "personal stamp or vision" can be readily recognised. The key point for investors to keep in mind is that the political situation will continue to remain stable for the foreseeable future.

Sino-US Relations

Of all the foreign relations China maintains, clearly the most important and at times most turbulent is with the US. Singaporean Prime Minister Goh Chok Tong summed it up best by saying, "... the US-China relationship will be the defining factor in global economics and politics in the coming decades."[15] When Sino-US relations are good, American companies can benefit; when relations are poor, European and Japanese investors can hope to gain – just look at the billion-dollar deals negotiated between Boeing and Airbus. Overall though, healthy Sino-US relations are good for the world economy. Constructive relationships are built through better understanding achieved by close high-level talks. When President Clinton first took office in 1992, relations with China were poor. However, during Clinton's second term, high-level exchanges were conducted, relations improved, trade blossomed, and the historic WTO agreement was eventually struck between the US and China. In spite of the sale of arms to Taiwan and the clash over the US spy plane incident over Hainan Island, the encouraging sign with the Bush administration since taking office is that Bush has already been to China twice and high-level state visits by both sides continue as a welcome sign that

---

[15] Singapore Prime Minister Goh Chok Tong's National Day address at the National University of Singapore, 19 August 2001. See Web link for the full speech: http://www.gov.sg/singov/announce/NDR.htm

better understanding will lead to better relations. For those in the US who criticise China for its human rights abuses and repression of political dissidents, my hope is that they come to China to see firsthand the changes taking place. Only through a closer exchange and understanding will trade flourish. Differences will continue, but the fact is that the US needs China and China needs the US. No one will benefit from an adversarial relationship (with the exception of the DPP).

The Role of Political Dissidents

Contrary to what some of the Western press and politicians may have the public believe, political dissidents play a very small role in China's society. There is no question that China has its fair share of challenges and its method of handling them may not be agreeable to all – especially when all means 1.3 billion. But Chinese dissidents should know, being Chinese, that direct confrontation rarely works in China – not in business and certainly not in politics. Because I don't know them personally, I cannot dispute the personal grievances certain Chinese dissidents may have against their government, but what I am more concerned about is the effects their claims or demands may have on the overall society. For example, trying to impose full Western-style democracy on China today would be the same as trying to impose an immediate ban on all guns in the US. Good for the country and society as a whole in theory, but problems arising from the fear of the consequences would make implementation difficult if not impossible – chaos would ensue. Demands and threats by foreign politicians trying to impose their ideas that may work in their own country but untested in China will fail, since the Chinese are acutely sensitive about being pushed around by foreigners.

Rising Nationalism

The US spy plane incident over Hainan Island in 2001 highlights the growing tide of nationalism in China. When the news of the incident first broke, Chinese leaders kept the issue from reaching the front pages of Chinese newspapers, trying to avoid the mass outcry against America that took place after the NATO bombing of the Chinese Embassy in 1999. Eventually the issue did take centrestage and the leaders had to acknowledge the fact that ordinary Chinese citizens were enraged. Internet chat lines spoke of war with America and the harbingers of doom raised the spectre of Chinese nationalism becoming akin to the dangerous fuel the Nazis used to come to power. Adding to this fuel in the 90s, some local Chinese wrote a

China Streetsmart

book that translated as "China Can Say No" which was a pro-nation-alistic stance of China standing up to Western powers, especially the US (modelled after a Japanese book with similar anti-American sentiment). Nationalism can have positive benefits in rallying a country, such as that experienced in the US after the September 11 terrorist attacks on the Pentagon and World Trade Centers, but xeno-phobic nationalism (used by the Nazis) is dangerous in any society. The best way to avoid xenophobic nationalism from arising in China is through closer interaction with the West. The West has many benefits to share with China and only through open constructive engagement will Chinese citizens learn that the West aims to work with, not subjugate, China. This is the main reason why a policy of containment and isolating China, advocated by some politicians, is dangerous and will have the opposite effect intended.

Controlling Pollution

China's environment continues to suffer at the expense of economic development. Already China has seven of the top ten most polluted cities in the world.[14] Measures to combat pollution are under way, but since China's energy demands still remain 70–80% reliant on thermal (coal burning) energy, it will be some time before this problem shows signs of improvement. The government realises that fighting pollution is an increasing priority and has begun measures to combat this, but clearly could use help. This need could represent an opportunity for Western environmental companies with advanced methods of fighting pollution. China has pledged to hold a "green" Olympics and has invited bids from leading international environmental organisations to help resolve its problem – one of which is the heavy amount of coal dust in the air causing respiratory problems.

Reforming China's Deteriorating Healthcare System

Pollution causing respiratory problems in Beijing and around China, for example, coupled with its aging population, will increase the

---

[14] World Health Organisation, 1998 report.

strain on the healthcare system. The World Bank estimates almost 300,000 deaths could be avoided if air pollution levels were reduced to meet existing Chinese legal standards.[15] Cigarette advertising has been banned since 1996, but the government needs to do more in the area of healthcare as poorly funded government-run hospitals continue to deteriorate. One possible answer is the role privatised healthcare may play in China's future. Tests in privatising hospitals are now under way. In one instance, I heard of a new five-star service maternity hospital being set up to cater to China's growing elite. The logic is that since most Chinese families can have only one child, they plan on making that experience the best possible and those who can afford the best will pay. However, for the millions of those who cannot pay these exorbitant premiums, the government will continue to need assistance and those companies experienced with providing low-cost private healthcare may find opportunities in China. Medical insurance was once all paid for by government work units; now the costs are shared, and private medical insurance schemes are now available for purchase.

Curbing Separatists

The recent war in Afghanistan has stirred up some of the Xinjiang Muslim separatist groups, some of which have been linked to the Taliban and Al Qaeda. The negative scenario is that these separatist groups will grow in strength, leading to increased bombings and civil unrest. This in turn will lead to the government clamping down hard on them, further suppressing individual rights and freedom. A tough response has always been China's answer to any group that threatens its sovereignty and national security and is similar to what the FBI did in the US after the September 11 terrorist attacks. As history has shown, economic prosperity is one factor that can quell unrest and the "Go West" development campaign the central government is promoting is intended to achieve just that (see Figure 28.4).

---

[15] Supachai Panitchpakdi and Mark L. Clifford, 2002, *China and the WTO*, pp. 26–27, Singapore: John Wiley & Sons.

☐ Western China

Figure 28.4   China's Western Region

In September 1999, the government announced its "Go West" or Western Development Strategy (WDS). In March 2000, the Western Regional Development Office (WRDO) under the State Development Planning Commission was formally set up to coordinate large infrastructure projects and attract foreign investment through proven incentives that are being phased out in the coastal regions. The development of the western provinces is aimed at promoting social stability and is a key pillar of China's Tenth Five-Year Plan (2001–2005). Investors looking for attractive investment incentives will find them in the western regions, but careful study should be conducted, as Action Step 3 (Be Patient and Thorough) dictates, to ensure all the critical needs are met, such as transportation links and a good supply of qualified labour. Government projects to improve these needs are currently under way.

29 | China's Long-Term Silver Linings

Encouraging Trends and Endless Opportunities

Within these emerging positive and negative trends are endless opportunities awaiting the investor.

What many of China's critics and harbingers of doom rarely acknowledge are the encouraging trends in China. Simultaneously growing positive and negative trends are what make the China market so dynamic. As noted earlier, whether one treats an issue as a serious problem or an opportunity depends on

wei ji = Crisis

Opportunity = ji hui

one's view. In Chinese the word for crisis is *weiji* (pronounced "way-jee" in Mandarin) and the word for opportunity is *jihui* (pronounced "jee-hway" in Mandarin); the character *ji* (pronounced "jee" in Mandarin) in both words is the same, which is why the Chinese believe that where there is a crisis there are also opportunities. As discussed in the previous chapter, within the dangers there may also be opportunities, such as the role international environmental and healthcare experts may play in helping China tackle its serious issues in these two fields. **Effective Streetsmart investors are often cautious optimists.** Cautious suggesting the need to understand the risks and challenges one faces, but also optimistic suggesting that within each crisis and emerging trend are distinct opportunities to be capitalised on. Listed below are but a few of the more positive trends in China the Streetsmart investor should consider before deciding how to plan his or her long-term China strategy.

China, Inc. – The Growing Role of Private Enterprises

Economic liberalisation can be clearly seen in the steady increase in privatisation, growing from 5% of total gross domestic product back in 1990 to now, over 30% as of 2001. Official statistics, considered conservative by many estimates, count more than 1.7 million private enterprises with an investment of 132 billion USD employing 27 million people.[1] What's more impressive is to see this growth in the face of obstacles many of these private businessmen have had to overcome. The lack of capital availability, for example, is a big obstacle for private Chinese businesspeople. Even though their ability and track record of paying back loans are often far higher than state-owned enterprises (SOEs), many of the banks have no choice but to take their limited funds and lend it to SOEs as directed by the government to keep the SOEs afloat and people employed. To mitigate this obstacle, China has now created special policy lending institutions to alleviate the burden on China's commercial banks, but capital still remains tight for most private Chinese enterprises. While the government acknowledges the benefits of privatisation as a cornerstone in their strategy to create new employment as a result of China's entry into the World Trade Organisation (WTO), the lack of funding creates an enormous opportunity for foreign private equity funds to find the many promising Chinese companies in search of needed capital to bring them to the next stage of development. Given the enormous upside growth potential, venture capitalists could find more riches in China's private sector than the dot-com boom ever offered. Already, I am starting to see and consult for foreign companies setting up funds for this specific need. Prior to the availability of these private international funds, the luckier private Chinese companies could only raise funds through a public listing, but there are thousands of companies not quite at this stage still waiting for the influx of capital to bring it to the next level.

Civilian Rule and Control

Central to maintaining a good investment climate is the ability of a civilian-led government to control its military. Since the era of Jiang

---

[1] Amcham China brief, "China's Awakening Private Sector", June 2002, p. 11.

Zemin's leadership, several key reforms point to the fact that the civilian government is more in control of the military than ever before. In 1995, the government released a Defence White Paper called "China's Arms Control and Disarmament", the first of its kind in China, followed up five years later with another White Paper called "China's National Defence in 2000".[2] International critics applauded these papers and international peace groups urged other countries to do the same, for example, to state publicly under what conditions they would use nuclear weapons. Not all countries, including the US, have complied.

Perhaps the biggest test of civilian control over the military came in July 1998, when Jiang Zemin ordered the military out of its involvement in commercial enterprises. Over the years, the military had built up a sizable commercial business generating revenue estimated at 25 billion involving 15,000 enterprises ranging from hotels and bars to telecom companies.[3] Stories of corruption, illegal smuggling and shady accounting practices among People's Liberation Army (PLA) officers were rife. Certain PLA officers, including potentially high-ranking officers, were benefiting from these enterprises, but for the PLA to adhere to these civilian orders and willingly stop and divest itself from these lucrative ventures is an extremely encouraging sign of professionalism.

The PLA continues to undergo reform to create a more professional force. Since the opening of China's doors in 1979, it has reduced its personnel by half to about 1.5 million (still the world's largest army) and allowed its procurement and development of weaponry to come under civilian control through the State Commission on Science and Technology for National Defence (COSTIND).[4]

Commercial Ease and Transparency

China has now had more than two decades of Western influence and its commercial laws continue to improve on its efficiency and

---

[2] You can view the report online by following the Web link: http://www.chinadaily.com.cn/cndydb/2000/10/d1-6re~1.a17.html

[3] The Economist Intelligence Unit, July 2000, "Chapter 1: Politics, Economy, and Basic Data", *China Hand*, p. 16.

[4] Ibid.

transparency. Just ten years ago you had to wait months and be a "China expert" with extensive contacts in the government to set up a simple representative office, but today, the process is far quicker and simpler. Businesses can be set up in a matter of weeks and the range of different investment options, such as a wholly owned foreign enterprise (WOFE), will only expand as the full implementation of WTO comes into effect. Companies will soon be able to import goods at lowered tariffs and set up their own marketing, sales and distribution arms without having to invest in physical "brick-and-mortar" factories, as they were regulated in the past. Lawsuits of foreign enterprises against local companies are no longer as one-sided as they used to be. In the brewing industry we were successful in working with the local Administration for Industry and Commerce (AIC) officials who closed down distributors, padlocked their warehouses and confiscated their goods if they were grossly delinquent in their payments or caught selling counterfeit goods. As noted earlier, the degree of commercial ease and business transparency varies across China, so do not misunderstand that this positive situation is happening everywhere. Establishing close relations with local government officials will continue to be a *China Streetsmart* practice, but in major centres like Shanghai the degree one needs to "get cozy" with local officials diminishes. As a result, early reports indicate that major centres like Shanghai, especially Pudong, which do largely follow international practices, are getting the majority of foreign investment.

Developing Talent

During the 50s and 60s, people like my Beijing in-laws were encouraged to study Russian. However today, China realises its future in successfully capturing the benefits of WTO will rely on its ability to communicate in English. Unprecedented waves of people from businesspeople and politicians (including Jiang Zemin) to Chinese children, beginning as early as 3–4 years old, have begun taking English lessons. This new S-generation of China, i.e., children of the one-child policy, increases the pressure on that single child to obtain every competitive advantage possible to succeed. Children remain the traditional insurance policy parents seek when they grow old; as a result, it is not uncommon for many local Chinese parents and grandparents to spend a large portion of their salary (50% or more) and savings on extra courses for their children. Supplementary schooling and private training courses are in full bloom. Weekend and night classes are filled with hopeful students and employees wanting to improve their English and computer skills, for example.

Scenes like this gentleman diligently studying the latest computer manual are common all across China. Even those who work for state-run enterprises understand knowledge and training are the keys to the future. While many may feel the opportunities for retraining are too late for themselves, they are determined that their children do not share the same fate. As a result, parents are willing to spend whatever it takes to give their children every competitive advantage they can possibly afford.

Photograph by John L. Chan

Grace Cheng, the Managing Director for Korn Ferry's Beijing office, strongly believes that returnees will be the driving force that will lead China into the future. More Chinese students than ever are now studying and working abroad and even those who left after the Tiananmen incident are now coming back to China because they perceive greater opportunities here, and I agree with these perceptions. Larry Wang, another well-known executive in China's executive search industry and regular commentator in the Chinese media on developing China's human capital, has written several books regarding this phenomena. His most recent book called *Know the Game Play the Game* is a guide for local Chinese staff on how to work with foreign multinational firms. This increasing breadth of talent will only increase and continue to improve on China's opening up and understanding of Western business practices.

Stable Currency

The Asian financial crisis showed Chinese leaders, bankers and economists the dangers of opening up their currency to international speculators. A key factor triggering the crisis was the ability for short-term monies to flow out of the country; however, in China,

China Streetsmart

the State Administration of Foreign Exchange (SAFE) strictly controls the money flow making any attacks by speculators very difficult. China's currency remains basically pegged to the US dollar, allowing it to trade within a very narrow controlled range each day (see Table C.12 in Appendix C). For years, economists and journalists have been speculating whether the Chinese yuan or *renminbi* (RMB) (pronounced "ren-men-bee" in Mandarin, meaning "people's money") was going to float freely or remain managed (roughly pegged) in relation to the US dollar. Camps began to emerge speculating whether the RMB was going to appreciate because of confidence in a strong Chinese economy, inflow of international risk capital to China after September 11, and strong foreign currency reserves, or depreciate because of negative impacts due to falling exports and regional currency pressures. Experts believe that over the next few years, the currency trading band will expand, but following its key policy of maintaining stability, the government will not allow the Chinese currency to become "freely convertible". The economy has grown strongly using the pegged system and with current low rates in the US dollar, exports have not been adversely affected.

Stanford's International Economics Professor Ronald McKinnon, who has written extensively on Asian foreign exchange policies and the Asian financial crisis, supports Dai Xianglong, the Governor of the People's Bank of China's policy of continuing to maintain a managed peg. Using Japan's historical development as an example, he says that a stable exchange rate preserves confidence in the currency as the economy becomes more open and can act as a natural anchor for domestic monetary policy in a high-growth economy whose long-term capital market is not yet well developed. The Japanese yen remained fixed to the US dollar from 1949 to 1971 and the confidence in the stable exchange helped facilitate economic growth of 6–12% per year, unlike what China is experiencing today.[5] China's foreign currency reserves are over 286 billion USD, making it the world's second largest, next to Japan. Such strong reserves and diversification into euros, as well as yen, should keep the Chinese

---

[5] Ronald McKinnon, "China's Financial Policies upon Accession to the WTO", *Perspectives*, Vol. 2, No.1. Web link: http://www.oycf.org/Perspectives/7_083100/China_rm.htm

currency stable, free from economic volatility for some time. This stability is a good sign for investors who want to avoid the situation of having their investments being negatively affected by wide uncontrollable swings, as happened with Korea and the other Southeast Asian economies in the late 90s.

Technological Leapfrogging and Adoption

While I was a director at Asia Online, my main focus was on Greater China and I got to work firsthand with the leading technological companies that were taking advantage of the impressive growth in China. Mike Hall, Director at International Data Corp. (IDC), another long-time China hand and one of the few Western expats who speaks fluent Shanghainese, predicts that China's spending on information technology (IT) will lead the region in growth and Chinese leaders will continue to keep technology at the forefront of their drive for modernisation. Almost all technology investments fall under the "encouraged" category of foreign investment with favourable incentives to attract foreign companies to invest. A key advantage China has over developed Western countries is that it can adopt new technology faster without having to worry about what to do with old outdated proprietary-based (legacy) systems such as in the telecommunications sector.

The adoption and implementation of fibre optics is a good example. In the West, including developed centres like Hong Kong, fibre-optic cabling is being laid throughout the streets, connecting buildings. The implication of installing fibre-optic cabling is significant. Ethernet technologies, which rely on fibre-optic cabling, known as Cat 5, can achieve speeds 50–100 times faster than current digital subscriber line (DSL) technologies using the current copper phone lines. The real problem is the high cost of broad wiring existing buildings (i.e., each room) with the fibre-optic Cat 5 cables because walls need to be opened and new holes drilled, but since most of China's building are new and just being built, they are able to start broad wiring the buildings at the beginning and the cost is no more than the cost of putting in electrical wiring.

Beijing's Zhongguancun district, symbolised by the golden double helix, and home to the Chinese Academy of Sciences, responsible for everything from developing China's nuclear energy to founding the Chinese computer giant Legend Computers, aims to be the centre for China's high-tech industry. Surrounding the double helix is massive construction as new high-tech centres are being constructed.

Jerry Hamilton, Vice President of Mindspeed (Asia Pacific), a subsidiary of Conexant (a Rockwell spin-off) which focuses on supplying "semi-conductor solutions" for China's telecommunications and Internet infrastructure, informs me that by 2005, China's telecommunications services revenue will grow to an estimated 120 billion USD and the IT industry will account for another 110 billion as targeted in China's Tenth Five-Year Plan. This target appears to be well on its way to being achieved. As of 2001, China's exports of electronics and IT products have already surpassed 65 billion USD. China has the largest number of fixed-line and mobile users in the world, over 400 million split roughly 50/50 between fixed line and mobile.[6] As a result, perhaps the most exciting area of China's technological development will be in cutting-edge wireless technologies with the rollout of the general packet radio system (GPRS) and the impending arrival of 3G. The personal computer (PC) and Internet sectors are booming as well. According to the China Internet Network Information Centre, as of 2002, China's Internet population is 59.1 million, having grown 75% over the previous year, and has been rated the second most active Web audience in the world. Christian Morales, the Vice President for Intel (Asia Pacific) said that

---

[6] North Asia News, Bloomberg, 11 December 2002, "China Aims for 500 Mln Phone Users by 2005, Wu Says (Update1)", http://quote.bloomberg.com/fgcgi?ptitle=North%20Asia%20News&tp=nornew&T=as_storypage

in 2002 China had overtaken Japan in the PC market (1–2 years ahead of original estimates).[7]

Like a proud father, Jerry Hamilton, Vice President of Mindspeed (Asia Pacific) insisted that I take a picture with his staff. He gives his staff the respect they deserve and in return, all of his staff have been loyal and have been with him since he first set up Mindspeed, a division of Conexant (a Rockwell spin-off) in China back in 1997. From left to right: Jean Wu, John Wei, Rui Wang, Lily Wang, Jerry Hamilton, Andy Lai and Wei Jiang.

Improving Customer Service

Customer service has long been a problem in China and quite frankly still is. But I am happy to report the trend is definitely improving. China's up-and-coming generations will not have the same state-owned "do only as much as you have to" mentality and they are beginning to know that customer service is key to making the sale.

---

[7] *China Daily*, 1 August 2002. "China Becomes World's No. 2 Market for Web and PCs". Web link: http://www1.chinadaily.com.cn/news/2002-08-01/80333.html Also note that of the 45.8 million Internet users, the split between men and women is roughly 60/40; 16 million computers had access to the Web; and people aged between 18 and 24 make up 37.2% of China's Internet users, while those between 25 and 30 account for 16.9%. The 31 to 35 age group accounts for 11.6%. More than 40% of China Web users were concentrated in three cities: Beijing, Guangzhou and Shanghai. Web link: http://www1.chinadaily.com.cn/news/2002-07-23/78950.html

China Streetsmart

Increasing competitiveness dictates that customer service will only improve. Given the cheapness of labour, delivery and installation are often free of charge. "800" service toll-free phone numbers and national help desks are being set up at impressive speeds. Companies like Aquarius have sophisticated call centres where if I call in the morning I can get my water delivered to my home or office within several hours. Many call centre help desks, such as those used by telecommunications companies, now quote operator help codes to identify who you were talking to so you can call back with a complaint if you are unhappy with their service. I was quite frankly shocked when I had my kitchen exhaust fan installed by a joint-venture company called Vantage based in Guangdong, where the fan cost no more than 250 RMB or around 30 USD. Two weeks after installation, I received an unsolicited phone call from their company thanking me for buying their product and asking me if I was happy with the installation service I received. Just a few years ago this was highly unlikely and a decade ago this would have been considered pure fantasy. Admittedly, I am less familiar with the other areas of China compared to Shanghai, and my suspicion is that they are still far behind in terms of customer service. But, if Shanghai is the trend leader, China's future looks very promising.

Chinese Travellers Spreading the Wealth Globally

Hundreds of millions of nouveau riché Chinese will have a great positive impact on the world (see Figure 29.1). For example, as the travel restrictions on Mainland Chinese are freed up, this newfound wealth will be shared around the globe. More and more countries, like Australia, are beginning to sign arrangements with China, making their country the new destination of choice for these new travellers eager to see the rest of the world. In 1990 when Chinese tourists were first allowed to go abroad, they made 9 million trips. By 2020, China is estimated to be the fourth largest source of international travellers with 85–100 million annual trips. In Malaysia 2001, for example, Chinese tourists spent 500 million USD. As of 2002, there were 22 countries that had received Approved Destination Status from the Chinese government.[8] My own anecdotal evidence sup-

---

[8] Xinhua News Agency, 10 July 2002.

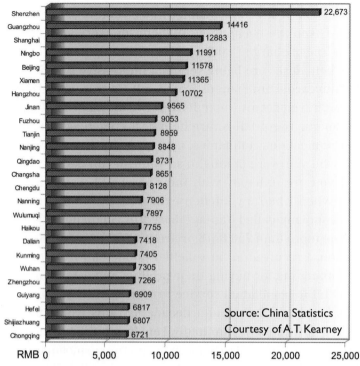

| RMB | 0 | 5,000 | 10,000 | 15,000 | 20,000 | 25,000 |

The annual disposable income in China remains relatively low compared to Western economies. However, the key to measuring the economic power of its consumers is to use the purchasing power parity (PPP) methodology. The PPP focuses on the relative buying power of consumers in each country to negate the impact of differing currencies. For example, although the wages are lower in China, the cost of living is also lower. A beer in China, for example, costs only about $0.30 USD and a Big Mac costs only $1.20 USD. Using this PPP method of measuring the economy, China's economy is approximately four times larger.

Figure 29.1   China's Top 25 Cities, 2001: Per Capita Annual Disposable Income

ports this. When my wife and I spent our honeymoon in Paris back in 1998, we were walking around the musée du Louvre and throughout the quiet halls of the museum, I could hear the chattering away of Mandarin being spoke by dozens of Mainland Chinese – all tourists, all travelling abroad for their first time.

Crises and (Endless) Opportunities

Within these emerging trends lie an endless number of opportunities that the *China Streetsmart* investor can capitalise on. Those who can think out of the box will be the real winners in China's growth. For

China Streetsmart

example, it is well known that the foreign brewing industry in China is in crisis. Production capacity is many times over demand, prices remain depressed, and the overcapacity problem is not expected to alleviate itself for at least five years or longer. Foreign brewers who invested hundreds of millions of US dollars in state-of-the-art brewing and packaging equipment now have many of their equipment lines sitting idle. The opportunity could be for another beverage manufacturer to contract a deal with one of these under-utilised breweries to utilise their state-of-the-art packaging and bottling equipment and their ready-made distribution experience across China. Breweries would be glad to toll brew or pack and distribute a third party's product by setting up a new joint business venture that would help them better utilise their assets and share in the costs. In one case, a famous wine and spirits company has already started to package some of its mixed-drinks lines with one of these well-known foreign brewers.

Many other companies and industries are suffering the same fate of overcapacity as the breweries. Television manufacturers, for example, have warehouses full of excess television tubes as most families rich enough to afford a television set in China already have at least one set. A television set was the no. 1 big-ticket purchase item for Chinese families throughout the 80s – but not anymore. The opportunities could be for entrepreneurs to figure out different uses for these television tubes, such as in monitoring or surveillance uses for the medical or security industries, for example, and ship these to different parts of the world.

Utilising the huge pools of skilled labour also represents endless possibilities. The Hong Kong and Shanghai Banking Corporation (HSBC) has moved its call centre out of Hong Kong to Guangzhou. Hundreds, if not thousands, of training companies are setting up in China. The government encourages these types of companies to flourish, as a retrained workforce means more people will be employed and new jobs created. Training will be a huge requirement as part of the government's serious efforts to attract investment to the central and western regions of China. While Shanghai may be the safe option for companies new to China, the west, especially in areas like Chengdu, Chongqing and Xian, may attract great government incentives if negotiated properly. Xian, for example, has attracted a large number of software developers who are well

Photograph by John L. Chan

Wanted: English Specialists
What's wrong with this picture? Pointing out spelling errors on public signs like this one at one of China's international airports is not meant to embarrass local officials, rather to illustrate that a language gap still exists which stresses the need for improved English language training. Foreign companies such as the Wall Street Institute for teaching English have set up in China and as you may suspect, business is booming.

trained but willing to work at lower rates than those in Shanghai and Beijing – let alone western countries.

China's radically changing demographics must also be noted. During the 50s and 60s, when Mao said to his people, "Go forth and multiply", women were giving birth to five–six children on average, according to a UN study on demographic trends. My grandmothers on my mother's and mother-in-law's side had 11 and 7 children respectively. Today, the fertility rate is down to around two. What this means for the demographics 10, 20 and 50 years from now will be significant. Currently, China's population is 1.3 billion and over the next 50 years it is expected to peak at around 1.5 billion. The extra 200 million people will grow due to shear population momentum, but as the baby boomers pass their childbearing years and continue to grow older, and the one-child policy holds in effect, China's demographics will be significantly skewed to an aging population (see Table 29.1). While this is the general trend throughout the world, China is especially skewed. By 2050, there will be twice as many people over the age of 50 as there will be infants and teenagers. Given these trends, it's not surprising that according to ACNielsen, eight out of the top ten advertisers in China in 2001 were pharmaceutical companies.

These changing demographics also entail huge social implications for marketers to consider. Children of single-child families known as the S-generation are materially spoilt, having grown up in a time of economic prosperity and rising expectations. The choices available to them are greater than their parents ever had and they constantly seek the latest fads and fashions. As a professional mar-

China Streetsmart

keter based in Shanghai, I was acutely aware of this trend. Companies that offer goods and services aimed at this insatiable appetite for "new things" will be the real benefactors.

Table 29.1   United Nations Population Projections for China[9] (in millions)

Period / Age	1950		1995		2010		2025		2050	
0–4	76.2	14%	103.7	8%	92.7	7%	86.3	6%	78.1	5%
5–19	165.0	30%	319.6	26%	290.4	21%	278.1	19%	245.6	17%
20–49	228.4	41%	594.7	48%	665.0	48%	597.9	40%	529.7	36%
50+	87.1	16%	208.8	17%	332.0	24%	525.8	35%	631.0	43%
Total	**556.7**	100%	**1,226.8**	100%	**1,380.1**	100%	**1,488.1**	100%	**1,484.4**	100%

Photograph by John L. Chan

Western Influences – Tai Chi or Cha Cha? Chinese citizens continue to enjoy habits and lifestyles imported from the West. Twenty years ago these ordinary Chinese citizens would be practising Tai Chi in the park, but the ballroom dancing craze has swept all of China. Furthermore, note that this generation of Chinese pictured here are not the ones to inherit and direct the new China. Go to any disco in China and you will see how the West is influencing the future generations of Chinese leaders.

---

[9] United Nations report 1998. Web link: http://www.iiasa.ac.at/Research/LUC/ChinaFood/data/pop/pop_7.htm

30 | Conclusion

Tying all the information together for the China Streetsmart *investor.*

I was giving a presentation at a national China Logistics Conference when Guy Chambers, General Manager of Customer Development with Swire Beverages, China's largest Coca-Cola bottler (and seventh largest in the world), later came back to me with a riddle posed by American playwright and comedian Woody Allen: "What can you sleep on, drive in, and brush your teeth with?" Answer: "A bed. A car. And a toothbrush." Said Guy, "We try and overcomplicate life by looking for a single answer to big questions, whereas we should just give in to the fact that life is full of inconsistencies and we should accept multiple, simple answers. Your speech reminded me of this, because the 'What is the secret to China?' question is just too complex a question to get an intelligent answer to. Common sense, smaller questions – like 'What do we need to do in Meizhou?' (a small town in Guangdong province as an example) – are probably far more practical."

As a result, *China Streetsmart* was written on this basis of practicality. While China can be incredibly complex, the approach to tackling this complex market does not need to be difficult to understand or implement. Sticking to basic business principles and consistently carrying out the six easy-to-remember action steps outlined in Part I can be incredibly effective in setting up and running an effective and profitable business in China. One does not need to be a Confucian expert at practising the art of developing *guanxi* or be fluent in the local language to reach this goal. Many companies, like Portola, have been successful for years in China. In fact, **according to surveys conducted by various Chambers of Commerce and its members, the majority of foreign invested enterprises do make money in China.** Many of these companies are smaller and less visible to the press and media, but they have been making money happily for years in China. "Why should we tell you our secrets?" retorted Erwin Hardy, who is an ex-banker and Chairman of the Austrian Chamber of Commerce based in Hong Kong. Mr Hardy operates several successful business ventures in China. "We've worked hard to achieve what we have so why should we want to share it? I asked my business partner if he would come and speak with you and he respectfully declined." Although his partner declined, Mr Hardy was gracious enough to share with me some of his "secrets" – which sum up the book: "The biggest secret to doing business in China is there is no secret; it's simple common business sense."

However, to be effective at making the right long-term strategic decisions for your business in China does require a deeper understanding of the macro issues. As noted in Chapter 28, the risks and challenges China faces are numerous and **this book has really only scratched the surface of what one really needs to know to fully appreciate the risks, challenges and opportunities. Given the limitation of a single book aimed at such a broad topic like doing business in China, the intent of *China Streetsmart* is to stimulate your thinking and encourage you to go beyond the brief information presented**, to do your own due diligence on each of the important issues that could affect your business. You do not need to be a Chinese political historian or economist to be a smart investor, but the more you know and understand, the better your chances of making the right strategic decisions. Some of the key warning signs to watch out for will be unemployment (even though it can only measure specific urban unemployment figures); retail sales and the consumer price index (CPI) as a measure of consumer confidence; debt to gross domestic product ratio (including those liabilities held by asset management companies) and the government's ability to increase revenue collection and/or reduce spending; trade balance to gauge the effects of the World Trade Organisation and pressure on the local currency; and foreign direct investment (FDI) as a measure of foreign investor confidence.

No one can accurately predict where China will be decades from now, but it is important to understand that we all have the ability to help shape that future. **Constructive engagement is the best way to mould and positively influence what a socialist market economy with Chinese characteristics eventually looks like.** FDI has the positive effect of steering China's development to be more open to the world. I look at people like Michael Colozzi of Portola, Emil Schlumpf of Siemens and Mark DeCocinis of the Ritz-Carlton as just a few examples of model Westerners that can help build a China beneficial to all through constructive engagement. These gentlemen truly love and respect their local staff and their staff returns the same respect in the way of loyalty and productivity. It is not surprising that their businesses are leaders in their class, as their leadership is able to harness the power and capitalise on opportunities that exist in China today. These business leaders are positively influencing China's new generation in what it means to work with the West and be open to Western values and ideas. In time, the Chinese will learn from this interaction to determine which Western practices are most relevant to their needs. At the same time, the West will also be able to learn from China and how to adjust to accommodate this emerging powerhouse.

A robust and healthy Chinese economy is good for the world. Currently, the Japanese and American economies are down, but the Chinese economy remains buoyant, less reliant on exports compared to its Southeast Asian neighbours, and the Chinese government predicts still more healthy growth figures. Foreign companies operating in China like Shanghai Portola Packaging and Siemens Switchgear continue to overflow with orders. Restaurant chains like McDonald's and Kentucky Fried Chicken are expanding their development teams. Wal-Mart just announced they were opening up new superstores throughout China. Whether to expand is the big-

Photograph courtesy of Portman Ritz-Carlton

Mark DeCocinis, General Manager of the Portman Ritz-Carlton, stands proudly with his staff shortly after the Portman Ritz-Carlton won the Best Employer Award in Asia for 2001, the first ever for a China-based company. From front to back are Irene Yang, Barbara Zhuang, Carrie Ni, Kelly Yu, Mark DeCocinis, Michael Lu, Bill Yu and Tony Wang.

China Streetsmart

gest question on the minds of these executives and if they do, the income they generate will be good for the world economy. Foreign executives are listening. In September 2002, A.T. Kearney completed their annual FDI Confidence Index which surveys executives of the world's top 1,000 companies, and China grew in confidence to fin-

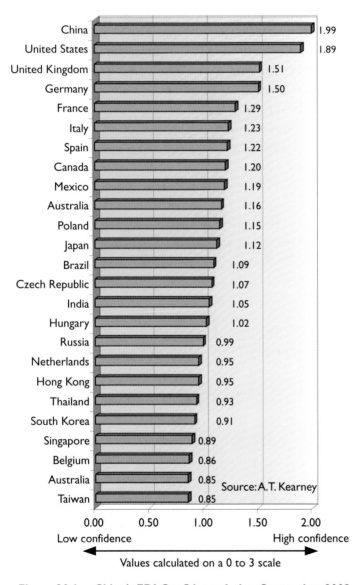

Figure 30.1   China's FDI Confidence Index, September 2002

ish no. 1, surpassing the US for the first time (see Figure 30.1). 2002 marked the highest level of FDI in China and analysts predict the future amounts of FDI to only increase to 100 billion USD within the next five years in spite of the world slowdown. According to the World Bank, by 2020 China's share of world trade will more than triple to 10%. Using the purchasing power parity method of calculating global output, China will be the second largest economy in the world with 8% of the world's total, second only to the US, which is expected to account for 19%.[1] In the future, the hope is that China's newly emerging economy will hopefully act as a spark to keep the global economic engine moving to buttress the slowdown in other markets, which will not only benefit China but the world.

---

[1] Supachai Panitchpakdi and Mark L. Clifford, 2002, *China and the WTO*, pp. 33–34, Singapore: John Wiley & Sons.

Epilogue

At a recent conference I was asked to speak, I asked this one attendee if he had set up operations in China yet, to which he sheepishly replied, "Uh no … I'm a latecomer. I guess I am a bit late." I laughed when I heard him say this and responded, "This is the same as the American pioneer saying he was late in America's development because he wasn't a pilgrim on the Mayflower!" China's economic development is still in its early stages and its entry into the World Trade Organisation marks the first time China will play on an even international playing field. The *China Streetsmart* investor needs to watch these developments closely because as the challenges arise so will the unique opportunities. The key is to begin learning now. Begin asking questions and analyse the information received through the *China Streetsmart* approach. Look into setting up a representative office to begin formal exploration. Seek those knowledgeable executives who can help you plan your strategy and realise your bottom-line objectives. Hopefully, reading *China Streetsmart* will be just the beginning of your exciting and rewarding journey.

Afterword

Just before the book went to print I had a chance to re-visit the people at Shanghai Portola Packaging Co., Ltd. and received an update, which is worth mentioning. The business continues to perform very well. The senior management team has tentatively approved expansion plans pending the closing of several large supply contracts that will allow them to begin expansion as early as April 2003. The expansion will more than physically double their size by absorbing the adjacent lots and triple their production capacity.

Driving this expansion plan are new initiatives Michael and his team have been working on since I last visited the plant. The Advanced Moulding Division, which was just starting to become operational when I last spoke with them, is now in full production and broke even during its second month of operation. Further growth in the new division is being limited by the current physical restrictions of the existing facilities. Since Portola's current capacity is already fully utilised with long-term supplier contracts, the Portola sales force is concentrating their efforts on securing new customers and orders to justify their expansion, i.e., securing future orders so they can continue to run at full capacity once their expansion plans are complete. Michael Colozzi was hesitant about revealing his other new product initiatives, not wanting to alert his competition, but he assures me that if his new global customers agree to his proposals "the sky's the limit", he says with a massive grin.

Not wanting to sit on their laurels, the people at Shanghai Portola continue to find new ways of improving efficiencies, such as implementing a new just-in-time (JIT) supplier arrangement with major suppliers such as Exxon Chemical, that supplies a lot of the high-quality resins used in their products. "There's still plenty to improve on," claims Michael. "Like everything we have been doing since we started, we will prioritise what's most important for the business and go about improving our company one step at a time", echoing

271

the words of another successful business executive in China, Hank Greenberg, Chairman of AIG.

Their employee base will also expand from 50 employees to eventually 120. With this new expansion, two of his existing local directors will be promoted to Deputy General Manager. I jokingly said to Michael who remains firmly at the helm that with all the publicity the book will create, his people will become obvious targets for headhunters. He replied, "Let them call; my guys get a call every week and they aren't going anywhere. They see the way we are growing and as promised they are growing as the company grows. They love it here!"

Spoken like a true *China Streetsmart* executive. What more can I say?

Appendices

The appendices provide supplemental information that the investor may find useful to develop a deeper understanding of China, specifically:

- How to find more information about China and more importantly which of these sources are more relevant to their needs.

- What are some relevant historical facts an investor, not a historian, would need to know to help improve his or her understanding of why the China government and its citizens behave the way they do.

- What are some basic statistical facts and figures investors may want to know about China.

Appendix A

Information Sources on China

The amount of information sources available on China is staggering, but more important is deciding what is relevant. Relevance is determined by using the same *China Streetsmart* filtering process as outlined in Chapter 1. Listed below are just a few of the information sources I would recommend to new investors to begin their understanding.

Start with Your Government – The Free Option

There is a lot of useful free information available on China. Since China is one of the most exciting and dynamic markets to be in, almost every government's trade development section will have useful free information – the key is to make sure that the information is up to date. Information older than three years really should be treated with caution. I took the opportunity to visit different countries' trade consular sections and was impressed with the amount of free information available. What is surprising, though, is the number of companies that come to China and do not bother taking advantage of these free but useful services.

During my visits to these trade consular offices I also took the opportunity to talk with some of the trade counsellors to understand their views and opinions about investing in China. As expected, everyone had a strong opinion (since it is supposed to be their job to know what they are talking about), yet the responses and views were very mixed, which could easily confuse the inexperienced China investor – be forewarned! Some were very experienced trade officials and as a free service, you will probably find no better place to start your understanding of the market. On the other hand, I also encountered a lot of inexperienced government people to China and the advice I received was, for lack of a better word, awful. Many had not spent a lot of time in China and saw China merely as another foreign posting. A former counsellor from the British Embassy in Beijing, for example, later admitted to me that she was often giving advice which she really should not have – given her lack of experience – yet she and her colleagues were all advising British companies on what to do. Many of these government officials seldom have real industry experience working in China. Government officials, even the most capable, often only see a certain side of the business transaction process so it is important to keep in mind the frames of reference and experience or lack of experience they may have, and employ the process of vetting information outlined in Chapter 2 on how to interpret the stories you hear. Nevertheless, the information and advice are free and remain the best value in town.

Online Information

There are countless information sources available online that can help companies learn more about China. Here are just a few of the sites available I used regularly during my research.

URL	Description
http://www.chinabiz.org	This privately run site is one of my favourites since the information is free. You can subscribe to a newsletter which gives you daily updates on news headlines concerning China from publications such as *Bloomberg, International Herald Tribune, China Daily*, etc.
http://www.chinaupdates.com	Another site with news headlines links is run by Professor Wang Pien from the National University of Singapore's Business School. You can also subscribe to her newsletter.
http://www.uschina.org	This is the official site of the US China Business Council and has information such as the China's WTO commitments as outlined in the US-China WTO Agreement. Also, you can look for past articles of their publication, the *US China Business Review*.

URL	Description
http://www.stats.gov.cn/english/	The China Statistical Information Network is run by the National Bureau of Statistics. If you need to look up basic information such as demographic statistics, you will find the information here.
http://english.people.com.cn	*The People's Daily* is China's national newspaper. This English edition is available online and you can find information, including the English version of the constitution of the People's Republic of China and profiles of all the top leaders in China.
http://www1.chinadaily.com.cn/	*The China Daily* is China's official English newspaper and has an excellent business section that keeps up on all the latest corporate news in China.

These are just a few of the sites that are readily available. China Online (www.chinaonline.com) is another useful site that has a lot of information and newspaper headline links, but it is a prepaid subscription-based site. I have not used it, but know others who have. A lot of the information in China Online is available free from other sources if you are willing to take the time to find it. The Google search engine (www.google.com) is a good place to start.

Local Business Forums and Groups

For a small fee, there are many very useful organisations available, which can really help you understand the market. By joining these organisations, you will be able to network with other business people who have real *China Streetsmart* experience. For example, joining some of the local chambers of commerce is an excellent way to start. The American Chamber of Commerce (Amcham) in Shanghai, for example, costs as little as 500 USD per year and gives you access to their members' directory listing companies by name, industry and individual members. Amcham regularly hosts special events and periodically invites guest speakers on a host of topics.

The Economist Conferences is another excellent organisation to join and is highly recommended as one of your primary sources for basic reliable information. The group holds monthly business

Long-time China hand Lois Dougan-Tretiak chairs a business forum run by the Economist Corporate Networks, flanked by then Mayor of Shanghai, Mr Xu Kuangdi.

group forums in Beijing, Shanghai and Hong Kong to discuss relevant business issues that could affect your business, and special annual forums like the Government Round Table where leaders of the Chinese government are invited to speak with the foreign business community. Having attended these business group forums myself over the past four years, I can attest firsthand that they are not only valuable sources of information, but also an excellent networking opportunity to learn more from others about how they are coping with real life issues they face in China today. The group's business forums are headed up by Lois Dougan-Tretiak, Vice President of the Economist Conferences and the Chief Representative for the Economist Group in China. Lois is a very *China Streetsmart* person with 25 years living and working in Hong Kong and China. She first visited China in January 1972, a month before Nixon. A wealth of information, she can bring a great perspective to your business if you have a chance to talk with her – and she will always make herself available for a chat. The Economist Group's Economist Intelligence Unit (EIU), publishes three very China-specific reports that I would highly recommend: *Business China*, an informative newsletter published every two weeks on some of China's most current issues; *Country Reports and Forecast*, which are updated quarterly; and the *China Hand*, a large three-volume comprehensive refer-

China Streetsmart

The Economist Corporate Networks' breakfast briefings can attract well over a hundred corporate attendees from some of the largest and most prominent companies operating in China. This photo is of a conference covering the important topic "How to Develop China's Human Capital" held at the Grand Hyatt in Shanghai.

ence work that is updated monthly and is a must for any executive who wants to keep informed of changing business rules and practices in China.

If you are an American company, you definitely should join the US China Business Council (USCBC), which is the principal organization of US corporations engaged in business relations with China. It is a private, non-profit, member-supported entity headquartered in Washington, DC with two offices in China (Canada and the UK, for example, also have their own equivalents). Unlike Amcham, your company (not necessarily yourself) must have a legal presence in the US to be a USCBC member. The USCBC also produces a bi-monthly publication called the *US China Business Review* and the magazine is available to anyone. Each issue features a major theme or current industry topic, such as telecommunications, agriculture, banking and insurance.

Unlike most other chambers and councils, USCBC offers real-time business advisory and advocacy services to its members and essentially functions as consultants to its members, which include many of America's best-known firms as well as small- to medium-sized enterprises (SMEs). Like the EIU's *Business China*, the writers for the *US China Business Review* are often directly involved with China businesses and represent some of the best-known companies in China today. Many of the people I interviewed for this book were once contributors to both these publications. I spoke with Patrick Powers, the local Director for the USCBC based in Beijing and told him that my biggest criticism of his publication was the fact that more companies did not know of the good work they did.

Each nationality, such as the German, Canadian and Dutch for example, has its own relevant and useful business groups, especially if you are interested in issues pertinent to each country, such as when a head of state or other trade missions arrive. However, the American organisations remain one of the best-funded and well-run business organisations in China. Many of the non-American Westerners chose, or only chose, to be members of the American Chamber as it often does have the best programmes, and to quote one Canadian government official, "It's good value."

Appendix B

A Historical *China Streetsmart* Primer

For a people to be without history, or to be ignorant of its history, is as for a man to be without memory – condemned forever to make the same discoveries that have been made in the past, invent the same techniques, wrestle with the same problems, commit the same errors; and condemned, too, to forfeit the rich pleasures of recollection.

Henry Steele Commager (1902–1998), US historian,
The Study of History.[1]

A joke I learned early on about China was: "Question: What's the best thing about China? Answer: 5,000 years of history. Question: What's the worst thing about China? Answer: 5,000 years of history." No question, China has one of the, or arguably the, richest civilised history on the planet. Chances are, if you do not mention China's 5,000 years of history while doing business in China your Chinese counterpart certainly will. An understanding of the relevant historical points that impact China will definitely help the *China Streetsmart* executive.

Advantages of Understanding Chinese History

In marketing and advertising, a good knowledge of history and historical figures can be very useful. Tiger Beer in 2000 launched a popular beer campaign in China called "Where's the Tiger?" (*Laohu zai nar li?*) after the legendary story of Wu Song who hunted this mythical Tiger during the Song Dynasty more than 1,000 years ago. Everyone in China knows the tale, and the campaign captured the

---

[1] *Encarta Book of Quotations* © 1999, 2000, Microsoft Corp. All rights reserved. Developed for Microsoft by Bloomsbury Publishing Plc.

imagination of the Chinese public. Phil Davis, the Managing Director for Anheuser-Busch for Asia, is a historian by training. Although he cannot speak the language, he is often able to break the ice and win the confidence of distributors by pointing out that their surnames are the same as this Emperor or that Emperor, which always impresses the distributors.

This Shanghai bus ad simply reads, "The Tiger is here!" Asia Pacific Breweries, brewers of the award-winning Tiger Beer, created this campaign after the mythical hero Wu Song who battles a tiger. This historical story has been told throughout China over the past thousand years, similar in the West to the biblical story of Samson and the Lion.

China Streetsmart is not a History Book

There are many great China historians from the West: John King Fairbank (Harvard); Jonathan Spence (Yale); Kenneth Leiberthal (Michigan); Lucien Pye (MIT); etc., which I would encourage you to read if you have a real interest in China. However, to make the point that you do not have to be a China historian, I chose to source a lot of the information which is presented here not from these excellent historians, rather from Microsoft's *Encarta*, to illustrate that these historical facts are readily available to anyone. There are at least 17 dynasties in China, each lasting several hundred years (some overlapping), but I won't mention any of them except the last one – the Qing Dynasty, since the others are not critically relevant to the objective of understanding the modern Chinese psyche and actions of its citizens and government influencing China's outlook.

The Qing Dynasty (1644–1911) – China's Last Imperial Dynasty[2]

The most relevant part of China's 5,000 years of history the *China Streetsmart* executive needs to know is focused on the past 200 years

---

[2] Microsoft Encarta 2001, Microsoft Corp.

– since the end of the 18th century. Chinese history, like the history of any other civilisation, has had its ups and downs. A late adopter of modern economic and military advances brought to the West during the Industrial Revolution caused the later part of the Qing Dynasty (1800–1911) to be weak and on the decline. However, prior to this period (1644–1800), China's territorial influence was at its highest point, with territory ranging from Tibet in the southwest to parts of Kyrgyzstan, Kazakhstan, all of Mongolia in the northwest, and the Korean Peninsula going into parts of modern day Eastern Russia in the northeast (see Figure B.1). Interestingly, if you look at a map of China in some Taiwan textbooks, you will see that the Guomindang or Nationalist Party of Taiwan, which technically ruled China from 1912 to 1949, still recognises Mongolia as belonging to China.

The Qing Dynasty was ruled by the Manchus, a group originating from northeast China in former Manchuria. Hence their language is where the term Mandarin derives from. In China, they do not call Mandarin, Mandarin (*manzhou hua*), rather simply *guoyu* (national language) or *putonghua* (common language). The

Figure B.1   Qing Dynasty, 1644–1911

Manchus were the first rulers to experience the dynamics of foreign trade on a truly international scale, since early trading partners from the Silk Road era were basically from the Middle East. International trade now included Britain, France and the US. Prior to this period, China was always self-sufficient and not that interested in trading with the West, but grudgingly opened up Guangzhou (or Canton) at the end of the 18th century. Britain's desire for China's tea and other goods created a trade imbalance with China. The one product the British found they could trade successfully in China was opium being grown in British-controlled India. The Chinese government, however, was against the burgeoning opium trade since it created a huge drain on China's financial reserves, let alone the negative social impact the opium drug had on Chinese society. The issue came to a head in 1839, when the British refused to restrict the importation of opium. Chinese officials subsequently confiscated and destroyed large amounts of opium, setting off the First Opium War (1839–1842). The Chinese protest actions were similar to the American's Boston Tea Party (where, incidentally, Chinese tea leaves were thrown into the harbour).

Western Domination (1839–1911) – Period of Unequal Treaties[5]

The Manchus, still using swords on horseback, were ill-equipped to fight the modern industrialised armies of the British and other Western powers. Their financial reserves were low, given the high cost of maintaining control over such a huge empire, which prevented the military from modernising. The Treaty of Nanking (called Nanjing today) in 1842, was a treaty of concessions made to Britain, with France and the US extracting similar concessions shortly thereafter. It was during this treaty that China was forced to cede Hong Kong Island to Britain. The Chinese government, obviously reluctant to comply with these unequal, forced treaties, only grudgingly complied and often refused, to the point that 14 years later, another war erupted known as the Second Opium War (1856–1860). During the Second Opium War, the Chinese again lost to the better-equipped

---

[5] Ibid.

Summer Palace – Beijing

Photograph by John L. Chan

文昌閣

Wenchang Ge (Wenchang Tower)

Plaque from Xiangshan – Beijing ➤ The temple was aggressively destroyed in the year 1860 by the Anglo-French Allied Forces and in the year 1900 by the Eight-power Allied Expedition. Only something like Zhile Moat, Sal Trees, the Stone Screen and the Imperial Monument survived and remained till today. In the year 1991, the base of the temple was cleared.

foreign powers and further concessions were made in Tianjin in 1858. When the Chinese refused to comply, a Joint British-French Expeditionary Force went into Beijing and destroyed the Summer Palace, burning it to the ground. This period of Chinese History is simply known as the Unequal Treaties.

To be fair, one could also argue that the Western period of domination of the "treaty ports" also had its benefits. It brought China into the industrial age, with Hong Kong's impressive development being the most glaring example. Shanghai's famous Bund, home to many of the leading international banks and insurance companies then and now, were mostly built with British architecture. Modern schooling and medical systems were also set in place in China and some of China's most prominent leaders, such as Dr Sun Yat-Sen, Chiang Kai Shek, Zhou Enlai and Deng Xiaoping, all received Western education either in Western-run schools or abroad. For example, Zhou Enlai and Deng Xiaoping both studied in Paris in the early part of the 20th century (which is when they first learned about communism). In terms of industry, China's famous Tsingtao Beer for example, the largest beer brand in China, was started by the Germans and comes from the city of Qingdao (formerly spelled Tsingtao) since this was the treaty port the Germans had extracted concessions from. The White Cat brand of household detergents and soaps, one of the largest brands in China, took over the Unilever factory after all industries were nationalised in 1949, and is one of the joint venture partners of Unilever today. In fact, if you look back far enough, many of the large state-run companies in China today had foreign roots and/or investment.

However, regardless of the benefits, this period is significant in that it explains a lot of the feelings of resentment and suspicion that the Chinese have towards the West. When I go back to the West and tell my friends that historically, Britain, France, the US and many of the other major foreign powers at the time, including Germany, Russia and Japan, were the biggest proponents of the "drug trade" on the planet, most find it almost impossible to believe. Some refuse to believe altogether. But I encourage everyone to read about this period of history, to discover for themselves what really happened. When you go to Beijing and visit the ancient imperial palaces, there are plaques all over citing these buildings as "restored replacements" since the original buildings were burnt to the ground by the imperialist powers led by the British and French. If you have a chance to visit Yuanming Yuan (Park), also in Beijing, the site of one of China's greatest imperial palaces, what you will find are beautiful trees covering marbled ruined palace grounds that would rival the Acropolis in Athens, destroyed by Western imperial forces. A museum has been erected in the park reminding citizens of the atrocities committed against China by foreign powers. Ancient cultural treasures looted during this period still reside in foreign museums. China also has its own holocaust museum, which shows the atrocities the Japa-

Photograph by John L. Chan

The ancient palace ruins of the imperial palace in Beijing's Yuanmingyuan (Park) destroyed by Western powers twice, once in 1860 and again in 1900, act as a reminder to modern-day Chinese of the importance of never again bowing to foreign powers. On the site is a museum, which documents the destruction, including a famous letter written by the famous French writer Victor Hugo condemning his own government's actions.

China Streetsmart

nese committed against the Chinese people during the Sino-Japanese War of 1936–1945. Since every student and citizen of China is aware of these periods, you should be too.

Taiping Rebellion (1850–1864) and Boxer Rebellion (1900–1901)[4] – Predecessor to the Falun Dafa?

Another interesting period in Chinese history which has some relevance today is the Taiping Rebellion of 1850–1864. Given the weakness of the Manchu government to protect the Chinese people from Western suppression, a Cantonese schoolmaster called Hong Xiuquan, discontent with the government, started a popular uprising to overthrow the Manchu government. Believing he was the younger brother of Jesus Christ, he had visions of establishing a new state called the Taiping or Heavenly Kingdom and pronounced himself King. Ordinary Chinese, whether believing in his own derivative of Christianity or not, but disenchanted with authorities, joined the movement to overthrow the Chinese government. Ironically, it was American and British generals that saved the Manchu government by defeating the Taipings. **During the Taiping Rebellion, an estimated 20 million Chinese are said to have died.**

The Boxer Rebellion in 1900 was another uprising that resulted in millions of deaths. During this period, China was rampant with secret societies, such as the White Lotus Society and the Small Sword Society, all of which were determined to overthrow the Manchu government. The Fists of Harmony Society was a secret sect that practised martial arts. They believed their martial arts exercises would help heal the body and eventually "make them invincible to bullets". Many people at the time were suffering from starvation and used these meditative exercises to help them overcome the hardship and misery of the time. The foreigners witnessing these people practise their martial arts exercises referred to them as "Boxers". The Boxers were determined to overthrow the Manchu government, expel all the foreigners, Christian missionaries and Chinese converts whom they believed were all destroying China. The uprising culminated in a dramatic standoff in Beijing's foreign legation near

---

[4] Ibid.

the Forbidden City when an international force consisting of forces from eight foreign powers freed the foreigners barricaded in their compounds, and then proceeded to loot and ransack various imperial palaces. Once again, the foreign powers demanded reparation and concessions from the Chinese government.

These periods in history go a long way towards helping us understand why the Chinese government is suspicious and overly conservative when it comes to allowing any organised gathering of groups of people in China. Even innocuous groups like the Rotary Club, Toastmasters or business groups are supposed to register with the authorities or risk the possibility of being declared illegal and shut down. Westerners may see this need to register as ridiculous or going overboard, and the government is learning to turn a blind eye to those obviously innocuous cases. They know they are not secret societies, but it is hard for locals unfamiliar with these Western groups to make the clear distinction between these and truly unauthorised movements, such as the Falun Dafa (or Falungong), which do make the government genuinely nervous. Like the Boxers before them, the Falun Dafa practise martial arts (qigong) and its members include a lot of disenchanted displaced workers as a result of the reform of state-owned enterprises.

Although there are thousands of followers around the world who could honestly claim that they are merely practising spiritual meditation, many of the followers in China join because they are disillusioned with society and government and find the meditative exercises useful in forgetting about their troubles. Whether one believes that Liu Hongzhi, the self-proclaimed spiritual leader of the Falun Dafa, is another Hong Xiuquan, running a religion or a cult that aims to overthrow the government, the similarities with the past, such as his ability to attract large numbers of disaffected people and rallying them together for organised protests through sophisticated means such as the Internet, or even interrupting satellite transmissions during the national television broadcast of the World Cup, is enough to make the central government very nervous. The Falun Dafa was in existence for years, but the government did not crack down hard on them until 25 April 1999, and this was only after they rallied some 10,000 followers to stage a protest in front of the Zhongnanhai compound where China's top leaders live and work.

Although the protest was relatively peaceful, the central government saw this as a direct challenge. Whether the Falun Dafa's aim is to ultimately overthrow the government or not, China certainly does not need another Taiping or Boxer Rebellion. Twenty million deaths in 1850 would translate into more than 100 million today.

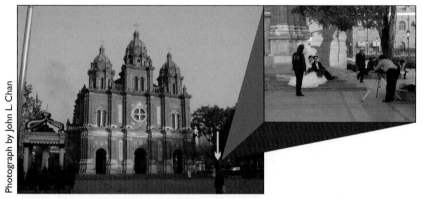

Photograph by John L. Chan

The area around Beijing's Wangfujing Cathedral, as it is known today, was once the scene of a famous siege during the Boxer Rebellion and now 100 years later is a peaceful place where Chinese couples can go to get their picture taken.

The Republican and Warlord Period (1912–1949)[5] – A Weak but Emerging China

The Manchu government, weakened by foreign powers and uprisings, such as the Taiping and Boxer Rebellions, was destined to fall. As China continued to fall into decay throughout the 19th century, many movements alongside the secret societies were trying to overthrow the Manchus' Qing Dynasty. Eventually the Western-educated Dr Sun Yat-Sen, founder of the Nationalist Party called the Guomindang (Kuomintang or KMT), gathered enough power to declare China a republic in 1912. However, in doing so, Dr Sun had to step down from the Presidency as a compromise to the leading military (warlord) figure at the time named Yuan Shi Kai. Although China from 1912 to 1949 was known as the Republic of China, it was never really ruled by one central government, rather a nationalist party

---

[5] Microsoft Encarta 2001, Microsoft Corp.

weakened by corruption, constantly fighting regional warlords that had sprung up after the fall of the Manchu government – similar to the situation in Afghanistan today. In fact, Yuan Shi Kai at one point tried to dissolve the National Assembly and declare himself the new Emperor of China. He died prematurely in 1916 before this was to materialise. The point for Westerners to note about this period is that while China was struggling to find its footing as a new nation, having eliminated dynastic rule after more than 4,000 years, it was weak, highly fragmented, and plagued by constant wars, externally with the Japanese and internally among competing warlords and political factions. During this period, once again, millions of Chinese died.

World War II (1939–1945)[6] –
The True Allies and Defenders of China

Before talking about the Chinese Communist Party (CCP) and their takeover of China following the 1949 Revolution, it is important to note what happened during World War II between China and the American-led Allied forces. It is widely known that China, the US and Britain fought alongside each other against the Japanese during World War II, but what is not as well known is that the real Chinese forces fighting the Japanese were most often the Chinese communists, not the Nationalist government at that time led by Generalissimo Chiang Kai Shek (later President of Taiwan). American General George Stillwell, the general in charge of Allied forces in China against Japan, was constantly frustrated with Chiang's decision to fight the Chinese communists, who were in fact helping the Americans oppose the Japanese. American historian and writer Barbara Tuchman later wrote a book based on Stillwell's diaries and won the Pulitzer Prize highlighting these facts.

An American colonel, David Barrett, under orders from President Roosevelt, headed a military mission to visit the Chinese communists. They called the mission Dixie (as was the American reference to the Chinese communists) and were accompanied by reporters representing major international news groups such as the *New*

---

[6] Barbara W. Tuchman, 1971, *Stillwell and the American Experience in China, 1911–45*, New York: The Grove Press.

York Times, the London Times, Associated Press, United Press International and the Christian Science Monitor. What they reported enthusiastically was a Chinese government led by Mao Zedong, that controlled an area the size of Japan and governed 54 million people. The CCP's armies were highly motivated, better fed and clothed than the KMT, and had a strong sense of purpose that they were all building a better China. In fact, the London Times wrote an article called "Yenan, a Chinese Wonderland City" after the famous communist base in Shaanxi province during the war. The mission made the recommendation that the American government support Mao Zedong who had openly welcomed a coalition between the CCP and the US. After much political haggling, Washington declined to work with the CCP and the US lost the chance to help constructively steer the course of China's post-war development.

One of the reasons the Chinese communists were victorious over the Nationalists during the Chinese Revolution in 1945–1949 was the fact that they could claim the moral right as the true legitimate defenders of China against the Japanese. Their soldiers joined voluntarily, in contrast to the KMT who often resorted to conscription and would literally bring in peasants "with their hands tied". Therefore, it was no surprise that mass defections from the KMT to the CCP took place during the war. Furthermore, because the Chinese communists were closest to the Japanese frontlines, when Japan surrendered their arms in 1945, they easily snapped up most of the Japanese military equipment, which they later used to win decisive victories in the revolution against the KMT Nationalists. The CCP victory over the KMT followed the lines of a "classic Hollywood storyline" where the poor ill-equipped underdog, using justice, triumphs over the unjust, corrupt, well-equipped establishment. In fact, many in the Western press and American writers like Edgar Snow captured the spirit of the Chinese Revolution in print. Edgar Snow was able to develop a close friendship with Mao and the CCP and maintained contact throughout the 50s and 60s, even when it was illegal for Americans to do so. Thankfully, his continued relationship with Mao sparked Secretary of State Henry Kissinger's secret trip to China in 1971, which led to the historical reestablishment of relations between the US and China, culminating in the Shanghai Communiqué during Nixon's visit to China in 1972.

The Force for Good

The Chinese Communist Party, in 1949, was the first force in over 150 years to truly unite China and eventually bring peace and stability to the land. One could cite the disastrous mistakes of the Great Leap Forward (1957–1960) and the Cultural Revolution (1966–1978) as periods of huge social upheaval, which they certainly were, but the country since 1949, has remained united and at peace from any major war (with the exception of the Korean conflict and border skirmishes with India, Russia and Vietnam during the 60s and 70s). Prior to the communist takeover, China's government and society were full of corruption, organised crime, opium dens and brothels. Dubious characters such as gangsters, opium merchants and prostitutes were what made Shanghai so colourful during its

The Godfather of Shanghai, Du Yuesheng

heyday in the 1930s. The stories, for example, of Du Yuesheng (an ally of Chiang Kai Shek), and the Green Gang, the infamous mobster that ruled Shanghai, could have easily matched Al Capone in reputation. Organised crime, brothels and opium dens were eliminated by the CCP after 1949. The triads, whose history coincided with the secret societies in China, escaped to Hong Kong and other overseas Chinese communities around the world – hence the emergence of the "Chinese Mafia" in Chinatown. However, now that the doors to the West have re-opened 30 years later, many of the former vices such as the triads, prostitution and corruption have returned. As Deng Xiaoping once remarked, "When you open the door, a few flies are bound to come in."

A Historical Perspective of China's Modern Leadership – Gradual Re-Emergence of China

Since 1949, China has had at least eight different leaders that one could argue were running China, namely, Mao Zedong, Liu Shaoqi, Hua Guofeng, Deng Xiaoping, Hu Yaobang, Zhao Ziyang, Jiang Zemin and currently, Hu Jintao. Arguably, Lin Biao and the Gang of Four headed by Jiang Qing, Mao's wife, could also be thrown onto the list, but for practical purposes, China's modern leadership need only be divided into three eras, characterised by distinct periods of leadership, style and objectives for China, namely, Mao, Deng and Jiang. Each era has unique meaning and significance for the foreign investor today and all three influence China's current outlook.

The Mao era from 1949 to 1978 (even though Mao passed away in 1976) helps the foreign investor understand the thinking and experience of China's current government and business leaders. This generation of leaders all grew up during the Mao era and in spite of the vast shift away from Mao's experimentation with Marxist socialist theory, Jiang is very much revitalising some of the key teachings of Mao as the spiritual leader of the party.

The Mao era acts as a cautious reminder to today's leaders of what can happen when sweeping economic reforms are made too quickly. Historians describe Mao as a great leader and military commander, but arguably a poor economist. Ambitious, but misguided, economic reforms gave rise to disasters such as the Great Leap Forward. The Cultural Revolution was another ambitious disaster; its purpose was to re-educate the masses but it re-

Latest currency issue.

sulted in an entire generation losing any formal education as universities and schools were shut down. Yet in spite of the black marks during Mao's leadership, he is still highly regarded in China. The fact that the new issue of currency bills all have Mao's portrait is a small example of the symbolic value the central government still

Photograph by John L. Chan

Mao's legendary status remains alive and well among Chinese citizens. Unlike the statues of Lenin that were torn down and replaced when the Soviet Union collapsed, Mao statues continue to stand proudly at the gates of most universities in China like the one pictured opposite in Beijing's Haidian (University) District.

sees in **Mao's contribution as the person who unified and liberated China and reinstated the Chinese people on the world stage.**

The Deng Era (1979–1997) – The Re-Opening of China

The Deng era, from 1979 to 1997, assures today's foreign investor that the reform process of opening up to the West will not be turned back and has given business executives a new framework to work in. He will best be known as the Chief Architect of Reform, but to fully appreciate his efforts, one needs to understand his skill at controlling the hardliners and reconciling conflicting ideologies of moving from a socialist system to an open market economy. "Building socialism with Chinese characteristics" was his answer, and is the centrepiece of Deng Xiaoping Theory. Foreign executives need to understand what this theory implies and how China's eventual economic model will likely be very different from other Western economies. Deng's work of transforming the economy is very much unfinished. But what he did was to provide the roadmap for resolving China's long-standing problems. His system of "One country, two systems" adopted by Hong Kong and Macau, for example, is his proposed framework on how Taiwan and the rest of Mainland China may peacefully reunite.

Another aspect of Deng's leadership, which signals a progressive shift to a modern China, is the move away from the cult personality or the overreliance on a single leader. Deng, a very private man, was very much against becoming another Mao in terms of the cult popularity Mao enjoyed during the late 60s and 70s. Before he passed away in February 1997, he gave instructions that his body was to be cremated and his ashes spread over the sea leaving no visible monument to worship – unlike Mao, whose body (replica?) still lies in state in Tiananmen Square. His monuments are really the modern cities, such as Shenzhen, that sprung up as a result of his reforms. Deng was at the height of his power only after he officially retired. His Southern Inspection Tour (or *Nanxun*) in 1992 was a watershed in modern Chinese history, since during his tour when he proclaimed, "To get rich is glorious", growth spurred to unprecedented levels and the wealth and prosperity of ordinary Chinese citizens grew to unprecedented levels. These thriving cities remain very positive and progressive signs of the future of China.

China Streetsmart

The third era of China's modern leadership is the era of Jiang Zemin, which is where we are today. Jiang represents a new era of leadership in China. Unlike Mao or Deng, he does not have a military or revolutionary background. He also represents the new leadership of China in the sense that, like President Kennedy in the 60s, Jiang is China's first real television leader. He demonstrates a good command of the media and the importance it plays in China. Almost every night Chinese citizens can see Jiang shaking the hands of world leaders, handing out food packets in disaster-stricken areas and patting the backs of the People's Liberation Army (PLA) soldiers. His demonstrated English skills have impressed the Western media, such as when he sang Elvis Presley's karaoke version of *Love Me Tender* with then Philippine President Fidel Ramos in front of the world press. However, he understands the foreign press well enough to keep his distance and is not afraid to challenge or even scold the foreign press, as he did a group of Hong Kong reporters, if he feels they are not covering the relevant issues.

The Jiang era represents for the foreign investor a new generation of leaders whose backgrounds contain little revolutionary or military credentials. Jiang officially took over the CCP as General Secretary in 1989, just weeks after the Tiananmen crackdown, when disgraced leader Zhao Ziyang was forced to step down. Shortly after, he also assumed the posts of Head of State, as President of China, and eventually the key position as Chairman of the Central Military Commission (CMC). In spite of holding concurrent positions in all three of the key posts, something which not even Deng was able to achieve, he really was not able to start branding his own vision of China until Deng passed away – eight years into his leadership. As many political experts point out, Jiang Zemin's eulogy at Deng's funeral in 1997 was one of his most important speeches ever. Part of the speech was a tribute to Deng, but the rest of the eulogy was devoted to his platform for moving China forward.

When Jiang first stepped into power, many people referred to him as an "interim" leader. However, over the years, he has proven to be more resilient than most analysts, including his political opponents, have given him credit for. Most people in the West are unaware of the internal power struggles and victories Jiang had to win over his opponents behind the walls of Zhongnanhai (China's version of the Kremlin); one by one, over the past decade, Yang Shangkun, Chen Xitong and Qiao Shi, to name but a few opponents of Jiang, have been swept aside. There used to be a saying that "If the river runs dry all that remains will be the stones". This saying was referring to Jiang, which means river, and Shi, which means Stone, would have Qiao Shi, then head of the National People's Congress (NPC) replace Jiang Zemin should the latter fall from power. However, Jiang has not fallen and Qiao Shi has now left the political scene. Jiang's demonstrated mastery at building consensus and support for his policies within the inner ranks is demonstrated by the visible fact that he has remained in power for so long – something which Hu Yaobang and Zhao Ziyang, his predecessors, did not do.

More conservative than Deng, he has solidified his power by carefully bringing in thousands of like-minded leaders to take up key posts throughout the government. These leaders included Zhu Rongji, the former Premier of China and Wu Bangguo, Vice Premier of China, both of whom used to hold Jiang's old position as Mayor of Shanghai. Furthermore, for more than a decade Jiang, who also holds the top seat as Chairman of the CMC, has been able to appoint generals loyal to him as old generals retire.

Understanding Jiang Zemin's vision for China is important for the foreign investor. The core of Jiang's vision is a revitalisation of nationalism mixed with socialistic ideology, which is set out in his ideological campaigns called the Three Stresses and the Three Representatives. Even with Hu Jintao (Jiang's handpicked successor) stepping into power, now that Jiang has stepped down from his posts as President of China and General Party Secretary of the CCP, Jiang's vision will remain the dominant theme for some time to come.

Appendix C

China Facts and Figures

Author's note: To get a better understanding of China facts and figures, please make sure you have read Chapter 27 first.

Table C.1   Population, 2001 Data

Province/Region	Millions	Per capita/sq km		
Henan	95.55	572.2	Population growth rate	0.88%
Shandong	90.41	577.0		
Sichuan	86.40	177.0	Percentage male	51.46%
Guangdong	77.83	437.2	Percentage female	48.54%
Jiangsu	73.55	716.9		
Hebei	66.99	360.4	Percentage urban	37.66%
Hunan	65.96	311.1	Percentage rural	62.34%
Anhui	63.28	452.0		
Hubei	59.75	318.3	Percentage aged 0–14	22.90%
Guangxi	47.88	202.3	Percentage aged 15–24	15.90%
Zhejiang	46.13	453.1	Percentage aged 25–39	28.49%
Yunnan	42.87	108.8	Percentage aged 40–65	25.60%
Liaoning	41.94	287.3	Percentage aged 65 and over	7.09%
Jiangxi	41.86	251.3	* Based on 2000 Census	
Heilongjiang	38.11	81.3		
Guizhou	37.99	218.3	Percentage Han nationality	93.94%
Shaanxi	36.59	178.0	Percentage minority nationality	6.06%
Shanxi	36.59	234.6		
Fujian	34.40	282.7	Number of households (millions)	351
Chongqing	30.97	377.7		
Jilin	26.91	143.6	Literacy rate	84%
Gansu	25.75	56.7		
Inner Mongolia	23.77	19.8	Total employment (millions)	730
Xinjiang	18.76	11.7		
Shanghai	16.14	2,545.7	10 cities across China (millions)	
Beijing	13.83	823.2	Chongqing	31.0
Tianjin	10.04	888.5	Shanghai	16.1
Hainan	7.96	234.5	Beijing	13.8
Ningxia	5.63	84.8	Chengdu	10.2
Qinghai	5.23	7.3	Tianjin	10.0
Tibet	2.63	2.1	Guangzhou	9.9
Other (E.g. Military)	4.57 * Not included in regions		Harbin	9.4
			Qingdao	7.0
NATIONAL TOTAL	1,276.27	133.0	Wuhan	8.3
			Xian	6.2

Source: *China Statistical Yearbook 2002*

Table C.2   Transportation, 2000 Data

Length of land transportation	(kilometres)
Railway routes in operation	58,656
Extension length of the trunk lines	81,736
Length of navigable inland waterways	119,325
Total length of roadways (breakdown)	1,402,698
Expressway	16,314
Class I and II	154,760
Class III and IV	1,044,939
Roadway below class IV	186,685

Source: *China Statistical Yearbook 2001, 2002*

Freight Traffic 2001 Data
(Total: 7.46 billion tonnes)
- The railway (18% of total volume) is typically the cheapest method, but also has the highest rate of damages and loss and is not as reliable as roads.
- Waterways (10% of total volume) are cheap and reliable but slow. 2% of Waterways is actually pipeline traffic.
- Roads (72% of total volume) are the fastest growing, but road conditions remain poor. Western-standard expressways are only 1% of total roads. Class I and II are also good, but account for no more than 11%. Class III and IV remain in poor condition and anything below class IV you can expect dirt roads or worse.
- Air freight (<1% of total volume) remains small due to cost. Total 2001 volume was only 200,000 tonnes.

Table C.3   Consumer Price Index

	Consumer price index (CPI)	Year over year increase
1985	(Base year) 100.0	N/A
1986	106.5	6.5%
1987	114.3	7.3%
1988	135.8	18.8%
1989	160.2	18.0%
1990	165.2	3.1%
1991	170.8	3.4%
1992	181.7	6.4%
1993	208.4	14.7%
1994	258.6	24.1%
1995	302.8	17.1%
1996	327.9	8.3%
1997	337.1	2.8%
1998	334.4	−0.8%
1999	329.7	−1.4%
2000	331.0	0.4%
2001	333.3	0.7%
2002 Estimate	331.0	−0.7%

Source: *China Statistical Yearbook 2002*

China Streetsmart

Table C.4   Living Expenditure Breakdown, Urban Households 2001 Survey

Living expenditure breakdown	Percentage of expenditure			
	National average	Lowest income earners (lowest 10%)	Middle income earners (third quintile)	Highest income earners (highest 10%)
Food	37.94	48.35	39.61	29.71
Recreation, education and cultural services	13.00	11.78	12.88	12.95
Residence	10.32	12.36	10.31	9.88
Clothing	10.05	7.43	10.30	10.40
Transport, post and communication services	8.61	6.09	8.21	10.42
Household facilities, articles and services	8.27	4.49	7.37	12.64
Medicine and medical services	6.47	6.26	6.54	6.60
Miscellaneous commodities and services	5.35	3.24	4.78	7.41

Number of TV sets per 100 households in urban areas	120.5
Number of TV sets per 100 households in rural areas	105.2
TV covering rate of population	94.2%

Source: *China Statistical Yearbook 2002*

Table C.5   Retail Sales (in billions)

	RMB	USD	Year over year % change
1952	26.3	3.2	
1953	32.9	4.0	25%
1954	35.6	4.3	8%
1955	36.4	4.4	2%
1956	42.4	5.1	16%
1957	44.2	5.3	4%
1958	48.1	5.8	9%
1959	55.7	6.7	16%
1960	59.5	7.2	7%
1961	53.8	6.5	−10%
1962	54.4	6.6	1%
1963	54.5	6.6	0%
1964	57.3	6.9	5%
1965	59.0	7.1	3%
1966	63.3	7.6	7%
1967	67.9	8.2	7%
1968	64.9	7.8	−4%
1969	69.8	8.4	8%
1970	72.9	8.8	4%
1971	77.7	9.4	7%
1972	85.4	10.3	10%
1973	91.8	11.1	8%
1974	96.7	11.7	5%
1975	104.6	12.6	8%
1976	109.9	13.3	5%
1977	117.4	14.2	7%
1978	126.5	15.3	8%
1979	147.6	17.8	17%
1980	179.4	21.7	22%
1981	200.3	24.2	12%
1982	218.2	26.3	9%
1983	242.6	29.3	11%
1984	289.9	35.0	20%
1985	430.5	52.0	48%
1986	495.0	59.8	15%
1987	582.0	70.3	18%
1988	744.0	89.9	28%
1989	810.1	97.8	9%
1990	830.0	100.2	2%
1991	941.6	113.7	13%
1992	1,099.4	132.8	17%
1993	1,246.2	150.5	13%
1994	1,626.5	196.4	31%
1995	2,062.0	249.0	27%
1996	2,477.4	299.2	20%
1997	2,729.9	329.7	10%
1998	2,915.3	352.1	7%
1999	3,113.5	376.0	7%
2000	3,415.3	412.5	10%
2001*	3,759.5	454.0	10%
2002*	4,088.8	493.8	9%

Exchange rate: 1 USD = 8.28 RMB

* Estimate

Source: CEIC

China Streetsmart

Table C.6   China Trade

	Exports (USD billions)	Year over year % change	Imports	Year over year % change	Total Trade (USD billions)	Year over year % change	Balance (USD billions)
1950	0.550		0.580		1.130		−0.030
1951	0.760	38%	1.200	107%	1.960	73%	−0.440
1952	0.820	8%	1.120	−7%	1.940	−1%	−0.300
1953	1.020	24%	1.350	21%	2.370	22%	−0.330
1954	1.150	13%	1.290	−4%	2.440	3%	−0.140
1955	1.410	23%	1.730	34%	3.140	29%	−0.320
1956	1.650	17%	1.560	−10%	3.210	2%	0.090
1957	1.600	−3%	1.500	−4%	3.100	−3%	0.100
1958	1.980	24%	1.890	26%	3.870	25%	0.090
1959	2.260	14%	2.120	12%	4.380	13%	0.140
1960	1.860	−18%	1.950	−8%	3.810	−13%	−0.090
1961	1.490	−20%	1.450	−26%	2.940	−23%	0.040
1962	1.490	0%	1.170	−19%	2.660	−10%	0.320
1963	1.650	11%	1.270	9%	2.920	10%	0.380
1964	1.920	16%	1.550	22%	3.470	19%	0.370
1965	2.230	16%	2.020	30%	4.250	22%	0.210
1966	2.370	6%	2.250	11%	4.620	9%	0.120
1967	2.140	−10%	2.020	−10%	4.160	−10%	0.120
1968	2.100	−2%	1.950	−3%	4.050	−3%	0.150
1969	2.200	5%	1.830	−6%	4.030	0%	0.370
1970	2.260	3%	2.330	27%	4.590	14%	−0.070
1971	2.640	17%	2.200	−6%	4.840	5%	0.440
1972	3.440	30%	2.860	30%	6.300	30%	0.580
1973	5.820	69%	5.160	80%	10.980	74%	0.660
1974	6.950	19%	7.620	48%	14.570	33%	−0.670
1975	7.260	4%	7.490	−2%	14.750	1%	−0.230
1976	6.850	−6%	6.580	−12%	13.430	−9%	0.270
1977	7.590	11%	7.210	10%	14.800	10%	0.380
1978	9.750	28%	10.890	51%	20.640	39%	−1.140
1979	13.660	40%	15.670	44%	29.330	42%	−2.010
1980	18.120	33%	20.020	28%	38.140	30%	−1.900
1981	22.007	21%	22.015	10%	44.022	15%	−0.008
1982	22.321	1%	19.285	−12%	41.606	−5%	3.036
1983	22.226	0%	21.390	11%	43.616	5%	0.836
1984	26.139	18%	27.410	28%	53.549	23%	−1.271
1985	27.350	5%	42.252	54%	69.602	30%	−14.902
1986	30.942	13%	42.904	2%	73.846	6%	−11.962
1987	39.437	27%	43.216	1%	82.653	12%	−3.779
1988	47.516	20%	55.268	28%	102.784	24%	−7.752
1989	52.538	11%	59.140	7%	111.678	9%	−6.602
1990	62.091	18%	53.345	−10%	115.436	3%	8.746
1991	71.840	16%	63.791	20%	135.631	17%	8.049
1992	84.940	18%	80.585	26%	165.525	22%	4.355
1993	91.744	8%	103.959	29%	195.703	18%	−12.215
1994	121.006	32%	115.615	11%	236.621	21%	5.391
1995	148.780	23%	132.080	14%	280.860	19%	16.700
1996	151.048	2%	138.833	5%	289.881	3%	12.215
1997	182.790	21%	142.361	3%	325.151	12%	40.429
1998	183.810	1%	140.240	−1%	324.050	0%	43.570
1999	194.930	6%	165.700	18%	360.630	11%	29.230
2000	249.200	28%	225.090	36%	474.290	32%	24.110
2001	266.160	7%	243.610	8%	509.770	7%	22.550
2002	325.570	22%	295.220	21%	620.790	22%	30.350

Source: CEIC

Appendix C

Table C.7 China's Top 50 Trading Partners

USD millions TOTAL TRADE	2000 Total	2000 Exports	2000 Imports	2001 Total	2001 Exports	2001 Imports	Market Share
Region	**474,296**	**249,203**	**225,094**	**509,768**	**266,155**	**243,613**	
Asia	273,650	132,308	141,342	288,139	140,957	147,183	57%
Europe	86,266	45,482	40,784	97,641	49,239	48,402	19%
North America	81,393	55,274	26,120	87,882	57,641	30,241	17%
Latin America	12,595	7,185	5,410	14,939	8,237	6,702	3%
Africa	10,597	5,042	5,555	10,800	6,007	4,793	2%
Oceanic and Pacific Islands	9,788	3,910	5,877	10,367	4,074	6,293	2%
Others	7	2	5	0	0	0	0%
Rank							
1 Japan	83,164	41,654	41,510	87,754	44,958	42,797	17%
2 United States	74,462	52,099	22,363	80,485	54,283	26,202	16%
3 Hong Kong	53,947	44,518	9,429	55,970	46,547	9,423	11%
4 Republic of Korea (South)	34,500	11,292	23,207	35,910	12,521	23,389	7%
5 Taiwan, China	30,533	5,039	25,494	32,340	5,000	27,339	6%
6 Germany	19,687	9,278	10,409	23,526	9,754	13,772	5%
7 Singapore	10,821	5,761	5,060	10,934	5,792	5,143	2%
8 Russia	8,003	2,233	5,770	10,671	2,711	7,959	2%
9 United Kingdom	9,903	6,310	3,592	10,308	6,780	3,527	2%
10 Malaysia	8,045	2,565	5,480	9,425	3,220	6,205	2%
11 Australia	8,453	3,429	5,024	8,997	3,570	5,426	2%
12 Netherlands	7,923	6,687	1,236	8,739	7,282	1,457	2%
13 France	7,655	3,705	3,950	7,790	3,686	4,105	2%
14 Italy	6,880	3,802	3,078	7,782	3,993	3,789	2%
15 Canada	6,909	3,158	3,751	7,375	3,346	4,028	1%
16 Thailand	6,624	2,243	4,381	7,050	2,337	4,713	1%
17 Indonesia	7,464	3,062	4,402	6,725	2,837	3,888	1%
18 Belgium	3,687	2,301	1,386	4,251	2,530	1,721	1%
19 Saudi Arabia	3,098	1,145	1,954	4,075	1,354	2,721	1%
20 Brazil	2,845	1,224	1,621	3,698	1,351	2,347	1%
21 India	2,914	1,561	1,353	3,596	1,896	1,700	1%
22 Philippines	3,142	1,464	1,677	3,566	1,620	1,945	1%
23 Iran	2,487	713	1,773	3,313	889	2,424	1%
24 Finland	3,190	837	2,353	3,287	910	2,376	1%
25 Sweden	3,503	828	2,675	3,105	932	2,173	1%
26 Spain	2,747	2,124	623	2,976	2,262	714	1%
27 United Arab Emirates	2,495	2,078	416	2,825	2,377	448	1%
28 Vietnam	2,466	1,537	929	2,815	1,804	1,011	1%
29 Mexico	1,824	1,335	488	2,551	1,790	761	1%
30 Switzerland	2,209	748	1,461	2,382	652	1,730	0%
31 South Africa	2,051	1,014	1,037	2,222	1,049	1,173	0%
32 Chile	2,122	784	1,339	2,118	815	1,303	0%
33 Antigua and Barbuda	1,540	610	930	1,855	574	1,281	0%
34 Oman	3,321	60	3,262	1,676	67	1,610	0%
35 Denmark	1,334	782	552	1,524	899	626	0%
36 Pakistan	1,163	670	492	1,397	815	582	0%
37 Israel	1,054	719	335	1,316	833	483	0%
38 Kazakhstan	1,557	599	958	1,288	328	961	0%
39 Poland	960	860	100	1,243	1,016	226	0%
40 Panama	1,291	1,290	1	1,242	1,240	2	0%
41 New Zealand	1,054	416	638	1,172	435	737	0%
42 Hungary	997	897	100	1,161	1,031	130	0%
43 Sudan	890	158	732	1,158	220	938	0%
44 Nigeria	856	549	307	1,145	917	227	0%
45 Ireland	714	336	377	1,143	530	613	0%
46 Austria	781	309	472	1,016	354	662	0%
47 Norway	1,097	487	611	982	411	571	0%
48 Bangladesh	918	900	19	972	955	17	0%
49 Egypt	907	805	102	953	873	80	0%
50 Turkey	1,205	1,078	127	905	674	231	0%

Source: *China Statistical Yearbook 2002*

China Streetsmart

Table C.8   Foreign Direct Investiment (FDI)

	Realised (USD billions)	Contractual (USD billions)
1979–1982	1.769	4.958
1983	0.916	1.917
1984	1.419	2.875
1985	1.956	6.333
1986	2.244	3.330
1987	2.314	3.709
1988	3.194	5.297
1989	3.393	5.600
1990	3.487	6.596
1991	4.366	11.977
1992	11.008	58.124
1993	27.515	111.436
1994	33.767	82.680
1995	37.521	91.282
1996	41.726	73.276
1997	45.257	51.003
1998	45.463	52.102
1999	40.400	41.200
2000	40.772	62.657
2001	46.850	69.191
2002	52.743	82.768

Source: CEIC

Table C.9   FDI Investors by Country

	1999 (USD billions)	Market share (%)	2000 (USD billions)	Market share (%)
Hong Kong	16.400	40.6%	15.500	38.0%
Rest of World	5.800	14.4%	7.247	17.8%
United States	4.200	10.4%	4.384	10.8%
Japan	3.000	7.4%	2.916	7.2%
Taiwan	2.600	6.4%	2.296	5.6%
Singapore	2.600	6.4%	2.173	5.3%
South Korea	1.300	3.2%	1.490	3.7%
Other European Union	1.200	3.0%	1.708	4.2%
United Kingdom	1.000	2.5%	1.164	2.9%
Germany	1.400	3.5%	1.041	2.6%
France	0.900	2.2%	0.853	2.1%
European Union Total	4.500	11.1%	4.766	11.7%
	40.400	100.0%	40.772	100.0%

Source: CEIC

China Streetsmart

Table C.10   FDI Breakdown by Province, 2000 Data

Province	FDI (USD millions)	Market share
Guangdong	12,835	31%
Jiangsu	6,426	15%
Fujian	3,432	8%
Shanghai	3,160	8%
Shandong	3,028	7%
Liaoning	2,044	5%
Beijing	1,684	4%
Zhejiang	1,613	4%
Tianjin	1,166	3%
Hubei	1,036	2%
Hebei	683	2%
Hunan	678	2%
Henan	564	1%
Guangxi	528	1%
Sichuan	437	1%
Hainan	431	1%
Jilin	337	1%
Anhui	318	1%
Heilongjiang	301	1%
Shaanxi	288	1%
Chongqing	246	1%
Jiangxi	227	1%
Shanxi	225	1%
Yunnan	128	0%
Inner Mongolia	106	0%
Gansu	62	0%
Guizhou	25	0%
Xinjiang	19	0%
Ningxia	17	0%
Qinghai	0	0%
Tibet	0	0%
TOTAL	42,044	

Note: FDI breakdown by province shown here includes "other investments" such as cash deposits held by foreign companies, which totalled about 1.272 billion USD nationally. Actual FDI for 2000 was only 40.772 billion USD.
Source: CEIC

Table C.11   Income Breakdown by City, 2001 Data

		Yearly disposable income (RMB)	Yearly living expenditure (RMB)	Yearly income (RMB)
	National	**9,141**	**7,272**	**9,128**
1	Shenzhen	22,673	18,006	22,947
2	Guangzhou	14,416	11,137	14,734
3	Shanghai	12,883	9,336	12,982
4	Ningbo	11,991	9,463	12,057
5	Beijing	11,578	8,923	11,659
6	Xiamen	11,365	8,490	11,507
7	Hangzhou	10,702	9,150	10,810
8	Jinan	9,565	7,465	9,673
9	Fuzhou	9,053	6,493	9,148
10	Tianjin	8,959	6,987	8,999
11	Nanjing	8,848	7,326	8,884
12	Qingdao	8,731	6,849	8,783
13	Changsha	8,651	7,683	8,742
14	Chengdu	8,128	6,801	8,182
15	Nanning	7,906	7,107	7,994
16	Wulumuqi	7,897	6,066	7,944
17	Haikou	7,755	6,154	7,803
18	Dalian	7,418	6,512	7,448
19	Kunming	7,405	5,974	7,463
20	Wuhan	7,305	6,342	7,325
21	Zhengzhou	7,266	5,894	7,325
22	Guiyang	6,909	5,776	6,924
23	Hefei	6,817	5,599	6,871
24	Shijiazhuang	6,805	5,579	6,899
25	Chongqing	6,721	5,874	6,755
26	Xian	6,705	5,816	6,744
27	Taiyuan	6,500	5,165	6,530
28	Harbin	6,407	5,045	6,444
29	Shenyang	6,386	5,515	6,427
30	Changchun	6,339	5,595	6,363
31	Lanzhou	6,325	5,239	6,359
32	Yinchun	6,257	5,508	6,302
33	Nanchang	6,206	4,294	6,300
34	Hohohot	6,182	4,866	6,203
35	Xining	6,041	4,775	6,070

Source: A.T. Kearney

Table C.12   Exchange Rate History

	Average rates, Foreign Currency to RMB		
	US dollar	**Japanese yen**	**Hong Kong dollar**
1985	2.9366	0.0125	0.3757
1986	3.4528	0.0207	0.4422
1987	3.7221	0.0258	0.4774
1988	3.7221	0.0291	0.4770
1989	3.7651	0.0274	0.4828
1990	4.7832	0.0332	0.6139
1991	5.3233	0.0396	0.6845
1992	5.5146	0.0436	0.7124
1993	5.7620	0.0520	0.7441
1994	8.6187	0.0844	1.1153
1995	8.3510	0.0892	1.0796
1996	8.3142	0.0764	1.0751
1997	8.2898	0.0686	1.0709
1998	8.2791	0.0635	1.0688
1999	8.2783	0.0729	1.0666
2000	8.2784	0.0769	1.0618
2001	8.2770	0.0681	1.0608

Source: *China Statistical Yearbook 2002*

Notes

- In 1993 the dual currency, using RMB and foreign exchange certificates (FECs), was abandoned in favour of a unified currency, i.e. the RMB.
- Since 1997, the RMB has traded in a very narrow band of roughly 8.2770 to 8.2800 USD. Recently, however, the People's Bank of China, China's state bank, has occasionally allowed the RMB to surpass this band. For example, on 12 April 2002 the RMB was allowed to close at 8.2830 and on 26 June 2002, the RMB closed at 8.2768. These fluctuations have drawn speculation that the RMB will be allowed to float freely but experts disagree. While the trading range will likely widen over the coming years, most experts do not foresee a fully convertible currency for the next five years or more.

Foreign Exchange Certificate (1979–1993)

FRONT

BACK

Collector's Item

When foreigners first went to China between 1979 and 1993, they were officially not allowed to use ordinary Chinese currency (RMB) and instead were issued FECs, which technically were equivalent in value to the RMB, but on the black market FECs could be exchanged for RMB at rates far higher than 1:1, since local Chinese could use FECs to buy, then scarce, Western-imported goods in friendship stores, which accepted only FECs.

Table C.13   Country Comparisons, 2000 Data

Country	Population	GDP USD	GDP/Capita	Area sq km	Pop density/sq km
Greater China	1,296,995,000	1,610,678,956,100	1,242	9,637,094	135
China	1,267,430,000	1,159,033,726,100	914	9,600,000	132
India	1,005,960,000	425,627,190,000	423	2,974,000	338
US	281,550,000	9,872,900,000,000	35,066	9,373,000	30
Indonesia	210,420,000	128,201,800,000	609	1,905,000	110
Russian Federation	145,560,000	229,289,080,000	1,575	17,075,000	9
Japan	126,870,000	4,220,535,550,800	33,267	378,000	336
Germany	82,150,000	2,023,069,400,000	24,627	357,000	230
Philippines	75,580,000	62,419,140,000	826	300,000	252
UK	59,740,000	1,476,878,700,000	24,722	242,000	247
France	58,890,000	1,406,709,920,000	23,887	552,000	107
Italy	57,690,000	1,163,402,240,000	20,166	301,000	192
South Korea	47,280,000	417,567,360,000	8,832	99,000	478
Canada	30,750,000	677,740,800,000	22,040	9,971,000	3
Malaysia	23,270,000	89,638,170,000	3,852	330,000	71
Taiwan	22,406,000	281,477,330,000	12,563	36,000	622
Australia	19,180,000	367,537,500,000	19,163	7,682,000	2
Hong Kong	6,725,000	163,967,800,000	24,382	1,070	6,285
Singapore	4,020,000	91,143,000,000	22,672	600	6,700
Macau	434,000	6,200,100,000	14,286	24	18,390

China Streetsmart

Table C.13   (continued)

Rank	Country	GDP (USD)
1	US	9,872,900,000,000
2	Japan	4,220,535,550,800
3	Germany	2,023,069,400,000
4	Greater China	1,610,678,956,100
5	UK	1,476,878,700,000
6	France	1,406,709,920,000
7	Italy	1,163,402,240,000
8	China	1,159,033,726,100
9	Canada	677,740,800,000
10	India	425,627,190,000
11	South Korea	417,567,360,000
12	Australia	367,537,500,000
13	Taiwan	281,477,330,000
14	Russian Federation	229,289,080,000
15	Hong Kong	163,967,800,000
16	Indonesia	128,201,800,000
17	Singapore	91,143,000,000
18	Malaysia	89,638,170,000
19	Philippines	62,419,140,000
20	Macau	6,200,100,000

Rank	Country	GDP/Capita (USD)
1	US	35,066
2	Japan	33,267
3	UK	24,722
4	Germany	24,627
5	Hong Kong	24,382
6	France	23,887
7	Singapore	22,672
8	Canada	22,040
9	Italy	20,166
10	Australia	19,163
11	Macau	14,286
12	Taiwan	12,563
13	South Korea	8,832
14	Malaysia	3,852
15	Russian Federation	1,575
16	Greater China	1,242
17	China	914
18	Philippines	826
19	Indonesia	609
20	India	423

Rank	Country	Area sq km
1	Russian Federation	17,075,000
2	Canada	9,971,000
3	Greater China	9,637,094
4	China	9,600,000
5	US	9,373,000
6	Australia	7,682,000
7	India	2,974,000
8	Indonesia	1,905,000
9	France	552,000
10	Japan	378,000
11	Germany	357,000
12	Malaysia	330,000
13	Italy	301,000
14	Philippines	300,000
15	UK	242,000
16	South Korea	99,000
17	Taiwan	36,000
18	Hong Kong	1,070
19	Singapore	600
20	Macau	24

Rank	Country	Pop density/sq km
1	Macau	18,390
2	Singapore	6,700
3	Hong Kong	6,285
4	Taiwan	622
5	South Korea	478
6	India	338
7	Japan	336
8	Philippines	252
9	UK	247
10	Germany	230
11	Italy	192
12	Greater China	135
13	China	132
14	Indonesia	110
15	France	107
16	Malaysia	71
17	US	30
18	Russian Federation	9
19	Canada	3
20	Australia	2

Note: Greater China includes Hong Kong, Macau and Taiwan.

Source: *China Statistical Yearbook 2002*

Index